THE PEARSON CUSTOM LIBRARY OF

American Literature

Duke Talent Identification Program
The Reader's Journey, Volume 1

Pearson Learning Solutions

New York   Boston   San Francisco
London   Toronto   Sydney   Tokyo   Singapore   Madrid
Mexico City   Munich   Paris   Cape Town   Hong Kong   Montreal

Senior Vice President, Editorial and Marketing: Patrick F. Boles
Senior Sponsoring Editor: Natalie Danner
Development Editor: Mary Kate Paris
Assistant Editor: Jill Johnson
Operations Manager: Eric M. Kenney
Production Manager: Jennifer Berry
Rights Manager: Jillian Santos
Art Director and Cover Designer: Renée Sartell

Cover Art: "Gloucester Landscape" by Greg Nikas; "Washington Landscape" by
Darrell Gulin; "Utah Landscape" and "Great Smokey Mountain National Park" by
David Muench; "Red Sunset Over Twin Cities" by Richard Hamilton Smith; and
"New York City Tenements" by Alan Schein Photography, Inc. All courtesy of
Corbis Images.

Printed in the United States of America.

V092

Please visit our website at www.pearsoncustom.com.

Attention bookstores: For permission to return any unsold stock, contact us at
pe-uscustomreturns@pearson.com.

Pearson Learning Solutions, 501 Boylston Street, Suite 900, Boston, MA 02116
A Pearson Education Company
www.pearsoned.com

ISBN 10: 0-558-15850-1
ISBN 13: 978-0-558-15850-7

Acknowledgments

The idea of a customizable set of Anchor Volumes drawn from a comprehensive library of American literary texts that is both representative and flexible in its offerings of the canonical and new, and which would be assembled by a group of innovative and experienced scholars, was first conceived by Virginia Blanford and John Bryant in 1993. The project was brought to Pearson Custom Publishing by acquisitions editor Ellen Kuhl and freelance development editor Janice Wiggins, who advanced its growth with the help of in-house development editor Katherine Gehan and editorial assistant Amy Hurd. Sponsoring editor Natalie Danner joined the project in 2002 and, along with production manager Kathleen Masse, copyeditor Lydia Stuart Horton, Jim O'Malley at Stratford, permissions editors Karl Christian Krumpholtz and Deborah Schwartz, and designer Renée Sartell, squired the project through its final phases of production. Marketing manager Annabel Cellini conceived and implemented the plan for bringing the project intelligently and effectively into the hands of sales representatives, bookstores, faculty, and students. From the beginning, the project received enthusiastic support from executives at Pearson including President of Pearson Custom Publishing, Don Kilburn, Vice President: Editorial, Marketing and Media, Patrick Boles, and in particular Assistant Vice President and Director of Database Publishing, Michael Payne, who along with the previously mentioned individuals has, with patience and insight, contributed to the intellectual scope as well as practical dimensions of the Pearson Custom Library of American Literature.

The five editors of PCLAL worked closely in developing the table of contents, in selecting and editing texts, and in writing period introductions, author head notes, and textual annotations as well as special pedagogical features for over three hundred authors and more than 1700 texts. They could not have completed these tasks without the help and feedback of numerous scholars. They wish to thank Jane Aldrich, Kevin Armitage, Ralph Bauer, Dennis Berthold, Bruce Bickley, Virginia Blanford, Joanna Brooks, Eliza Bryant, Christy Burns, Kathy Cain, Gregg Camfield, Beth Widmaier Capo, Barbara Clonts, Stanley Corkin, Robert Dawidoff, Richard Dillman, John Ernest, Antonia Garcia-Orozco, Ann Gilmartin, Walter Graffin, Nancy L. Gray, Jane C. Harred, Sharon Harris, Henry W. Hart, Robert Hass, Beverly Haviland, John Hildebidle, Sue E. Houchins, Ken Johnson, David Kadlec, David Kann, Jim Kinney, Lucinda Kriete, Jasmin L. Lambert, Elaine Limbaugh, Bennett Lovett-Graff, Richard Lowry, Lucy Maddox, Joseph Malof, William Marling, Darlene McElfresh, Susan McKay, Janice Neuleib, Margaret Darlene O'Dell, John Parks, Catherine E. Paul, Michael Pearson, Kimberley Phillips, Hermine D. Pinson, Victoria Ramirez,

Bethany Reid, Paige Reynolds, David Robinson, James Rocks, Lois Rudnick, Stephen Ruffus, Maria Sanchez, Jonathan Smith, Steve Spence, Suzette A. Spencer, Andrew Stambuk, Judith Stanford, Elizabeth Sumner, Sheila Teahan, Donald Weber, Shira Wolosky, Hilary Wyss, John Young, and Lee Zimmerman.

Contents

HARRIET BEECHER STOWE
[1811–1896]

One of the most famous and influential novels in American literary history began with a vision—at least according to its author, Harriet Beecher Stowe, who would later explain the novel's success and power by ascribing its author-ship to God. While in church in Brunswick, Maine, Stowe had a vision of a slave being beaten to death—and from that vision grew the central narrative line in Stowe's antislavery novel Uncle Tom's Cabin *(1852), in which an enslaved man is beaten to death in a scene that depicts the slave "Uncle" Tom as a Christian martyr to the evils of slavery. There were, of course, other influences—including Stowe's deeply religious upbringing, her experience in centers of pro- and antislavery struggle, and the passing of the Compromise of 1850, which included the Fugitive Slave Law, requiring (among other things) Northerners to assist in the apprehension of runaway slaves. But Stowe's reporting of the novel's visionary origins captures well, perhaps, what is for many readers at once powerful and deeply troubling about the novel. Stowe's image of Christian suffering can be, for some, a strong indictment against a culture in which both Christianity and the system of slavery played central roles, a culture dangerously blind to its own philosophical and moral contra-dictions. But Stowe's portrayal of Tom as a man whose religious beliefs lead him to submission, suffering, and forgiveness is, for others, a distorted and abstracted representation of the experience of enslavement, and one in which black suffering can be staged as the occasion for white benevolence and pity. If God wrote this novel, many might say, then why does the divine being seem so incapable of representing life from the perspective of the oppressed, and why do the characters in this novel seem to match so closely the racial stereotypes of white Americans in the nineteenth century?*

Whatever the reader may think of Uncle Tom's Cabin, *it is an unavoidable presence in American literary and cultural history—even in a country that for so many years successfully avoided recognizing Stowe as a major author. This novel, along with Stowe's other antislavery publications, heightened the pas-sions behind various divisions over slavery, both regional and ideological, and it inspired a number of both proslavery and antislavery publications, as writers from across the political spectrum tried variously to support, undermine, or* shift the terms of debates tied closely to the arguments presented in Uncle Tom's Cabin. But even beyond her most notorious publication, Stowe's presence in the American literary landscape is formidable. Stowe wrote sketches and historical novels that promoted regional customs and sensibilities—for example, The Mayflower (1843) and The Pearl of Orr's Island (1862), the latter a historical novel about rural life in Maine. In The Minister's Wooing (1859), she challenged the theological rigidity of Calvinism while embracing Christian principles and high standards of individual integrity. In novels such as My Wife and I (1871) and Pink and White Tyranny (1871), Stowe explored the developing culture of mass consumption. Moreover, while she was known for her commentary on the great issues of the day, Stowe was respected also as an adviser in the home. She published household advice in the respected magazine the Atlantic, collected and republished in Household Papers and Stories in 1865, and she co-authored with her sister Catherine Beecher the domestic manual An American Woman's Home (1869), in which the order of the home, of individual character, and of society generally are linked. Stowe's reach was impressive, and her influence extensive and lasting.

Stowe's writing was, in many ways, a natural extension of her upbringing in a family in which both religion and education defined her role and her expectations for life. She worked in schools founded by her sister Catherine, and over the course of her life she was daughter, sister, wife, and mother to clergymen. She was born in Litchfield, Connecticut, in 1811, the daughter of Roxanna Foote and Lyman Beecher. Her mother died when Harriet was five, and Harriet's life was shaped significantly by her sister Catherine, by her strict father, and by the trials of girlhood in a family never very financially secure. To be sure, both her father and her sister saw to it that Harriet was educated far beyond the level expected of or encouraged in women at the time (and beyond the level achieved by most men as well), but Harriet's life was filled by significant domestic duties as well. When Catherine established the Hartford Female Seminary in 1824, Harriet worked with her. Following the family's move to Cincinnati, Ohio, Harriet worked with her sister again when Catherine formed the Western Female Institute. Somehow, Harriet managed to find time to write in addition to her other responsibilities, and began her publishing career while living in Cincinnati—regional sketches first published in magazines and republished in her book The Mayflower in 1843. The money Stowe earned from her writing was especially welcome after she married biblical scholar Calvin Ellis Stowe in 1836.

Stowe's years in Cincinnati were formative in other ways as well. The family had moved there in 1832 when Harriet's father became president of Lane Theological Seminary. It was here that Harriet met the man who became her husband, but it was also here that the young writer, wife, and mother (Harriet gave birth to seven children between 1836 and 1850) encountered the realities of slavery. Cincinnati, a city positioned at the borders of slave and *free states, was accordingly a center of often explosive tensions between proslavery and antislavery advocates, and a center as well of white racist attempts to restrict the rights and social mobility of the city's free black population. When the Board of Trustees for Lane Theological Seminary ruled that students could neither live with nor work on behalf of African Americans in Cincinnati, a significant number of students left the institution (adding to the financial problems of its faculty, which included Harriet's husband). The intimacy of the problem of slavery was brought home further by anti-abolitionist riots in Cincinnati in 1836. Stowe, affected by such events and by local efforts of antislavery activists (including those involved in the Underground Railroad who would play a significant role in the plot of* Uncle Tom's Cabin*), responded in 1845 with her first sketch on slavery, "Immediate Emancipation," in which she pushed beyond more gradualist approaches to ending slavery (like those of her father).*

In 1850, Calvin and Harriet Stowe moved to Brunswick, Maine, when Calvin secured a position on the faculty of Bowdoin College, and it was here that Stowe envisioned and wrote her most famous work, Uncle Tom's Cabin. *She was inspired by her background, her vision, and the passing of the Compromise of 1850. The Compromise of 1850 included the Fugitive Slave Law, a renewal and extension of existing fugitive slave laws that posed new dangers to all fugitives in the North, endangered the security of even those African Americans born free in the North, and required the participation of white Americans in the North in securing the capture of fugitives from slavery. Initially envisioned as a series of sketches,* Uncle Tom's Cabin *was serialized in the* National Era, *with the subtitle* The Man That Was a Thing. *Reader response was so great that Stowe continued the series, which ran from 1851 to 1852. Published in 1852 with the title* Uncle Tom's Cabin; or, Life Among the Lowly, *Stowe's novel was an immediate and unprecedented success, selling over 300,000 in its first year, and has since been translated into roughly forty languages. The novel did not present any new arguments against slavery, but it brought those arguments home to readers with renewed vividness and framed them in a complex portrait of a Christian republic that was in danger of sacrificing its most revered political principles and its most sacred beliefs to the maintenance of the system of slavery.*

Uncle Tom's Cabin *had an immediate effect on cultural debates about slavery—shifting the discourse and tone of the debates and heightening the political tensions between those engaged in the debates. Parents named their children after the angelic white character Eva; a commercial industry produced various items associated (often loosely) with the novel, including everything from wallpaper depicting scenes from the novel to a card game based on the novel's principal characters. Other writers produced both antislavery and proslavery novels to support or refute Stowe's portrayal of the system of slavery; at least one public burning of Stowe's novel was staged in the South; and* reviewers on all sides of the debate weighed in on the merits of both the novel and its author. "Mrs. Stowe betrays a malignity so remarkable," wrote one prominent Southern writer, "that the petticoat lifts of itself, and we see the hoof of the beast under the table." In response to questions about the accuracy of her fictional portrayal, and to support and extend the novel's indictment of slavery, Stowe published in 1853 a compilation of articles from various newspapers, antislavery poetry, biographies, and commentary titled A Key to Uncle Tom's Cabin. In 1856, she tried to extend her argument further, and compensate for her own limited vision in Uncle Tom's Cabin, in another novel Dred: A Tale of the Dismal Swamp, though this novel failed to achieve the extensive influence of the earlier work.

The fame of Uncle Tom's Cabin made Stowe an international celebrity, and she soon became her family's primary source of income. Her family moved to Andover, Massachusetts, in 1852, where they lived until 1864. In Andover, Stowe continued her antislavery writing (Dred), but moved increasingly toward historical fiction that explored an imagined, and somewhat idealized, New England. In many ways, though, this work was a continuation of her earlier work, including her antislavery fiction, for religion and regional character (as shaped by heritage, custom, and industry) remained her central concerns. The Minister's Wooing (1859) is a novel set in a New England town shortly after the American Revolution that mixes courtship and religion in a tale of love nearly lost, faith finally found, and lovers almost separated but finally reunited. The stereotypical depiction of African Americans (among others) that undermines Stowe's antislavery work remains a problem, however, in her later work—in the form of a deeply religious black servant, Candace, in The Minister's Wooing. In another novel published during her Andover years, The Pearl of Orr's Island (1862), Stowe tells a similar story of tangled relations and discovered loves set on the coast of Maine and featuring a biblical "pearl of great price," a young orphan girl who loves well but (like little Eva in Uncle Tom's Cabin) doesn't live to see the novel's end.

The Stowe family moved from Andover to Hartford, Connecticut, where Stowe was, for a time, a neighbor to Mark Twain, and where she lived for the rest of her life (though she spent a great deal of her time on a Florida plantation in her later years). Among the works published during these periods were books that highlighted the importance of the home. The domestic realm had always been an important part of Stowe's fiction (for her, the center of both social stability and social reform)—and thus Stowe's emphasis on Uncle Tom's cabin. Stowe's writing on domestic concerns included her articles offering household advice originally published in the Atlantic and then in Household Papers and Stories (1865). Moreover, Stowe co-authored with her sister Catherine Beecher a manual on the philosophy and science of domestic order, An American Woman's Home (1869). In her fiction, Stowe continued her *regionally-based historical fiction in* Oldtown Folks *(1869), the story of intertwined relations in a small town in post-Revolutionary Massachusetts—a story that sorts through the relations among religion, politics, regional identity, and the fragile fortunes of love.* Stowe's *reputation as a moral writer was damaged somewhat, however, when she told a tale of relations rather too tangled for the tastes of her readers—the nonfictional account of the British writer Lord Byron's incestuous relations with his sister that Stowe wrote in an attempt to defend the honor of Byron's wife and published as* Lady Byron Vindicated *(1870).*

Following this nonfiction scandal, Stowe turned her attention to social satire in the novel Pink and White Tyranny *(1871)—and then to explorations of the changing roles of women in a world increasingly removed from the comforting fireside of the New England fiction in such fictional works as* My Wife and I *(1871) and* We and Our Neighbors *(1875). Stowe never strayed far from that fireside, though, and she returned her readers to it in such books as* Poganuc People *(1878), based on her childhood, and she continued to promote her religious convictions, as in* Religious Poems *(1867). But increasingly the New England fireside grew dim and the times changed, and in 1873 Stowe published an account of her life in Florida, in many ways removed from the world she once knew, in* Palmetto-Leaves. *Stowe continued to write—her later work included hymns and children's stories—but her work lacked the power of her earlier publications. Her husband's death in 1886 was a sad chapter of a life serialized in the changing story of the national text. Still, the complexities of Stowe's religious visions from her younger days continued to form a subplot in the national story, even as Stowe's own vision faded in the Florida sunset of her death in 1896. For better and worse, Stowe's characters continue to play a central role in the national drama of race, transgression, sin, and redemption—in various stage versions of* Uncle Tom's Cabin, *in lingering stereotypes, and in the novel that still seems to provide a key to white American racial consciousness and the history of slavery.*

John Ernest
University of New Hampshire

For Further Reading

Primary Works

Uncle Tom's Cabin; or, Life Among the Lowly (1852); A Key to Uncle Tom's Cabin; Presenting the Original Facts and Documents upon Which the Story Is Founded. Together with Corroborative Statements Verifying the Truth of the Work (1853); Sunny Memories of Foreign Lands (1854); The May Flower and Miscellaneous Writings (1855); Dred: A Tale of the Great Dismal Swamp,

Together with Anti-Slavery Tales and Papers (1856); *The Minister's Wooing* (1859); *Agnes of Sorrento* (1862); *The Pearl of Orr's Island* (1862); *Household Papers and Stories* (1865–1867); *Little Foxes* (1866); *Oldtown Folks* (1869); *Lady Byron Vindicated: A History of the Byron Controversy, from Its Beginnings in 1816 to the Present Time* (1870); *Pink and White Tyranny* (1871); *My Wife and I; or, Harry Henderson's History* (1871); *Woman in Sacred History: A Series of Sketches Drawn from Scriptural, Historical, and Legendary Sources* (1874); *Poganuc People* (1878); *The Writings of Harriet Beecher Stowe* (1896); *Life and Letters of Harriet Beecher Stowe,* ed. Annie Fields (1897).

Biographies

Florine Thayer McCray, *The Life-Work of the Author of "Uncle Tom's Cabin"* (1889); Charles Edward Stowe, *Life of Harriet Beecher Stowe, Compiled from Her Letters and Journals* (1889); Charles Edward Stowe and Lyman Beecher Stowe, *Harriet Beecher Stowe: The Story of Her Life* (1911); Robert Forrest Wilson, *Crusader in Crinoline: The Life of Harriet Beecher Stowe* (1941); Margaret Holbrook, *Harriet Beecher Stowe: A Bibliography* (1976); Jean W. Ashton, *Harriet Beecher Stowe: A Reference Guide* (1977); Milton Rugoff, *The Beechers: An American Family in the Nineteenth Century* (1981); Joan D. Hedrick, *Harriet Beecher Stowe: A Life* (1994).

Secondary Works

Ann Douglas, *The Feminization of American Culture* (1977); Bruce E. Kirkham, *The Building of "Uncle Tom's Cabin"* (1977); Elizabeth Ammons, ed., *Critical Essays on Harriet Beecher Stowe* (1980); Mary Kelley, *Private Woman, Public Stage: Literary Domesticity in Nineteenth-Century America* (1984); Thomas F. Gossett, *"Uncle Tom's Cabin" and American Culture* (1985); Jane Tompkins, *Sensational Designs: The Cultural Work of American Fiction* (1985); Lawrence Buell, *New England Literary Culture* (1986); Eric Sundquist, ed., *New Essays on Uncle Tom's Cabin* (1986); Jeanne Boydston, Mary Kelley, and Anne Margolis, *The Limits of Sisterhood: The Beecher Sisters on Women's Rights and Women's Sphere* (1988); Gillian Brown, *Domestic Individualism* (1990); Susan Coultrap-McQuin, *Doing Literary Business: American Women Writers in the Nineteenth Century* (1990); Robert S. Levine, *Martin Delany, Frederick Douglass, and the Politics of Representative Identity* (1997); Audrey Fisch, *American Slaves in Victorian England: Abolitionist Politics in Popular Literature and Culture* (2000); Lyde Cullen Sizer, *The Political Work of Northern Women Writers and the Civil War, 1850–1872* (2000).

From Uncle Tom's Cabin; or, Life Among the Lowly[*]

HARRIET BEECHER STOWE

Preface

The scenes of this story, as its title indicates, lie among a race hitherto ignored by the associations of polite and refined society; an exotic race, whose ancestors, born beneath a tropic sun, brought with them, and perpetuated to their descendants, a character so essentially unlike the hard and dominant Anglo-Saxon race, as for many years to have won from it only misunderstanding and contempt.

---

[*]When it was published and ever since, Harriet Beecher Stowe's most famous novel has been controversial. Some praise the novel's presentation of a strong antislavery argument; some object to the limitations of that argument, particularly when, in the novel's concluding chapter, Stowe has her most revolutionary black character decide to move to Liberia, Africa—the country founded by American Colonization Society, an organization deeply distrusted by the great majority of African Americans of the time. Some praise Stowe's intricate application of a Christian perspective to the problem of slavery while others argue that the novel's religious core reduces it to a vaguely spiritual sentimentalism. Some praise Stowe's enlightened understanding while others argue that Stowe was typical among white writers in her assumptions about and characterizations of black identity. In these selections from *Uncle Tom's Cabin* readers may study these contrasts in a series of paired chapters: Stowe's Preface and Conclusion; the chapter on the white angelic girl Eva and the chapter on the black devilish girl Topsy; and the two chapters that occupy the novel's center, one ending volume one and the other beginning volume two, in which a white southern slaveholder and a white northern liberal discuss and debate the appropriate ethical response to the system of slavery.

The novel focuses on a number of characters, many of whom became cultural icons, and each of whom serves as a cultural representative of a nation shaped and divided by the system of slavery. "Uncle" Tom is a devoutly Christian enslaved man whose sense of honor and self-sacrifice leads eventually to his martyrdom to the system of slavery. Mr. and Mrs. Shelby, Tom's owners, are presented as relatively benevolent slaveholders, though financial difficulties still lead Mr. Shelby to sell Tom and other people on his plantation to Haley, the slave trader. Faced with the prospect of the sale of her son, an enslaved mulatto woman named Eliza escapes with her son by leaping across the ice floes on the Ohio River, after which she is reunited with her husband and the family is aided on their journey to Canada by way of the Underground Railroad. Tom is first sold to Augustine St. Clare, a slaveholder who has no illusions about the morality of slavery but who participates in it anyway, his conscience still alive but his moral courage all but dead. St. Clare presents some of the most forceful antislavery sentiments in the novel, though he largely fails to act upon those sentiments. Eva, the angelic daughter of Augustine St. Clare, manages, moments before her early death, to give voice to the novel's Christian message. Topsy, an

But, another and better day is dawning; every influence of literature, of poetry and of art, in our times, is becoming more and more in unison with the great master chord of Christianity, "good will to man."[1]

The poet, the painter, and the artist, now seek out and embellish the common and gentler humanities of life, and, under the allurements of fiction, breathe a humanizing and subduing influence, favorable to the development of the great principles of Christian brotherhood.

The hand of benevolence is everywhere stretched out, searching into abuses, righting wrongs, alleviating distresses, and bringing to the knowledge and sympathies of the world the lowly, the oppressed, and the forgotten.

In this general movement, unhappy Africa at last is remembered; Africa, who began the race of civilization and human progress in the dim, gray dawn of early time, but who, for centuries, has lain bound and bleeding at the foot of civilized and Christianized humanity, imploring compassion in vain.

But the heart of the dominant race, who have been her conquerors, her hard masters, has at length been turned towards her in mercy; and it has been seen how far nobler it is in nations to protect the feeble than to oppress them. Thanks be to God, the world has at last outlived the slave-trade![2]

The object of these sketches is to awaken sympathy and feeling for the African race, as they exist among us; to show their wrongs and sorrows, under a system so necessarily cruel and unjust as to defeat and do away the good effects of all that can be attempted for them, by their best friends, under it.

In doing this, the author can sincerely disclaim any invidious feeling toward those individuals who, often without any fault of their own, are involved in the trials and embarrassments of the legal relations of slavery.

Experience has shown her that some of the noblest of minds and hearts are often thus involved; and no one knows better than they do, that what may be gathered of the evils of slavery from sketches like these, is not the half that could be told, of the unspeakable whole.

In the northern states, these representations may, perhaps, be thought caricatures; in the southern states are witnesses who know their fidelity. What

---

enslaved young black girl who knows nothing of her parentage, is befriended by Eva and, from Eva's example, by Augustine St. Clare's cousin, a northerner with antislavery views but unselfconscious racial prejudices that she begins to learn to confront. Simon Legree, the man who eventually purchases Tom, is the novel's example of the most degraded and brutal of slaveholders, and it is on Legree's plantation that Tom is finally killed.

Uncle Tom's Cabin was serialized in the *National Era* from 1851 to 1852 with the subtitle *The Man That Was a Thing*. The novel was published in book form under the title *Uncle Tom's Cabin; or, Life Among the Lowly* by John P. Jewett and Company of Boston in 1852.

[1]Luke 2:14

[2]The importation of slaves into the United States was banned in 1808, though illegal trading continued. Great Britain abolished the slave trade in 1807; slavery was abolished in the British West Indies in 1833.

personal knowledge the author has had, of the truth of incidents such as are here related, will appear in its time.

It is a comfort to hope, as so many of the world's sorrows and wrongs have, from age to age, been lived down, so a time shall come when sketches similar to these shall be valuable only as memorials of what has long ceased to be.

When an enlightened and Christianized community shall have, on the shores of Africa, laws, language and literature, drawn from among us, may then the scenes of the house of bondage be to them like the remembrance of Egypt to the Israelite,[3]—a motive of thankfulness to Him who hath redeemed them!

For, while politicians contend, and men are swerved this way and that by conflicting tides of interest and passion, the great cause of human liberty is in the hands of one, of whom it is said:

"He shall not fail nor be discouraged
Till He have set judgment in the earth."
"He shall deliver the needy when he crieth,
The poor, and him that hath no helper."
"He shall redeem their soul from deceit and violence,
And precious shall their blood be in His sight."[4]

. . .

XIV.

Evangeline

"A young star! which shone
O'er life—too sweet an image for such glass!
A lovely being, scarcely formed or moulded;
A rose with all its sweetest leaves yet folded."[5]

The Mississippi! How, as by an enchanted wand, have its scenes been changed, since Chateaubriand[6] wrote his prose-poetic description of it, as a river of mighty, unbroken solitudes, rolling amid undreamed wonders of vegetable and animal existence.

But, as in an hour, this river of dreams and wild romance has emerged to a reality scarcely less visionary and splendid. What other river of the world bears on its bosom to the ocean the wealth and enterprise of such another country?—a country whose products embrace all between the tropics and

---

[3]Exodus 1–14
[4]Isaiah 42:4; Psalms 72:12 & 14
[5]From *Don Juan* (1818–1824) by English poet Lord Byron (1788–1824).
[6]French writer and statesman Vicomte François René de Chateaubriand (1768–1848) described the Mississippi River in "Les Natchez" (1826).

the poles! Those turbid waters, hurrying, foaming, tearing along, an apt resemblance of that headlong tide of business which is poured along its wave by a race more vehement and energetic than any the old world ever saw. Ah! would that they did not also bear along a more fearful freight,—the tears of the oppressed, the sighs of the helpless, the bitter prayers of poor, ignorant hearts to an unknown God—unknown, unseen and silent, but who will yet "come out of his place to save all the poor of the earth!"

The slanting light of the setting sun quivers on the sea–like expanse of the river; the shivery canes, and the tall, dark cypress, hung with wreaths of dark, funereal moss, glow in the golden ray, as the heavily laden steamboat marches onward.

Piled with cotton–bales, from many a plantation, up over deck and sides, till she seems in the distance a square, massive block of gray, she moves heavily onward to the nearing mart. We must look some time among its crowded decks before we shall find again our humble friend Tom. High on the upper deck, in a little nook among the everywhere predominant cotton–bales, at last we may find him.

Partly from confidence inspired by Mr. Shelby's representations, and partly from the remarkably inoffensive and quiet character of the man, Tom had insensibly won his way far into the confidence even of such a man as Haley.

At first he had watched him narrowly through the day, and never allowed him to sleep at night unfettered; but the uncomplaining patience and apparent contentment of Tom's manner led him gradually to discontinue these restraints, and for some time Tom had enjoyed a sort of parole of honor, being permitted to come and go freely where he pleased on the boat.

Ever quiet and obliging, and more than ready to lend a hand in every emergency which occurred among the workmen below, he had won the good opinion of all the hands, and spent many hours in helping them with as hearty a good will as ever he worked on a Kentucky farm.

When there seemed to be nothing for him to do, he would climb to a nook among the cotton–bales of the upper deck, and busy himself in studying over his Bible,—and it is there we see him now.

For a hundred or more miles above New Orleans, the river is higher than the surrounding country, and rolls its tremendous volume between massive levees twenty feet in height. The traveller from the deck of the steamer, as from some floating castle top, overlooks the whole country for miles and miles around. Tom, therefore, had spread out full before him, in plantation after plantation, a map of the life to which he was approaching.

He saw the distant slaves at their toil; he saw afar their villages of huts gleaming out in long rows on many a plantation, distant from the stately mansions and pleasure–grounds of the master;—and as the moving picture passed on, his poor, foolish heart would be turning backward to the Kentucky farm, with its old shadowy beeches,—to the master's house, with its wide, cool halls, and, near by, the little cabin, overgrown with the multiflora and bigno-nia. There he seemed to see familiar faces of comrades, who had grown up with him from infancy; he saw his busy wife, bustling in her preparations for his evening meals; he heard the merry laugh of his boys at their play, and the chirrup of the baby at his knee; and then, with a start, all faded, and he saw again the cane–brakes[7] and cypresses and gliding plantations, and heard again the creaking and groaning of the machinery, all telling him too plainly that all that phase of life had gone by forever.

In such a case, you write to your wife, and send messages to your chil-dren; but Tom could not write,—the mail for him had no existence, and the gulf of separation was unbridged by even a friendly word or signal.

Is it strange, then, that some tears fall on the pages of his Bible, as he lays it on the cotton–bale, and, with patient finger, threading his slow way from word to word, traces out its promises? Having learned late in life, Tom was but a slow reader, and passed on laboriously from verse to verse. Fortunate for him was it that the book he was intent on was one which slow reading cannot injure,— nay, one whose words, like ingots of gold, seem often to need to be weighed separately, that the mind may take in their priceless value. Let us follow him a moment, as, pointing to each word, and pronouncing each half aloud, he reads,

"Let—not—your—heart—be—troubled.   In—my—Father's—house— are—many—mansions. I—go—to—prepare—a—place—for—you."[8]

Cicero,[9] when he buried his darling and only daughter, had a heart as full of honest grief as poor Tom's,—perhaps no fuller, for both were only men;— but Cicero could pause over no such sublime words of hope, and look to no such future reünion; and if he *had* seen them, ten to one he would not have believed,—he must fill his head first with a thousand questions of authentic-ity of manuscript, and correctness of translation. But, to poor Tom, there it lay, just what he needed, so evidently true and divine that the possibility of a question never entered his simple head. It must be true; for, if not true, how could he live?

As for Tom's Bible, though it had no annotations and helps in margin from learned commentators, still it had been embellished with certain way–marks and guide–boards of Tom's own invention, and which helped him more than the most learned expositions could have done. It had been his custom to get the Bible read to him by his master's children, in particular by young Master George; and, as they read, he would designate, by bold, strong marks and dashes, with pen and ink, the passages which more particularly gratified his ear or affected his heart. His Bible was thus marked through, from one end to

---

[7]Cane-brakes are thickets of cane, a woody stem like that of bamboo.
[8]John 14:1-2
[9]Roman statesman Marcus Tullius Cicero (106–43 B.C.E.).

the other, with a variety of styles and designations; so he could in a moment seize upon his favorite passages, without the labor of spelling out what lay between them;—and while it lay there before him, every passage breathing of some old home scene, and recalling some past enjoyment, his Bible seemed to him all of this life that remained, as well as the promise of a future one.

Among the passengers on the boat was a young gentleman of fortune and family, resident in New Orleans, who bore the name of St. Clare. He had with him a daughter between five and six years of age, together with a lady who seemed to claim relationship to both, and to have the little one especially under her charge.

Tom had often caught glimpses of this little girl,—for she was one of those busy, tripping creatures, that can be no more contained in one place than a sunbeam or a summer breeze,—nor was she one that, once seen, could be easily forgotten.

Her form was the perfection of childish beauty, without its usual chubbiness and squareness of outline. There was about it an undulating and aërial grace, such as one might dream of for some mythic and allegorical being. Her face was remarkable less for its perfect beauty of feature than for a singular and dreamy earnestness of expression, which made the ideal start when they looked at her, and by which the dullest and most literal were impressed, without exactly knowing why. The shape of her head and the turn of her neck and bust was peculiarly noble, and the long golden–brown hair that floated like a cloud around it, the deep spiritual gravity of her violet blue eyes, shaded by heavy fringes of golden brown,—all marked her out from other children, and made every one turn and look after her, as she glided hither and thither on the boat. Nevertheless, the little one was not what you would have called either a grave child or a sad one. On the contrary, an airy and innocent playfulness seemed to flicker like the shadow of summer leaves over her childish face, and around her buoyant figure. She was always in motion, always with a half smile on her rosy mouth, flying hither and thither, with an undulating and cloud–like tread, singing to herself as she moved as in a happy dream. Her father and female guardian were incessantly busy in pursuit of her,—but, when caught, she melted from them again like a summer cloud; and as no word of chiding or reproof ever fell on her ear for whatever she chose to do, she pursued her own way all over the boat. Always dressed in white, she seemed to move like a shadow through all sorts of places, without contracting spot or stain; and there was not a corner or nook, above or below, where those fairy footsteps had not glided, and that visionary golden head, with its deep blue eyes, fleeted along.

The fireman, as he looked up from his sweaty toil, sometimes found those eyes looking wonderingly into the raging depths of the furnace, and fearfully and pityingly at him, as if she thought him in some dreadful danger. Anon the steersman at the wheel paused and smiled, as the picture–like head gleamed through the window of the round house, and in a moment was gone again. A thousand times a day rough voices blessed her, and smiles of unwonted softness stole over hard faces, as she passed; and when she tripped fearlessly over dangerous places, rough, sooty hands were stretched involuntarily out to save her, and smooth her path.

Tom, who had the soft, impressible nature of his kindly race, ever yearning toward the simple and childlike, watched the little creature with daily increasing interest. To him she seemed something almost divine; and whenever her golden head and deep blue eyes peered out upon him from behind some dusky cotton–bale, or looked down upon him over some ridge of packages, he half believed that he saw one of the angels stepped out of his New Testament.

Often and often she walked mournfully round the place where Haley's gang of men and women sat in their chains. She would glide in among them, and look at them with an air of perplexed and sorrowful earnestness; and sometimes she would lift their chains with her slender hands, and then sigh wofully, as she glided away. Several times she appeared suddenly among them, with her hands full of candy, nuts, and oranges, which she would distribute joyfully to them, and then be gone again.

Tom watched the little lady a great deal, before he ventured on any overtures towards acquaintanceship. He knew an abundance of simple acts to propitiate and invite the approaches of the little people, and he resolved to play his part right skilfully. He could cut cunning little baskets out of cherry–stones, could make grotesque faces on hickory–nuts, or odd–jumping figures out of elder–pith, and he was a very Pan[10] in the manufacture of whistles of all sizes and sorts. His pockets were full of miscellaneous articles of attraction, which he had hoarded in days of old for his master's children, and which he now produced, with commendable prudence and economy, one by one, as overtures for acquaintance and friendship.

The little one was shy, for all her busy interest in everything going on, and it was not easy to tame her. For a while, she would perch like a canary–bird on some box or package near Tom, while busy in the little arts afore–named, and take from him, with a kind of grave bashfulness, the little articles he offered. But at last they got on quite confidential terms.

"What's little missy's name?" said Tom, at last, when he thought matters were ripe to push such an inquiry.

"Evangeline St. Clare," said the little one, "though papa and everybody else call me Eva. Now, what's your name?"

"My name's Tom; the little chil'en used to call me Uncle Tom, way back thar in Kentucky."

"Then I mean to call you Uncle Tom, because, you see, I like you," said Eva. "So, Uncle Tom, where are you going?"

---

[10]Pan was a flute-playing Greek god who had the legs of a goat.

"I don't know, Miss Eva."

"Don't know?" said Eva.

"No. I am going to be sold to somebody. I don't know who."

"My papa can buy you," said Eva, quickly; "and if he buys you, you will have good times. I mean to ask him to, this very day."

"Thank you, my little lady," said Tom.

The boat here stopped at a small landing to take in wood, and Eva, hearing her father's voice, bounded nimbly away. Tom rose up, and went forward to offer his service in wooding, and soon was busy among the hands.

Eva and her father were standing together by the railings to see the boat start from the landing–place, the wheel had made two or three revolutions in the water, when, by some sudden movement, the little one suddenly lost her balance, and fell sheer over the side of the boat into the water. Her father, scarce knowing what he did, was plunging in after her, but was held back by some behind him, who saw that more efficient aid had followed the child.

Tom was standing just under her on the lower deck, as she fell. He saw her strike the water, and sink, and was after her in a moment. A broad–chested, strong–armed fellow, it was nothing for him to keep afloat in the water, till, in a moment or two, the child rose to the surface, and he caught her in his arms, and, swimming with her to the boat–side, handed her up, all dripping, to the grasp of hundreds of hands, which, as if they had all belonged to one man, were stretched eagerly out to receive her. A few moments more, and her father bore her, dripping and senseless, to the ladies' cabin, where, as is usual in cases of the kind, there ensued a very well–meaning and kind–hearted strife among the female occupants generally, as to who should do the most things to make a disturbance, and to hinder her recovery in every way possible.

. . .

It was a sultry, close day, the next day, as the steamer drew near to New Orleans. A general bustle of expectation and preparation was spread through the boat; in the cabin, one and another were gathering their things together, and arranging them, preparatory to going ashore. The steward and chambermaid, and all, were busily engaged in cleaning, furbishing, and arranging the splendid boat, preparatory to a grand entree.

On the lower deck sat our friend Tom, with his arms folded, and anxiously, from time to time, turning his eyes towards a group on the other side of the boat.

There stood the fair Evangeline, a little paler than the day before, but otherwise exhibiting no traces of the accident which had befallen her. A graceful, elegantly–formed young man stood by her, carlessly leaning one elbow on a bale of cotton, while a large pocket–book lay open before him. It was quite evident, at a glance, that the gentleman was Eva's father. There was the same noble cast of head, the same large blue eyes, the same golden–brown hair; yet the expression was wholly different. In the large, clear blue eyes, though in form and color exactly similar, there was wanting that misty, dreamy depth of expression; all was clear, bold, and bright, but with a light wholly of this world: the beautifully cut mouth had a proud and somewhat sarcastic expression, while an air of free–and–easy superiority sat not ungracefully in every turn and movement of his fine form. He was listening, with a good–humored, negligent air, half comic, half contemptuous, to Haley, who was very volubly expatiating on the quality of the article for which they were bargaining.

"All the moral and Christian virtues bound in black morocco,[11] complete!" he said, when Haley had finished. "Well, now, my good fellow, what 's the damage, as they say in Kentucky; in short, what 's to be paid out for this business? How much are you going to cheat me, now? Out with it!"

"Wal," said Haley, "if I should say thirteen hundred dollars for that ar fellow, I should n't but just save myself; I should n't, now, re'ly."

"Poor fellow!" said the young man, fixing his keen, mocking blue eye on him; "but I suppose you 'd let me have him for that, out of a particular regard for me."

"Well, the young lady here seems to be sot on him, and nat'lly enough."

"O! certainly, there 's a call on your benevolence, my friend. Now, as a matter of Christian charity, how cheap could you afford to let him go, to oblige a young lady that 's particular sot on him?"

"Wal, now, just think on 't," said the trader; "just look at them limbs,— broad–chested, strong as a horse. Look at his head; them high forrads allays shows calculatin niggers, that 'll do any kind o' thing. I 've marked that ar. Now, a nigger of that ar heft and build is worth considerable, just, as you may say, for his body, supposin he 's stupid; but come to put in his calculatin faculties, and them which I can show he has oncommon, why, of course, it makes him come higher. What, that ar fellow managed his master's whole farm. He has a strornary talent for business."

"Bad, bad, very bad; knows altogether too much!" said the young man, with the same mocking smile playing about his mouth. "Never will do, in the world. Your smart fellows are always running off, stealing horses, and raising the devil generally. I think you 'll have to take off a couple of hundred for his smartness."

"Wal, there might be something in that ar, if it warnt for his character; but I can show recommends from his master and others, to prove his is one of your real pious,—the most humble, prayin, pious crittur ye ever did see. Why, he 's been called a preacher in them parts he came from."

"And I might use him for a family chaplain, possibly," added the young man, dryly. "That 's quite an idea. Religion is a remarkably scarce article at our house."

"You 're joking now."

---

[11] A fine leather.

15

"How do you know I am? Did n't you just warrant him for a preacher? Has he been examined by any synod or council? Come, hand over your papers."

If the trader had not been sure, by a certain good–humored twinkle in the large blue eye, that all this banter was sure, in the long run, to turn out a cash concern, he might have been somewhat out of patience; as it was, he laid down a greasy pocket–book on the cotton–bales, and began anxiously studying over certain papers in it, the young man standing by, the while, looking down on him with an air of careless, easy drollery.

"Papa, do buy him! it 's no matter what you pay," whispered Eva, softly, getting up on a package, and putting her arm around her father's neck. "You have money enough, I know. I want him."

"What for, pussy? Are you going to use him for a rattlebox, or a rocking-horse, or what?"

"I want to make him happy."

"An original reason, certainly."

Here the trader handed up a certificate, signed by Mr. Shelby, which the young man took with the tips of his long fingers, and glanced over carelessly.

"A gentlemanly hand," he said, "and well spelt, too. Well, now, but I 'm not sure, after all, about this religion," said he, the old wicked expression returning to his eye; "the country is almost ruined with pious white people: such pious politicians as we have just before elections, — such pious goings on in all departments of church and state, that a fellow does not know who 'll cheat him next. I don't know, either, about religion's being up in the market, just now. I have not looked in the papers lately, to see how it sells. How many hundred dollars, now, do you put on for this religion?"

"You like to be a jokin, now," said the trader; "but, then, there 's *sense* under all that ar. I know there 's differences in religion. Some kinds is mis-'rable: there 's your meetin pious; there 's your singin, roarin pious; them ar an't no account, in black or white; — but these rayly is; and I 've seen it in niggers as often as any, your rail softly, quiet, stiddy, honest, pious, that the hull world could n't tempt 'em to do nothing that they thinks is wrong; and ye see in this letter what Tom's old master says about him."

"Now," said the young man, stooping gravely over his book of bills, "if you can assure me that I really can buy *this* kind of pious, and that it will be set down to my account in the book up above, as something belonging to me, I would n't care if I did go a little extra for it. How d' ye say?"

"Wal, raily, I can't do that," said the trader. "I 'm a thinkin that every man 'll have to hang on his own hook, in them ar quarters."

"Rather hard on a fellow that pays extra on religion, and can't trade with it in the state where he wants it most, an't it, now?" said the young man, who had been making out a roll of bills while he was speaking. "There, count your money, old boy!" he added, as he handed the roll to the trader.

"All right," said Haley, his face beaming with delight; and pulling out an old inkhorn, he proceeded to fill out a bill of sale, which, in a few moments, he handed to the young man.

"I wonder, now, if I was divided up and inventoried," said the latter, as he ran over the paper, "how much I might bring. Say so much for the shape of my head, so much for a high forehead, so much for arms, and hands, and legs, and then so much for education, learning, talent, honesty, religion! Bless me! there would be small charge on that last, I 'm thinking. But come, Eva," he said; and taking the hand of his daughter, he stepped across the boat, and carelessly putting the tip of his finger under Tom's chin, said, good-humoredly, "Look up, Tom, and see how you like your new master."

Tom looked up. It was not in nature to look into that gay, young, handsome face, without a feeling of pleasure; and Tom felt the tears start in his eyes as he said, heartily, "God bless you, Mas'r!"

"Well, I hope he will. What 's your name? Tom? Quite as likely to do it for your asking as mine, from all accounts. Can you drive horses, Tom?"

"I 've been allays used to horses," said Tom. "Mas'r Shelby raised heaps on 'em."

"Well, I think I shall put you in coachy, on condition that you won't be drunk more than once a week, unless in cases of emergency, Tom."

Tom looked surprised, and rather hurt, and said, "I never drink, Mas'r."

"I 've heard that story before, Tom; but then we 'll see. It will be a special accommodation to all concerned, if you don't. Never mind, my boy," he added, good-humoredly, seeing Tom still looked grave; "I don't doubt you mean to do well."

"I sartin do, Mas'r," said Tom.

"And you shall have good times," said Eva. "Papa is very good to everybody, only he always will laugh at them."

"Papa is much obliged to you for his recommendation," said St. Clare, laughing, as he turned on his heel and walked away.

. . .

XVIII.

Miss Ophelia's Experiences and Opinions

Our friend Tom, in his own simple musings, often compared his more fortunate lot, in the bondage into which he was cast, with that of Joseph in Egypt;[12] and, in fact, as time went on, and he developed more and more under the eye of his master, the strength of the parallel increased.

---

[12]Genesis 37-50

St. Clare was indolent and careless of money. Hitherto the providing and marketing had been principally done by Adolph,[13] who was, to the full, as careless and extravagant as his master; and, between them both, they had carried on the dispersing process with great alacrity. Accustomed, for many years, to regard his master's property as his own care, Tom saw, with an uneasiness he could scarcely repress, the wasteful expenditure of the establishment; and, in the quiet, indirect way which his class often acquire, would sometimes make his own suggestions.

St. Clare at first employed him occasionally; but, struck with his soundness of mind and good business capacity, he confided in him more and more, till gradually all the marketing and providing for the family were intrusted to him.

"No, no, Adolph," he said, one day, as Adolph was deprecating the passing of power out of his hands; "let Tom alone. You only understand what you want; Tom understands cost and come to; and there may be some end to money, bye and bye if we don't let somebody do that."

Trusted to an unlimited extent by a careless master, who handed him a bill without looking at it, and pocketed the change without counting it, Tom had every facility and temptation to dishonesty; and nothing but an impregnable simplicity of nature, strengthened by Christian faith, could have kept him from it. But, to that nature, the very unbounded trust reposed in him was bond and seal for the most scrupulous accuracy.

With Adolph the case had been different. Thoughtless and self-indulgent, and unrestrained by a master who found it easier to indulge than to regulate, he had fallen into an absolute confusion as to *meum tuum*[14] with regard to himself and his master, which sometimes troubled even St. Clare. His own good sense taught him that such a training of his servants was unjust and dangerous. A sort of chronic remorse went with him everywhere, although not strong enough to make any decided change in his course; and this very remorse reäcted again into indulgence. He passed lightly over the most serious faults, because he told himself that, if he had done his part, his dependents had not fallen into them.

Tom regarded his gay, airy, handsome young master with an odd mixture of fealty, reverence, and fatherly solicitude. That he never read the Bible; never went to church; that he jested and made free with any and every thing that came in the way of his wit; that he spent his Sunday evenings at the opera or theatre; that he went to wine parties, and clubs, and suppers, oftener than was at all expedient,—were all things that Tom could see as plainly as anybody, and

---

[13]Adolph is the mulatto enslaved house servant of Augustine and Marie St. Clare.

[14]Stowe here refers to the phrase "*Quad tuum'st meum'st; omne est autem tuum*" (what is thine is mine, and all mine is thine) from *Trinummus* by Roman playwright Titus Maccius Plautus (254?–184 B.C.E.).

on which he based a conviction that "Mas'r was n't a Christian;"—a conviction, however, which he would have been very slow to express to any one else, but on which he founded many prayers, in his own simple fashion, when he was by himself in his little dormitory. Not that Tom had not his own way of speaking his mind occasionally, with something of the tact often observable in his class; as, for example, the very day after the Sabbath we have described, St. Clare was invited out to a convivial party of choice spirits, and was helped home, between one and two o'clock at night, in a condition when the physical had decided attained the upper hand of the intellectual. Tom and Adolph assisted to get him composed for the night, the latter in high spirits, evidently regarding the matter as a good joke, and laughing heartily at the rusticity of Tom's horror, who really was simple enough to lie awake most of the rest of the night, praying for his young master.

"Well, Tom, what are you waiting for?" said St. Clare, the next day, as he sat in his library, in dressing-gown and slippers. St. Clare had just been intrusting Tom with some money, and various commissions. "Is n't all right there, Tom?" he added, as Tom still stood waiting.

"I 'm 'fraid not, Mas'r," said Tom, with a grave face.

St. Clare laid down his paper, and set down his coffee-cup, and looked at Tom.

"Why, Tom, what 's the case? You look as solemn as a coffin."

"I feel very bad, Mas'r. I allays have thought that Mas'r would be good to everybody."

"Well, Tom, have n't I been? Come, now, what do you want? There 's something you have n't got, I suppose, and this is the preface."

"Mas'r allays been good to me. I have n't to complain of, on that head. But there is one that Mas'r is n't good to."

"Why, Tom, what 's got into you? Speak out; what do you mean?"

"Last night, between one and two, I thought so. I studied upon the matter then. Mas'r isn't good to *himself.*"

Tom said this with his back to his master, and his hand on the door-knob. St. Clare felt his face flush crimson, but he laughed.

"O, that's all, is it?" he said, gayly.

"All!" said Tom, turning suddenly round and falling on his knees. "O, my dear young Mas'r! I'm 'fraid it will be *loss of all—all—* body and soul. The good Book says, 'it biteth like a serpent and stingeth like an adder!'[15] my dear Mas'r!"

Tom's voice choked, and the tears ran down his cheeks.

"You poor, silly fool!" said St. Clare, with tears in his own eyes. "Get up, Tom. I 'm not worth crying over."

But Tom wouldn't rise, and looked imploring.

---

[15]Proverbs 23:31–32

"Well, I won't go to any more of their cursed nonsense, Tom," said St. Clare; "on my honor, I won't. I don't know why I have n't stopped long ago. I 've always despised *it*, and myself for it,—so now, Tom, wipe up your eyes, and go about your errands. Come, come," he added, "no blessings. I 'm not so wonderfully good, now," he said, as he gently pushed Tom to the door. "There, I 'll pledge my honor to you, Tom, you don't see me so again," he said; and Tom went off, wiping his eyes with great satisfaction.

"I 'll keep my faith with him, too," said St. Clare, as he closed the door.

And St. Clare did so,—for gross sensualism, in any form, was not the peculiar temptation of his nature.

But, all this time, who shall detail the tribulations manifold of our friend Miss Ophelia, who had begun the labors of a Southern housekeeper?

There is all the difference in the world in the servants of Southern establishments, according to the character and capacity of the mistresses who have brought them up.

South as well as north, there are women who have an extraordinary talent for command, and tact in educating. Such are enabled, with apparent ease, and without severity, to subject to their will, and bring into harmonious and systematic order, the various members of their small estate,—to regulate their peculiarities, and so balance and compensate the deficiencies of one by the excess of another, as to produce a harmonious and orderly system.

Such a housekeeper was Mrs. Shelby, whom we have already described; and such our readers may remember to have met with. If they are not common at the South, it is because they are not common in the world. They are to be found there as often as anywhere; and, when existing, find in that peculiar state of society a brilliant opportunity to exhibit their domestic talent.

Such a housekeeper Marie St. Clare was not, nor her mother before her. Indolent and childish, unsystematic and improvident, it was not to be expected that servants trained under her care should not be so likewise; and she had very justly described to Miss Ophelia the state of confusion she would find in the family, though she had not ascribed it to the proper cause.

The first morning of her regency, Miss Ophelia was up at four o'clock; and having attended to all the adjustments of her own chamber, as she had done ever since she came there, to the great amazement of the chamber-maid, she prepared for a vigorous onslaught on the cupboards and closets of the establishment of which she had the keys.

The store-room, the linen-presses, the china-closet, and kitchen and cellar, that day, all went under an awful review. Hidden things of darkness were brought to light to an extent that alarmed all the principalities and powers of kitchen and chamber, and caused many wonderings and murmurings about "dese yer northern ladies" from the domestic cabinet.

Old Dinah, the head cook, and principal of all rule and authority in the kitchen department, was filled with wrath at what she considered an invasion of privilege. No feudal baron in *Magna Charta*[16] times could have more thoroughly resented some incursion of the crown.

Dinah was a character in her own way, and it would be injustice to her memory not to give the reader a little idea of her. She was a native and essential cook, as much as Aunt Chloe,[17] — cooking being an indigenous talent of the African race; but Chloe was a trained and methodical one, who moved in an orderly domestic harness, while Dinah was a self-taught genius, and, like geniuses in general, was positive, opinionated and erratic, to the last degree.

Like a certain class of modern philosophers, Dinah perfectly scorned logic and reason in every shape, and always took refuge in intuitive certainty; and here she was perfectly impregnable. No possible amount of talent, or authority, or explanation, could ever make her believe that any other way was better than her own, or that the course she had pursued in the smallest matter could be in the least modified. This had been a conceded point with her old mistress, Marie's mother; and "Miss Marie," as Dinah always called her young mistress, even after her marriage, found it easier to submit than contend; and so Dinah had ruled supreme. This was the easier, in that she was perfect mistress of that diplomatic art which unites the utmost subservience of manner with the utmost inflexibility as to measure.

Dinah was mistress of the whole art and mystery of excuse-making, in all its branches. Indeed, it was an axiom with her that the cook can do no wrong; and a cook in a Southern kitchen finds abundance of heads and shoulders on which to lay off every sin and frailty, so as to maintain her own immaculateness entire. If any part of the dinner was a failure, there were fifty indisputably good reasons for it; and it was the fault undeniably of fifty other people, whom Dinah berated with unsparing zeal.

But it was very seldom that there was any failure in Dinah's last results. Though her mode of doing everything was peculiarly meandering and circuitous, and without any sort of calculation as to time and place,—though her kitchen generally looked as if it had been arranged by a hurricane blowing through it, and she had about as many places for each cooking utensil as there were days in the year,—yet, if one would have patience to wait her own good time, up would come her dinner in perfect order, and in a style of preparation with which an epicure[18] could find no fault.

It was now the season of incipient preparation for dinner. Dinah, who required large intervals of reflection and repose, and was studious of ease in all her arrangements, was seated on the kitchen floor, smoking a short, stumpy pipe, to which she was much addicted, and which she always kindled

---

[16]The *Magna Charta* (1215), a document from King John of England, indicated that people are legally protected from oppression by their king.

[17]"Aunt" Chloe is Tom's wife.

[18]An epicure is a person of fine taste in food and wine.

up, as a sort of censer, whenever she felt the need of an inspiration in her arrangements. It was Dinah's mode of invoking the domestic Muses.[19]

Seated around her were various members of that rising race with which a Southern household abounds, engaged in shelling peas, peeling potatoes, picking pin–feathers out of fowls, and other preparatory arrangements,— Dinah every once in a while interrupting her meditations to give a poke, or a rap on the head, to some of the young operators, with the pudding–stick that lay by her side. In fact, Dinah ruled over the woolly heads of the younger members with a rod of iron, and seemed to consider them born for no earthly purpose but to "save her steps," as she phrased it. It was the spirit of the system under which she had grown up, and she carried it out to its fullest extent.

Miss Ophelia, after passing on her reformatory tour through all the other parts of the establishment, now entered the kitchen. Dinah had heard, from various sources, what was going on, and resolved to stand on defensive and conservative ground,—mentally determined to oppose and ignore every new measure, without any actual and observable contest.

The kitchen was a large brick-floored apartment, with a great old-fashioned fireplace stretching along one side of it,—an arrangement which St. Clare had vainly tried to persuade Dinah to exchange for the convenience of a modern cookstove. Not she. No Puseyite,[20] or conservative of any school, was ever more inflexibly attached to time-honored inconveniencies than Dinah.

When St. Clare had first returned from the north, impressed with the system and order of his uncle's kitchen arrangements, he had largely provided his own with an array of cupboards, drawers, and various apparatus, to induce systematic regulation, under the sanguine illusion that it would be of any possible assistance to Dinah in her arrangements. He might as well have provided them for a squirrel or a magpie.[21] The more drawers and closets there were, the more hiding-holes could Dinah make for the accommodation of old rags, hair-combs, old shoes, ribbons, cast-off artificial flowers, and other articles of *vertu*,[22] wherein her soul delighted.

When Miss Ophelia entered the kitchen, Dinah did not rise, but smoked on in sublime tranquillity, regarding her movements obliquely out of the corner of her eye, but apparently intent only on the operations around her.

Miss Ophelia commenced opening a set of drawers.

---

[19]In Greek myth, the Muses are nine goddesses who oversee learning and creative arts.

[20]E. B. Pusey (1800–1882) was an English theologian who advocated a return to religious standards of the seventeenth century, and thus is associated with conservative, "high church" practices and doctrines.

[21]A magpie is a noisy bird of the crow family.

[22]*Vertu* signifies excellence in or excellent taste in art, or antiques—here used facetiously.

"What is this drawer for, Dinah?" she said.

"It 's handy for most anything, Missis," said Dinah. So it appeared to be. From the variety it contained, Miss Ophelia pulled out first a fine damask[23] table-cloth stained with blood, having evidently been used to envelop some raw meat.

"What 's this, Dinah? You don't wrap up meat in your mistress' best table-cloths?"

"O Lor, Missis, no; the towels was all a missin',—so I jest did it. I laid out to wash that ar,—that 's why I put it thar."

"Shif'less!" said Miss Ophelia to herself, proceeding to tumble over a drawer, where she found a nutmeg-grater and two or three nutmegs, a Methodist hymn-book, a couple of soiled Madras[24] handkerchiefs, some yarn and knitting-work, a paper of tobacco and a pipe, a few crackers, one or two gilded china-saucers with some pomade[25] in them, one or two thin old shoes, a piece of flannel carefully pinned up enclosing some small white onions, several damask table-napkins, some coarse crash[26] towels, some twine and darning-needles, and several broken papers, from which sundry sweet herbs were sifting into the drawer.

"Where do you keep your nutmegs, Dinah?" said Miss Ophelia, with the air of one who prayed for patience.

"Most anywhar, Missis; there 's some in that cracked teacup, up there, and there 's some over in that ar cupboard."

"Here are some in the grater," said Miss Ophelia, holding them up.

"Laws, yes, I put 'em there this morning,—I likes to keep my things handy," said Dinah. "You, Jake! what are you stopping for! You 'll cotch it! Be still, thar!" she added, with a dive of her stick at the criminal.

"What 's this?" said Miss Ophelia, holding up the saucer of pomade.

"Laws, it 's my har *grease;*—I put it thar to have it handy."

"Do you use your mistress' best saucers for that?"

"Law! it was cause I was driv, and in sich a hurry;—I was gwine to change it this very day."

"Here are two damask table-napkins."

"Them table-napkins I put thar, to get 'em washed out, some day."

"Don't you have some place here on purpose for things to be washed?"

"Well, Mas'r St. Clare got dat ar chest, he said, for dat; but I likes to mix up biscuit and hev my things on it some days, and then it an't handy a liftin' up the lid."

---

[23]Damask is a patterned silk fabric used for table linen.
[24]Madras is fine cotton fabric; the name comes from Madras, India.
[25]Pomade is a fragrant hair or scalp ointment.
[26]Crash is a coarse fabric.

"Why don't you mix your biscuits on the pastry-table, there?"

"Law, Missis, it gets sot so full of dishes, and one thing and another, der an't no room, noways—"

"But you should *wash* your dishes, and clear them right away."

"Wash my dishes!" said Dinah, in a high key, as her wrath began to rise over her habitual respect of manner; "what does ladies know 'bout work, I want to know? When 'd Mas'r ever get his dinner, if I was to spend all my time a washin' and a puttin' up dishes? Miss Marie never telled me so, nohow."

"Well, here are these onions."

"Laws, yes!" said Dinah; "thar *is* whar I put 'em, now. I could n't 'member. Them 's particular onions I was a savin' for dis yer very stew. I 'd forgot they was in dat ar old flannel."

Miss Ophelia lifted out the sifting papers of sweet herbs.

"I wish Missis would n't touch dem ar. I likes to keep my things where I knows whar to go to 'em," said Dinah, rather decidedly.

"But you don't want these holes in the papers."

"Them 's handy for siftin' on 't out," said Dinah.

"But you see it spills all over the drawer."

"Laws, yes! if Missis will go a tumblin' things all up so, it will. Missis has spilt lots dat ar way," said Dinah, coming uneasily to the drawers. "If Missis only will go up stars till my clarin' up time comes, I 'll have everything right; but I can't do nothin' when ladies is round, a henderin'. You, Sam, don't you gib the baby dat ar sugar-bowl! I 'll crack ye over, if ye don't mind!"

"I 'm going through the kitchen, and going to put everything in order, *once*, Dinah; and then I 'll expect you to *keep* it so."

"Lor, now! Miss Phelia; dat ar an't no way for ladies to do. I never did see ladies doin' no sich; my old Missis nor Miss Marie never did, and I don't see no kinder need on 't;" and Dinah stalked indignantly about, while Miss Ophelia piled and sorted dishes, emptied dozens of scattering bowls of sugar into one receptacle, sorted napkins, table-cloths, and towels, for washing; washing, wiping, and arranging with her own hands, and with a speed and alacrity which perfectly amazed Dinah.

"Lor, now! if dat ar de way dem northern ladies do, dey an't ladies, nohow," she said to some of her satellites, when at a safe hearing distance. "I has things as straight as anybody, when my clarin' up time comes; but I don't want ladies round, a henderin', and getting my things all where I can't find 'em."

To do Dinah justice, she had, at irregular periods, paroxysms of reformation and arrangement, which she called "clarin' up times," when she would begin with great zeal, and turn every drawer and closet wrong side outward, on to the floor or tables, and make the ordinary confusion seven-fold more confounded. Then she would light her pipe, and leisurely go over her arrangements, looking things over, and discoursing upon them; making all the young fry scour most vigorously on the tin things, and keeping up for several hours a most energetic state of confusion, which she would explain to the satisfaction of all inquirers, by the remark that she was a "clarin' up." "She could n't hev things a gwine on so as they had been, and she was gwine to make these yer young ones keep better order;" for Dinah herself, somehow, indulged the illusion that she, herself, was the soul of order, and it was only the *young uns,* and everybody else in the house, that were the cause of anything that fell short of perfection in this respect. When all the tins were scoured, and the tables scrubbed snowy white, and everything that could offend tucked out of sight in holes and corners, Dinah would dress herself up in a smart dress, clean apron, and high, brilliant Madras turban, and tell all marauding "young uns" to keep out of the kitchen, for she was gwine to have things kept nice. Indeed, these periodic seasons were often an inconvenience to the whole household; for Dinah would contract such an immoderate attachment to her scoured tin, as to insist upon it that it should n't be used again for any possible purpose—at least, till the ardor of the "clarin' up" period abated.

Miss Ophelia, in a few days, thoroughly reformed every department of the house to a systematic pattern; but her labors in all departments that depended on the coöperation of servants were like those of Sisyphus or the Danaides.[27] In despair, she one day appealed to St. Clare.

"There is no such thing as getting anything like system in this family!"

"To be sure, there is n't," said St. Clare.

"Such shiftless management, such waste, such confusion, I never saw!"

"I dare say you did n't."

"You would not take it so coolly, if you were housekeeper."

"My dear cousin, you may as well understand, once for all, that we masters are divided into two classes, oppressors and oppressed. We who are good-natured and hate severity make up our minds to a good deal of inconvenience. If we *will keep* a shambling, loose, untaught set in the community, for our convenience, why, we must take the consequence. Some rare cases I have seen, of persons, who, by a peculiar tact, can produce order and system without severity; but I 'm not one of them,—and so I made up my mind, long ago, to let things go just as they do. I will not have the poor devils thrashed and cut to pieces, and they know it,—and, of course, they know the staff is in their own hands."

"But to have no time, no place, no order,—all going on in this shiftless way!"

---

[27]In Greek myth, Sisyphus was the king of Corinth; in Hades he was forced to push uphill a heavy stone that would always roll back down. The Danaides were King Danaus's fifty daughters. Following their father's command, forty-nine of the daughters killed their husbands and were condemned to forever draw water with a sieve.

"My dear Vermont, you natives up by the North Pole set an extravagant value on time! What on earth is the use of time to a fellow who has twice as much of it as he knows what to do with? As to order and system, where there is nothing to be done but to lounge on the sofa and read, an hour sooner or later in breakfast or dinner is n't of much account. Now, there 's Dinah gets you a capital dinner,—soup, ragout, roast fowl, dessert, ice-creams and all,—and she creates it all out of chaos and old night down there, in that kitchen. I think it really sublime, the way she manages. But, Heaven bless us! if we are to go down there, and view all the smoking and squatting about, and hurryscurryation of the preparatory process, we should never eat more! My good cousin, absolve yourself from that! It 's more than a Catholic penance, and does no more good. You 'll only lose your own temper, and utterly confound Dinah. Let her go her own way."

"But, Augustine, you don't know how I found things."

"Don't I? Don't I know that the rolling-pin is under her bed, and the nutmeg-grinder in her pocket with her tobacco,—that there are sixty-five different sugar-bowls, one in every hole in the house,—that she washes dishes with a dinner-napkin one day, and with a fragment of an old petticoat the next? But the upshot is, she gets up glorious dinners, makes superb coffee; and you must judge her as warriors and statesmen are judged, by *her success.*"

"But the waste,—the expense!"

"O, well! Lock everything you can, and keep the key. Give out by driblets, and never inquire for odds and ends,—it is n't the best."

"That troubles me, Augustine. I can't help feeling as if these servants were not *strictly honest.* Are you sure they can be relied on?"

Augustine laughed immoderately at the grave and anxious face with which Miss Ophelia propounded the question.

"O, cousin, that 's too good,—*honest!*—as if that 's a thing to be expected! Honest!—why, of course, they arn't. Why should they be? What upon earth is to make them so?"

"Why don't you instruct?"

"Instruct! O, fiddlestick! What instructing do you think I should do? I look like it! As to Marie, she has spirit enough, to be sure, to kill off a whole plantation, if I 'd let her manage; but she would n't get the cheatery out of them."

"Are there no honest ones?"

"Well, now and then one, whom Nature makes so impracticably simple, truthful and faithful, that the worst possible influence can't destroy it. But, you see, from the mother's breast the colored child feels and sees that there are none but underhand ways open to it. It can get along no other way with its parents, its mistress, its young master and missie playfellows. Cunning and deception become necessary, inevitable habits. It is n't fair to expect anything else of him. He ought not to be punished for it. As to honesty, the slave is kept in that dependent, semi-childish state, that there is no making him realize the rights of property, or feel that his master's goods are not his own, if he can get them. For my part, I don't see how they *can* be honest. Such a fellow as Tom, here, is—is a moral miracle!"

"And what becomes of their souls?" said Miss Ophelia.

"That is n't my affair, as I know of," said St. Clare; "I am only dealing in facts of the present life. The fact is, that the whole race are pretty generally understood to be turned over to the devil, for our benefit, in this world, however it may turn out in another!"

"This is perfectly horrible!" said Miss Ophelia; "you ought to be ashamed of yourselves!"

"I don't know as I am. We are in pretty good company, for all that," said St. Clare, "as people in the broad road generally are. Look at the high and the low, all the world over, and it 's the same story,—the lower class used up, body, soul and spirit, for the good of the upper. It is so in England; it is so everywhere; and yet all Christendom stands aghast, with virtuous indignation, because we do the thing in a little different shape from what they do it."

"It is n't so in Vermont."

"Ah, well, in New England, and in the free States, you have the better of us, I grant. But there 's the bell; so, Cousin, let us for a while lay aside our sectional prejudices, and come out to dinner."

As Miss Ophelia was in the kitchen in the latter part of the afternoon, some of the sable children called out, "La, sakes! that 's Prue a coming, grunting along like she allers does."

A tall, bony colored woman now entered the kitchen, bearing on her head a basket of rusks[28] and hot rolls.

"Ho, Prue! you 've come," said Dinah.

Prue had a peculiar scowling expression of countenance, and a sullen, grumbling voice. She set down her basket, squatted herself down, and resting her elbows on her knees, said,

"O Lord! I wish 't I 's dead!"

"Why do you wish you were dead?" said Miss Ophelia.

"I 'd be out o' my misery," said the woman, gruffly, without taking her eyes from the floor.

"What need you getting drunk, then, and cutting up, Prue?" said a spruce quadroon chambermaid, dangling, as she spoke, a pair of coral ear-drops.

The woman looked at her with a sour, surly glance.

"Maybe you 'll come to it, one of these yer days. I 'd be glad to see you, I would; then you 'll be glad of a drop, like me, to forget your misery."

"Come, Prue," said Dinah, "let 's look at your rusks. Here 's Missis will pay for them."

---

[28]Rusks are soft, sweetened biscuits.

Miss Ophelia took out a couple of dozen.

"Thar 's some tickets in that ar old cracked jug on the top shelf," said Dinah. "You, Jake, climb up and get it down."

"Tickets, —what are they for?" said Miss Ophelia.

"We buys tickets of her Mas'r, and she gives us bread for 'em."

"And they counts my money and tickets, when I gets home, to see if I 's got the change; and if I han't, they half kills me."

"And serves you right," said Jane, the pert chambermaid, "if you will take their money to get drunk on. That 's what she does, Missis."

"And that 's what I *will* do, —I can't live no other ways, —drink and forget my misery."

"You are very wicked and very foolish," said Miss Ophelia, "to steal your master's money to make yourself a brute with."

"It 's mighty likely, Missis; but I will do it, —yes, I will. O Lord! I wish I 's dead, I do, —I wish I 's dead, and out of my misery!" and slowly and stiffly the old creature rose, and got her basket on her head again; but before she went out, she looked at the quadroon girl, who still stood playing with her ear-drops.

"Ye think ye 're mighty fine with them ar, frolickin' and a tossin' your head, and a lookin' down on everybody. Well, never mind, —you may live to be a poor, old, cut-up crittur, like me. Hope to the Lord ye will, I do; then see if ye won't drink, —drink, —drink, —yerself into torment; and sarve ye right, too —ugh!" and, with a malignant howl, the woman left the room.

"Disgusting old beast!" said Adolph, who was getting his master's shaving-water. "If I was her master, I 'd cut her up worse than she is."

"Ye could n't do that ar, no ways," said Dinah. "Her back 's a far sight now, —she can't never get a dress together over it."

"I think such low creatures ought not to be allowed to go round to gen-teel families," said Miss Jane. "What do you think, Mr. St. Clare?" she said, coquettishly tossing her head at Adolph.

It must be observed that, among other appropriations from his master's stock, Adolph was in the habit of adopting his name and address; and that the style under which he moved, among the colored circles of New Orleans, was that of *Mr. St. Clare.*

"I 'm certainly of your opinion, Miss Benoir," said Adolph.

Benoir was the name of Marie St. Clare's family, and Jane was one of her servants.

"Pray, Miss Benoir, may I be allowed to ask if those drops are for the ball, tomorrow night? They are certainly bewitching!"

"I wonder, now, Mr. St. Clare, what the impudence of you men will come to!" said Jane, tossing her pretty head till the ear-drops twinkled again. "I shan't dance with you for a whole evening, if you go to asking me any more questions."

"O, you could n't be so cruel, now! I was just dying to know whether you would appear in your pink tarletane,"[29] said Adolph.

"What is it?" said Rosa, a bright, piquant little quadroon, who came skipping down stairs at this moment.

"Why, Mr. St. Clare's so impudent!"

"On my honor," said Adolph, "I'll leave it to Miss Rosa, now."

"I know he's always a saucy creature," said Rosa, poising herself on one of her little feet, and looking maliciously at Adolph. "He's always getting me so angry with him."

"O! ladies, ladies, you will certainly break my heart, between you," said Adolph. "I shall be found dead in my bed, some morning, and you'll have it to answer for."

"Do hear the horrid creature talk!" said both ladies, laughing immoderately.

"Come, — clar out, you! I can't have you cluttering up the kitchen," said Dinah; "in my way, foolin' round here."

"Aunt Dinah's glum, because she can't go to the ball," said Rosa.

"Don't want none o' your light-colored balls," said Dinah; "cuttin' round, makin' b'lieve you's white folks. Arter all, you's niggers, much as I am."

"Aunt Dinah greases her wool stiff, every day, to make it lie straight," said Jane.

"And it will be wool, after all," said Rosa, maliciously shaking down her long, silky curls.

"Well, in the Lord's sight, an't wool as good as har, any time?" said Dinah. "I'd like to have Missis say which is worth the most, — a couple such as you, or one like me. Get out wid ye, ye trumpery, — I won't have ye round!"

Here the conversation was interrupted in a two-fold manner. St. Clare's voice was heard at the head of the stairs, asking Adolph if he meant to stay all night with his shaving-water; and Miss Ophelia, coming out of the dining–room, said,

"Jane and Rosa, what are you wasting your time for, here? Go in and attend to your muslins."[30]

Our friend Tom, who had been in the kitchen during the conversation with the old rusk-woman, had followed her out into the street. He saw her go on, giving every once in a while a suppressed groan. At last she set her basket down on a door-step, and began arranging the old, faded shawl which covered her shoulders.

"I'll carry your basket a piece," said Tom, compassionately.

"Why should ye?" said the woman. "I don't want no help."

---

[29]A tarletane is a dress made of a sheer cotton fabric.

[30]Muslin is a plain-woven cotton fabric.

"You seem to be sick, or in trouble, or somethin'," said Tom.

"I an't sick," said the woman, shortly.

"I wish," said Tom, looking at her earnestly,—"I wish I could persuade you to leave off drinking. Don't you know it will be the ruin of ye, body and soul?"

"I knows I'm gwine to torment," said the woman, sullenly. "Ye don't need to tell me that ar. I's ugly,—I's wicked,—I's gwine straight to torment. O, Lord! I wish I's thar!"

Tom shuddered at these frightful words, spoken with a sullen, impassioned earnestness.

"O, Lord have mercy on ye! poor crittur. Han't ye never heard of Jesus Christ?"

"Jesus Christ,—who's he?"

"Why, he's *the Lord*," said Tom.

"I think I've hearn tell o' the Lord, and the judgment and torment. I've heard o' that."

"But did n't anybody ever tell you of the Lord Jesus, that loved us poor sinners, and died for us?"

"Don't know nothin' 'bout that," said the woman; "nobody han't never loved me, since my old man died."

"Where was you raised?" said Tom.

"Up in Kentuck. A man kept me to breed chil'en for market, and sold 'em as fast as they got big enough; last of all, he sold me to a speculator, and my Mas'r got me o' him."

"What set you into this bad way of drinkin'?"

"To get shet o' my misery. I had one child after I come here; and I thought then I'd have one to raise, cause Mas'r was n't a speculator. It was de peartest little thing! and Missis she seemed to think a heap on 't, at first; it never cried,—it was likely and fat. But Missis tuck sick, and I tended her; and I tuck the fever, and my milk all left me, and the child it pined to skin and bone, and Missis would n't buy milk for it. She would n't hear to me, when I telled her I had n't milk. She said she knowed I could feed it on what other folks eat; and the child kinder pined, and cried, and cried, and cried, day and night, and got all gone to skin and bones, and Missis got sot agin it, and she said 't wan't nothin' but crossness. She wished it was dead, she said; and she would n't let me have it o' nights, cause, she said, it kept me awake, and made me good for nothing. She made me sleep in her room; and I had to put it away off in a little kind o' garret, and thar it cried itself to death, one night. It did; and I tuck to drinkin', to keep its crying out of my ears! I did,—and I will drink! I will, if I do go to torment for it! Mas'r says I shall go to torment, and I tell him I've got thar now!"

"O, ye poor crittur!" said Tom, "han't nobody never telled ye how the Lord Jesus loved ye, and died for ye? Han't they telled ye that he'll help ye, and ye can go to heaven, and have rest, at last?"

"I looks like gwine to heaven," said the woman; "an't thar where white folks is gwine? S'pose they'd have me thar? I'd rather go to torment, and get away from Mas'r and Missis. I had *so*," she said, as, with her usual groan, she got her basket on her head, and walked sullenly away.

Tom turned, and walked sorrowfully back to the house. In the court he met little Eva,—a crown of tuberoses[31] on her head, and her eyes radiant with delight.

"O, Tom! here you are. I'm glad I've found you. Papa says you may get out the ponies, and take me in my little new carriage," she said, catching his hand. "But what's the matter, Tom?—you look sober."

"I feel bad, Miss Eva," said Tom, sorrowfully. "But I'll get the horses for you."

"But do tell me, Tom, what is the matter. I saw you talking to cross old Prue."

Tom, in simple, earnest phrase, told Eva the woman's history. She did not exclaim, or wonder, or weep, as other children do. Her cheeks grew pale, and a deep, earnest shadow passed over her eyes. She laid both hands on her bosom, and sighed heavily.

Volume II

XIX.

Miss Ophelia's Experiences and Opinions, Continued

"Tom, you need n't get me the horses. I don't want to go," she said.

"Why not, Miss Eva?"

"These things sink into my heart, Tom," said Eva,—"they sink into my heart," she repeated, earnestly. "I don't want to go;" and she turned from Tom, and went into the house.

A few days after, another woman came, in old Prue's place, to bring the rusks; Miss Ophelia was in the kitchen.

"Lor!" said Dinah, "what's got Prue?"

"Prue isn't coming any more," said the woman, mysteriously.

"Why not?" said Dinah. "She an't dead, is she?"

"We does n't exactly know. She's down cellar," said the woman, glancing at Miss Ophelia.

After Miss Ophelia had taken the rusks, Dinah followed the woman to the door.

"What *has* got Prue, any how?" she said.

---

[31]A tuberose is a white, lilylike flower.

The woman seemed desirous, yet reluctant, to speak, and answered, in a low, mysterious tone.

"Well, you must n't tell nobody. Prue, she got drunk agin,—and they had her down cellar,—and thar they left her all day,—and I hearn 'em saying that the *flies had got to her,*—and *she 's dead!*"

Dinah held up her hands, and, turning, saw close by her side the spirit-like form of Evangeline, her large, mystic eyes dilated with horror, and every drop of blood driven from her lips and cheeks.

"Lor bless us! Miss Eva 's gwine to faint away! What got us all, to let her har such talk? Her pa 'll be rail mad."

"I shan't faint, Dinah," said the child, firmly; "and why should n't I hear it? It an't so much for me to hear it, as for poor Prue to suffer it."

"*Lor sakes!* it is n't for sweet, delicate young ladies like you,—these yer stories is n't; it 's enough to kill 'em!"

Eva sighed again, and walked up stairs with a slow and melancholy step.

Miss Ophelia anxiously inquired the woman's story. Dinah gave a very garrulous version of it, to which Tom added the particulars which he had drawn from her that morning.

"An abominable business,—perfectly horrible!" she exclaimed, as she entered the room where St. Clare lay reading his paper.

"Pray, what iniquity has turned up now?" said he.

"What now? why, those folks have whipped Prue to death!" said Miss Ophelia, going on, with great strength of detail, into the story, and enlarging on its most shocking particulars.

"I thought it would come to that, some time," said St. Clare, going on with his paper.

"Thought so!—an't you going to *do* anything about it?" said Miss Ophelia. "Have n't you got any *selectmen,*[32] or anybody, to interfere and look after such matters?"

"It 's commonly supposed that the *property* interest is a sufficient guard in these cases. If people choose to ruin their own possessions, I don't know what 's to be done. It seems the poor creature was a thief and a drunkard; and so there won't be much hope to get up sympathy for her."

"It is perfectly outrageous,—it is horrid, Augustine! It will certainly bring down vengeance upon you."

"My dear cousin, I did n't do it, and I can't help it; I would, if I could. If low-minded, brutal people will act like themselves, what am I to do? They have absolute control; they are irresponsible despots. There would be no use in interfering; there is no law that amounts to anything practically, for such a case. The best we can do is to shut our eyes and ears, and let it alone. It 's the only resource left us."

---

[32]A selectman is a town officer—associated with New England town practices.

"How can you shut your eyes and ears? How can you let such things alone?"

"My dear child, what do you expect? Here is a whole class,—debased, uneducated, indolent, provoking,—put, without any sort of terms or conditions, entirely into the hands of such people as the majority in our world are; people who have neither consideration nor self-control, who have n't even an enlightened regard to their own interest,—for that 's the case with the largest half of mankind. Of course, in a community so organized, what can a man of honorable and humane feelings do, but shut his eyes all he can, and harden his heart? I can't buy every poor wretch I see. I can't turn knight-errant, and undertake to redress every individual case of wrong in such a city as this. The most I can do is to try and keep out of the way of it."

St. Clare's fine countenance was for a moment overcast; he looked annoyed, but suddenly calling up a gay smile, he said,

"Come, cousin, don't stand there looking like one of the Fates;[33] you 've only seen a peep through the curtain,—a specimen of what is going on, the world over, in some shape or other. If we are to be prying and spying into all the dismals of life, we should have no heart to anything. 'T is like looking too close into the details of Dinah's kitchen;" and St. Clare lay back on the sofa, and busied himself with his paper.

Miss Ophelia sat down, and pulled out her knitting-work, and sat there grim with indignation. She knit and knit, but while she mused the fire burned; at last she broke out—

"I tell you, Augustine, I can't get over things so, if you can. It 's a perfect abomination for you to defend such a system,—that 's *my* mind!"

"What now?" said St. Clare, looking up. "At it again, hey?"

"I say it 's perfectly abominable for you to defend such a system!" said Miss Ophelia, with increasing warmth.

"*I* defend it, my dear lady? Who ever said I did defend it?" said St. Clare.

"Of course, you defend it,—you all do,—all you Southerners. What do you have slaves for, if you don't?"

"Are you such a sweet innocent as to suppose nobody in this world ever does what they don't think is right? Don't you, or did n't you ever, do anything that you did not think quite right?"

"If I do, I repent of it, I hope," said Miss Ophelia, rattling her needles with energy.

"So, do I," said St. Clare, peeling his orange; "I 'm repenting of it all the time."

"What do you keep on doing it for?"

"Did n't you ever keep on doing wrong, after you 'd repented, my good cousin?"

---

[33]In Greek and Roman myth, the three Fates were Clotho, Lachesis, and Atropos; they controlled human destiny.

"Well, only when I 've been very much tempted," said Miss Ophelia.

"Well, I 'm very much tempted," said St. Clare; "that 's just my difficulty."

"But I always resolve I won't, and I try to break off."

"Well, I have been resolving I won't, off and on, these ten years," said St. Clare; "but I have n't, some how, got clear. Have you got clear of all your sins, cousin?"

"Cousin Augustine," said Miss Ophelia, seriously, and laying down her knitting-work. "I suppose I deserve that you should reprove my short-comings. I know all you say is true enough; nobody else feels them more than I do; but it does seem to me, after all, there is some difference between me and you. It seems to me I would cut off my right hand sooner than keep on, from day to day, doing what I thought was wrong. But, then, my conduct is so inconsistent with my profession, I don't wonder you reprove me."

"O, now, cousin," said Augustine, sitting down on the floor, and laying his head back in her lap, "don't take on so awfully serious! You know what a good-for-nothing, saucy boy I always was. I love to poke you up,—that 's all,—just to see you get earnest. I do think you are desperately, distressingly good; it tires me to death to think of it."

"But this is a serious subject, my boy, Auguste," said Miss Ophelia, laying her hand on his forehead.

"Dismally so," said he; "and I—well, I never want to talk seriously in hot weather. What with mosquitos and all, a fellow can't get himself up to any very sublime moral flights; and I believe," said St. Clare, suddenly rousing himself up, "there 's a theory, now! I understand now why northern nations are always more virtuous than southern ones,—I see into that whole subject."

"O, Auguste, you are a sad rattle-brain!"

"Am I? Well, so I am, I suppose; but for once I will be serious, now; but you must hand me that basket of oranges;—you see, you 'll have to 'stay me with flagons and comfort me with apples,'[34] if I 'm going to make this effort. Now," said Augustine, drawing the basket up, "I 'll begin: When, in the course of human events,[35] it becomes necessary for a fellow to hold two or three dozen of his fellow-worms in captivity, a decent regard to the opinions of society requires—"

"I don't see that you are growing more serious," said Miss Ophelia.

"Wait,—I 'm coming on,—you 'll hear. The short of the matter is, cousin," said he, his handsome face suddenly settling into an earnest and serious expression, "on this abstract question of slavery there can, as I think, be but one opinion. Planters, who have money to make by it,—clergymen, who have planters to please,—politicians, who want to rule by it,—may warp and bend language and ethics to a degree that shall astonish the world at their

---

[34]Song of Solomon 2:5

[35]From the Declaration of Independence.

ingenuity; they can press nature and the Bible, and nobody knows what else, into the service; but, after all, neither they nor the world believe in it one particle the more. It comes from the devil, that 's the short of it;—and, to my mind, it 's a pretty respectable specimen of what he can do in his own line."

Miss Ophelia stopped her knitting, and looked surprised; and St. Clare, apparently enjoying her astonishment, went on.

"You seem to wonder; but if you will get me fairly at it, I 'll make a clean breast of it. This cursed business, accursed of God and man, what is it? Strip it of all its ornament, run it down to the root and nucleus of the whole, and what is it? Why, because my brother Quashy[36] is ignorant and weak, and I am intelligent and strong,—because I know how, and *can* do it,—therefore, I may steal all he has, keep it, and give him only such and so much as suits my fancy. Whatever is too hard, too dirty, too disagreeable, for me, I may set Quashy to doing. Because I don't like work, Quashy shall work. Because the sun burns me, Quashy shall stay in the sun. Quashy shall earn the money, and I will spend it. Quashy shall lie down in every puddle, that I may walk over dry-shod. Quashy shall do my will, and not his, all the days of his mortal life, and have such chance of getting to heaven, at last, as I find convenient. This I take to be about what slavery *is*. I defy anybody on earth to read our slave-code, as it stands in our law-books, and make anything else of it. Talk of the *abuses* of slavery! Humbug! The *thing itself* is the essence of all abuse! And the only reason why the land don't sink under it, like Sodom and Gomorrah,[37] is because it is *used* in a way infinitely better than it is. For pity's sake, for shame's sake, because we are men born of women, and not savage beasts, many of us do not, and dare not,—we would *scorn* to use the full power which our savage laws put into our hands. And he who goes the furthest, and does the worst, only uses within limits the power that the law gives him."

St. Clare had started up, and, as his manner was when excited, was walking, with hurried steps, up and down the floor. His fine face, classic as that of a Greek statue, seemed actually to burn with the fervor of his feelings. His large blue eyes flashed, and he gestured with an unconscious eagerness. Miss Ophelia had never seen him in this mood before, and she sat perfectly silent.

"I declare to you," said he, suddenly stopping before his cousin "(it 's no sort of use to talk or to feel on this subject), but I declare to you, there have been times when I have thought, if the whole country would sink, and hide all this injustice and misery from the light, I would willingly sink with it. When I have been travelling up and down on our boats, or about on my collecting tours, and reflected that every brutal, disgusting, mean, low–lived fellow I met, was allowed by our laws to become absolute despot of as many

---

[36]Quashy is a generic, racist designation, like Sambo, for enslaved black people.
[37]Genesis 18-19

35

men, women and children, as he could cheat, steal, or gamble money enough to buy,—when I have seen such men in actual ownership of helpless children, of young girls and women,—I have been ready to curse my country, to curse the human race!"

"Augustine! Augustine!" said Miss Ophelia, "I 'm sure you 've said enough. I never, in my life, heard anything like this, even at the North."

"At the North!" said St. Clare, with a sudden change of expression, and resuming something of his habitual careless tone. "Pooh! your northern folks are cold-blooded; you are cool in everything! You can't begin to curse up hill and down as we can, when we get fairly at it."

"Well, but the question is," said Miss Ophelia.

"O, yes, to be sure, the *question is*,—and a deuce of a question it is! How came *you* in this state of sin and misery? Well, I shall answer in the good old words you used to teach me, Sundays. I came so by ordinary generation. My servants were my father's, and, what is more, my mother's; and now they are mine, they and their increase, which bids fair to be a pretty considerable item. My father, you know, came first from New England; and he was just such another man as your father,—a regular old Roman[38]—upright, energetic, noble-minded, with an iron will. Your father settled down in New England, to rule over rocks and stones, and to force an existence out of Nature; and mine settled in Louisiana, to rule over men and women, and force existence out of them. My mother," said St. Clare, getting up and walking to a picture at the end of the room, and gazing upward with a face fervent with veneration, "*she* was *divine*! Don't look at me so!—you know what I mean! She probably was of mortal birth; but, as far as ever I could observe, there was no trace of any human weakness or error about her; and everybody that lives to remember her, whether bond or free, servant, acquaintance, relation, all say the same. Why, cousin, that mother has been all that has stood between me and utter unbelief for years. She was a direct embodiment and personification of the New Testament,—a living fact, to be accounted for, and to be accounted for in no other way than by its truth. O, mother! mother!" said St. Clare, clasping his hands, in a sort of transport; and then suddenly checking himself, he came back, and seating himself on an ottoman, he went on:

"My brother and I were twins; and they say, you know, that twins ought to resemble each other; but we were in all points a contrast. He had black, fiery eyes, coal-black hair, a strong, fine Roman profile, and a rich brown complexion. I had blue eyes, golden hair, a Greek outline, and fair complexion. He was active and observing, I dreamy and inactive. He was generous to his friends and equals, but proud, dominant, overbearing, to inferiors, and

---

[38]Augustine indicates what was usually meant by Roman: "upright, energetic, noble-minded, with an iron will." Strong but domineering.

utterly unmerciful to whatever set itself up against him. Truthful we both were; he from pride and courage, I from a sort of abstract ideality. We loved each other about as boys generally do,—off and on, and in general;—he was my father's pet, and I my mother's.

"There was a morbid sensitiveness and acuteness of feeling in me on all possible subjects, of which he and my father had no kind of understanding, and with which they could have no possible sympathy. But mother did; and so, when I had quarrelled with Alfred, and father looked sternly on me, I used to go off to mother's room, and sit by her. I remember just how she used to look, with her pale cheeks, her deep, soft, serious eyes, her white dress,—she always wore white; and I used to think of her whenever I read in Revelations about the saints that were arrayed in fine linen, clean and white. She had a great deal of genius of one sort and another, particularly in music; and she used to sit at her organ, playing fine old majestic music of the Catholic church, and singing with a voice more like an angel than a mortal woman; and I would lay my head down on her lap, and cry, and dream, and feel,—oh, immeasurably!—things that I had no language to say!

"In those days, this matter of slavery had never been canvassed as it has now; nobody dreamed of any harm in it.

"My father was a born aristocrat. I think, in some preëxistent state, he must have been in the higher circles of spirits, and brought all his old court pride along with him; for it was ingrain, bred in the bone, though he was originally of poor and not in any way of noble family. My brother was begotten in his image.

"Now, an aristocrat, you know, the world over, has no human sympathies, beyond a certain line in society. In England the line is in one place, in Burmah[39] in another, and in America in another; but the aristocrat of all these countries never goes over it. What would be hardship and distress and injustice in his own class, is a cool matter of course in another one. My father's dividing line was that of color. *Among his equals,* never was a man more just and generous; but he considered the negro, through all possible gradations of color, as an intermediate link between man and animals, and graded all his ideas of justice or generosity on this hypothesis. I suppose, to be sure, if anybody had asked him, plump and fair, whether they had human immortal souls, he might have hemmed and hawed, and said yes. But my father was not a man much troubled with spiritualism; religious sentiment he had none, beyond a veneration for God, as decidedly the head of the upper classes.

"Well, my father worked some five hundred negroes; he was an inflexible, driving, punctilious business man; everything was to move by system,—to be sustained with unfailing accuracy and precision. Now, if you take into account that all this was to be worked out by a set of lazy, twaddling,

---

[39] Burma is a country in southeast Asia.

shiftless laborers, who had grown up, all their lives, in the absence of every possible motive to learn how to do anything but 'shirk,' as you Vermonters say, and you'll see that there might naturally be, on his plantation, a great many things that looked horrible and distressing to a sensitive child, like me.

"Besides all, he had an overseer,—a great, tall, slab-sided, two-fisted renegade son of Vermont—(begging your pardon),—who had gone through a regular apprenticeship in hardness and brutality, and taken his degree to be admitted to practice. My mother never could endure him, nor I; but he obtained an entire ascendency over my father; and this man was the absolute despot of the estate.

"I was a little fellow then, but I had the same love that I have now for all kinds of human things,—a kind of passion for the study of humanity, come in what shape it would. I was found in the cabins and among the field-hands a great deal, and, of course, was a great favorite; and all sorts of complaints and grievances were breathed in my ear; and I told them to my mother, and we, between us, formed a sort of committee for a redress of grievances. We hindered and repressed a great deal of cruelty, and congratulated ourselves on doing a vast deal of good, till, as often happens, my zeal overacted. Stubbs complained to my father that he could n't manage the hands, and must resign his position. Father was a fond, indulgent husband, but a man that never flinched from anything that he thought necessary; and so he put down his foot, like a rock, between us and the field-hands. He told my mother, in language perfectly respectful and deferential, but quite explicit, that over the house-servants she should be entire mistress, but that with the field-hands he could allow no interference. He revered and respected her above all living beings; but he would have said it all the same to the virgin Mary herself, if she had come in the way of his system.

"I used sometimes to hear my mother reasoning cases with him,—endeavoring to excite his sympathies. He would listen to the most pathetic appeals with the most discouraging politeness and equanimity. 'It all resolves itself into this,' he would say; 'must I part with Stubbs, or keep him? Stubbs is the soul of punctuality, honesty, and efficiency,—a thorough business hand, and as humane as the general run. We can't have perfection; and if I keep him, I must sustain his administration as a *whole*, even if there are, now and then, things that are exceptionable. All government includes some necessary hardness. General rules will bear hard on particular cases.' This last maxim my father seemed to consider a settler in most alleged cases of cruelty. After he had said *that,* he commonly drew up his feet on the sofa, like a man that has disposed of a business, and betook himself to a nap, or the newspaper, as the case might be.

"The fact is, my father showed the exact sort of talent for a statesman. He could have divided Poland as easily as an orange, or trod on Ireland as quietly and systematically as any man living. At last my mother gave up, in despair. It never will be known, till the last account, what noble and sensitive natures like hers have felt, cast, utterly helpless, into what seems to them an abyss of injustice and cruelty, and which seems so to nobody about them. It has been an age of long sorrow of such natures, in such a hell-begotten sort of world as ours. What remained for her, but to train her children in her own views and sentiments? Well, after all you say about training, children will grow up substantially what they *are* by nature, and only that. From the cradle, Alfred was an aristocrat; and as he grew up, instinctively, all his sympathies and all his reasonings were in that line, and all mother's exhortations went to the winds. As to me, they sunk deep into me. She never contradicted, in form, anything that my father said, or seemed directly to differ from him; but she impressed, burnt into my very soul, with all the force of her deep, earnest nature, an idea of the dignity and worth of the meanest human soul. I have looked in her face with solemn awe, when she would point up to the stars in the evening, and say to me, 'See there, Auguste! the poorest, meanest soul on our place will be living, when all these stars are gone forever,—will live as long as God lives!'

"She had some fine old paintings; one, in particular, of Jesus healing a blind man.[40] They were very fine, and used to impress me strongly. 'See there, Auguste,' she would say; 'the blind man was a beggar, poor and loathsome; therefore, he would not heal him *afar off*! He called him to him, and put *his hands on him*! Remember this, my boy.' If I had lived to grow up under her care, she might have stimulated me to I know not what of enthusiasm. I might have been a saint, reformer, martyr,—but, alas! alas! I went from her when I was only thirteen, and I never saw her again!"

St. Clare rested his head on his hands, and did not speak for some minutes. After a while, he looked up, and went on:

"What poor, mean trash this whole business of human virtue is! A mere matter, for the most part, of latitude and longitude, and geographical position, acting with natural temperament. The greater part is nothing but an accident. Your father, for example, settles in Vermont, in a town where all are, in fact, free and equal; becomes a regular church member and deacon, and in due time joins an Abolition society, and thinks us all little better than heathens. Yet he is, for all the world, in constitution and habit, a duplicate of my father. I can see it leaking out in fifty different ways,—just that same strong, overbearing, dominant spirit. You know very well how impossible it is to persuade some of the folks in your village that Squire Sinclair does not feel above them. The fact is, though he has fallen on democratic times, and embraced a democratic theory, he is to the heart an aristocrat, as much as my father, who ruled over five or six hundred slaves."

---

[40]See John 9.

Miss Ophelia felt rather disposed to cavil at this picture, and was laying down her knitting to begin, but St. Clare stopped her.

"Now, I know every word you are going to say. I do not say they *were* alike, in fact. One fell into a condition where everything acted against the natural tendency, and the other where everything acted for it; and so one turned out a pretty wilful, stout, overbearing old democrat, and the other a wilful, stout old despot. If both had owned plantations in Louisiana, they would have been as like as two old bullets cast in the same mould."

"What an undutiful boy you are!" said Miss Ophelia.

"I don't mean them any disrespect," said St. Clare. "You know reverence is not my forte. But, to go back to my history:

"When father died, he left the whole property to us twin boys, to be divided as we should agree. There does not breathe on God's earth a nobler-souled, more generous fellow, than Alfred, in all that concerns his equals; and we got on admirably with this property question, without a single unbrotherly word or feeling. We undertook to work the plantation together; and Alfred, whose outward life and capabilities had double the strength of mine, became an enthusiastic planter, and a wonderfully successful one.

"But two years' trial satisfied me that I could not be a partner in that matter. To have a great gang of seven hundred, whom I could not know personally, or feel any individual interest in, bought and driven, housed, fed, worked like so many horned cattle, strained up to military precision,—the question of how little of life's commonest enjoyments would keep them in working order being a constantly recurring problem,—the *necessity* of drivers and overseers,—the ever-necessary whip, first, last, and only argument,—the whole thing was insufferably disgusting and loathsome to me; and when I thought of my mother's estimate of one poor human soul, it became even frightful!

"It's all nonsense to talk to me about slaves *enjoying* all this! To this day, I have no patience with the unutterable trash that some of your patronizing Northerners have made up, as in their zeal to apologize for our sins. We all know better. Tell me that any man living wants to work all his days, from day-dawn till dark, under the constant eye of a master, without the power of putting forth one irresponsible volition, on the same dreary, monotonous, unchanging toil, and all for two pairs of pantaloons and a pair of shoes a year, with enough food and shelter to keep him in working order! Any man who thinks that human beings can, as a general thing, be made about as comfortable that way as any other, I wish he might try it. I 'd buy the dog, and work him, with a clear conscience!"

"I always have supposed," said Miss Ophelia, "that you, all of you, approved of these things, and thought them *right*,—according to Scripture."

"Humbug! We are not quite reduced to that yet. Alfred, who is as determined a despot as ever walked, does not pretend to this kind of defence;—no, he stands, high and haughty, on that good old respectable ground, *the right of the strongest;* and he says, and I think quite sensibly, that the American planter is 'only doing, in another form, what the English aristocracy and capitalists are doing by the lower classes;' that is, I take it, *appropriating* them, body and bone, soul and spirit, to their use and convenience. He defends both,—and I think, at least, *consistently.* He says that there can be no high civilization without enslavement of the masses, either nominal or real. There must, he says, be a lower class, given up to physical toil and confined to an animal nature; and a higher one thereby acquires leisure and wealth for a more expanded intelligence and improvement, and becomes the directing soul of the lower. So he reasons, because, as I said, he is born an aristocrat;—so I don't believe, because I was born a democrat."

"How in the world can the two things be compared?" said Miss Ophelia. "The English laborer is not sold, traded, parted from his family, whipped."

"He is as much at the will of his employer as if he were sold to him. The slave-owner can whip his refractory slave to death,—the capitalist can starve him to death. As to family security, it is hard to say which is the worst,—to have one's children sold, or see them starve to death at home."

"But it 's no kind of apology for slavery, to prove that it is n't worse than some other bad thing."

"I did n't give it for one,—nay, I 'll say, besides, that ours is the more bold and palpable infringement of human rights; actually buying a man up, like a horse,—looking at his teeth, cracking his joints, and trying his paces, and then paying down for him,—having speculators, breeders, traders, and brokers in human bodies and souls,—sets the thing before the eyes of the civilized world in a more tangible form, though the thing done be, after all, in its nature, the same; that is, appropriating one set of human beings to the use and improvement of another, without any regard to their own."

"I never thought of the matter in this light," said Miss Ophelia.

"Well, I 've travelled in England some, and I 've looked over a good many documents as to the state of their lower classes; and I really think there is no denying Alfred, when he says that his slaves are better off than a large class of the population of England. You see, you must not infer, from what I have told you, that Alfred is what is called a hard master; for he is n't. He is despotic, and unmerciful to insubordination; he would shoot a fellow down with as little remorse as he would shoot a buck, if he opposed him. But, in general, he takes a sort of pride in having his slaves comfortably fed and accommodated.

"When I was with him, I insisted that he should do something for their instruction; and, to please me, he did get a chaplain, and used to have them catechized Sunday, though, I believe, in his heart, that he thought it would do about as much good to set a chaplain over his dogs and horses. And the fact is, that a mind stupefied and animalized by every bad influence from the

41

hour of birth, spending the whole of every week-day in unreflecting toil, cannot be done much with by a few hours on Sunday. The teachers of Sunday-schools among the manufacturing population of England, and among plantation-hands in our country, could perhaps testify to the same result, *there and here.* Yet some striking exceptions there are among us, from the fact that the negro is naturally more impressible to religious sentiment than the white."

"Well," said Miss Ophelia, "how came you to give up your plantation life?"

"Well, we jogged on together some time, till Alfred saw plainly that I was no planter. He thought it absurd, after he had reformed, and altered, and improved everywhere, to suit my notions, that I still remained unsatisfied. The fact was, it was, after all, the THING that I hated,—the using these men and women, the perpetuation of all this ignorance, brutality and vice,—just to make money for me!

"Besides, I was always interfering in the details. Being myself one of the laziest of mortals, I had altogether too much fellow-feeling for the lazy; and when poor, shiftless dogs put stones at the bottom of their cotton-baskets to make them weigh heavier, or filled their sacks with dirt, with cotton at the top, it seemed so exactly like what I should do if I were they, I could n't and would n't have them flogged for it. Well, of course, there was an end of plantation discipline; and Alf and I came to about the same point that I and my respected father did, years before. So he told me that I was a womanish sentimentalist, and would never do for business life; and advised me to take the bank-stock and the New Orleans family mansion, and go to writing poetry, and let him manage the plantation. So we parted, and I came here."

"But why did n't you free your slaves?"

"Well, I was n't up to that. To hold them as tools for money-making, I could not;—have them to help spend money, you know, did n't look quite so ugly to me. Some of them were old house–servants, to whom I was much attached; and the younger ones were children to the old. All were well satisfied to be as they were." He paused, and walked reflectively up and down the room.

"There was," said St. Clare, "a time in my life when I had plans and hopes of doing something in this world, more than to float and drift. I had vague, indistinct yearnings to be a sort of emancipator,—to free my native land from this spot and stain. All young man have had such fever-fits, I suppose, some time,—but then—"

"Why did n't you?" said Miss Ophelia;—"you ought not to put your hand to the plough, and look back."

"O, well, things did n't go with me as I expected, and I got the despair of living that Solomon did. I suppose it was a necessary incident to wisdom in us both; but, some how or other, instead of being actor and regenerator in society, I became a piece of drift-wood, and have been floating and eddying about, ever since. Alfred scolds me, every time we meet; and he has the better of me, I grant,—for he really does something; his life is a logical result of his opinions, and mine is a contemptible *non sequitur.* "[41]

"My dear cousin, can you be satisfied with such a way of spending your probation?"

"Satisfied! Was I not just telling you I despised it? But, then, to come back to this point,—we were on this liberation business. I don't think my feelings about slavery are peculiar. I find many men who, in their hearts, think of it just as I do. The land groans under it; and, bad as it is for the slave, it is worse, if anything, for the master. It takes no spectacles to see that a great class of vicious, improvident, degraded people, among us, are an evil to us, as well as to themselves. The capitalist and aristocrat of England cannot feel that as we do, because they do not mingle with the class they degrade as we do. They are in our houses; they are the associates of our children, and they form their minds faster than we can; for they are a race that children always will cling to and assimilate with. If Eva, now, was not more angel than ordinary, she would be ruined. We might as well allow the small-pox to run among them, and think our children would not take it, as to let them be uninstructed and vicious, and think our children will not be affected by that. Yet our laws positively and utterly forbid any efficient general educational system, and they do it wisely, too; for, just begin and thoroughly educate one generation, and the whole thing would be blown sky high. If we did not give them liberty, they would take it."

"And what do you think will be the end of this?" said Miss Ophelia.

"I don't know. One thing is certain,—that there is a mustering among the masses, the world over; and there is a *dies iræ*[42] coming on, sooner or later. The same thing is working in Europe, in England, and in this country. My mother used to tell me of a millennium that was coming, when Christ should reign, and all men should be free and happy. And she taught me, when I was a boy, to pray, 'Thy kingdom come.'[43] Sometimes I think all this sighing, and groaning, and stirring among the dry bones foretells what she used to tell me was coming. But who may abide the day of His appearing?"

"Augustine, sometimes I think you are not far from the kingdom," said Miss Ophelia, laying down her knitting, and looking anxiously at her cousin.

"Thank you for your good opinion; but it's up and down with me,—up to heaven's gate in theory, down in earth's dust in practice. But there's the tea-bell,—do let's go,—and don't say, now, I have n't had one downright serious talk, for once in my life."

---

[41]A non sequitur is something that doesn't follow the given premises or fit into an established logical pattern.

[42]Latin for "day of wrath."

[43]From the Lord's Prayer; see Matthew 6:9–13.

At table, Marie alluded to the incident of Prue. "I suppose you 'll think, cousin," she said, "that we are all barbarians."

"I think that 's a barbarous thing," said Miss Ophelia, "but I don't think you are all barbarians."

"Well, now," said Marie, "I know it 's impossible to get along with some of these creatures. They are so bad they ought not to live. I don't feel a particle of sympathy for such cases. If they 'd only behave themselves, it would not happen."

"But, mamma," said Eva, "the poor creature was unhappy; that 's what made her drink."

"O, fiddlestick! as if that were any excuse! I 'm unhappy, very often. I presume," she said, pensively, "that I 've had greater trials than ever she had. It 's just because they are so bad. There 's some of them that you cannot break in by any kind of severity. I remember father had a man that was so lazy he would run away just to get rid of work, and lie around in the swamps, stealing and doing all sorts of horrid things. That man was caught and whipped, time and again, and it never did him any good; and the last time he crawled off, though he couldn't but just go, and died in the swamp. There was no sort of reason for it, for father's hands were always treated kindly."

"I broke a fellow in, once," said St. Clare, "that all the overseers and masters had tried their hands on in vain."

"You!" said Marie; "well, I 'd be glad to know when *you* ever did anything of the sort."

"Well, he was a powerful, gigantic fellow,—a native-born African; and he appeared to have the rude instinct of freedom in him to an uncommon degree. He was a regular African lion. They called him Scipio. Nobody could do anything with him; and he was sold round from overseer to overseer, till at last Alfred bought him, because he thought he could manage him. Well, one day he knocked down the overseer, and was fairly off into the swamps. I was on a visit to Alf's plantation, for it was after we had dissolved partnership. Alfred was greatly exasperated; but I told him that it was his own fault, and laid him any wager that I could break the man; and finally it was agreed, that if I caught him, I should have him to experiment on. So they mustered out a party of some six or seven, with guns and dogs, for the hunt. People, you know, can get up just as much enthusiasm in hunting a man as a deer, if it is only customary; in fact, I got a little excited myself, though I had only put in as a sort of mediator, in case he was caught.

"Well, the dogs bayed and howled, and we rode and scampered, and finally we started him. He ran and bounded like a buck, and kept us well in the rear for some time; but at last he got caught in an impenetrable thicket of cane; then he turned to bay, and I tell you he fought the dogs right gallantly. He dashed them to right and left, and actually killed three of them with only his naked fists, when a shot from a gun brought him down, and he fell, wounded and bleeding, almost at my feet. The poor fellow looked up at me with manhood and despair both in his eye. I kept back the dogs and the party, as they came pressing up, and claimed him as my prisoner. It was all I could do to keep them from shooting him, in the flush of success; but I persisted in my bargain, and Alfred sold him to me. Well, I took him in hand, and in one fortnight I had him tamed down as submissive and tractable as heart could desire."

"What in the world did you do to him?" said Marie.

"Well, it was quite a simple process. I took him to my own room, had a good bed made for him, dressed his wounds, and tended him myself, until he got fairly on his feet again. And, in process of time, I had free papers made out for him, and told him he might go where he liked."

"And did he go?" said Miss Ophelia.

"No. The foolish fellow tore the paper in two, and absolutely refused to leave me. I never had a braver, better fellow,—trusty and true as steel. He embraced Christianity afterwards, and became as gentle as a child. He used to oversee my place on the lake, and did it capitally, too. I lost him the first cholera[44] season. In fact, he laid down his life for me. For I was sick, almost to death; and when, through the panic, everybody else fled, Scipio worked for me like a giant, and actually brought me back into life again. But, poor fellow! he was taken, right after, and there was no saving him. I never felt anybody's loss more."

Eva had come gradually nearer and nearer to her father, as he told the story,—her small lips apart, her eyes wide and earnest with absorbing interest.

As he finished, she suddenly threw her arms around his neck, burst into tears, and sobbed convulsively.

"Eva, dear child! what is the matter?" said St. Clare, as the child's small frame trembled and shook with the violence of her feelings. "This child," he added, "ought not to hear any of this kind of thing—she 's nervous."

"No, papa, I 'm not nervous," said Eva, controlling herself, suddenly, with a strength of resolution singular in such a child. "I 'm not nervous, but these things *sink into my heart.*"

"What do you mean, Eva?"

"I can't tell you, papa. I think a great many thoughts. Perhaps some day I shall tell you."

"Well, think away, dear,—only don't cry and worry your papa," said St. Clare. "Look here,—see what a beautiful peach I have got for you!"

Eva took it, and smiled, though there was still a nervous twitching about the corners of her mouth.

"Come, look at the gold-fish," said St. Clare, taking her hand and stepping on to the verandah. A few moments, and merry laughs were heard

---

[44]Cholera is a disease, usually fatal, and one that occasionally grew to epidemic proportions in the nineteenth century United States.

through the silken curtains, as Eva and St. Clare were pelting each other with roses, and chasing each other among the alleys of the court.

. . .

There is a danger that our humble friend Tom be neglected amid the adventures of the higher born; but, if our readers will accompany us up to a little loft over the stable, they may, perhaps, learn a little of his affairs. It was a decent room, containing a bed, a chair, and a small, rough stand, where lay Tom's Bible and hymn-book; and where he sits, at present, with his slate before him, intent on something that seems to cost him a great deal of anxious thought.

The fact was, that Tom's home-yearnings had become so strong, that he had begged a sheet of writing-paper of Eva, and, mustering up all his small stock of literary attainment acquired by Mas'r George's instructions, he conceived the bold idea of writing a letter; and he was busy now, on his slate, getting out his first draft. Tom was in a good deal of trouble, for the forms of some of the letters he had forgotten entirely; and of what he did remember, he did not know exactly which to use. And while he was working, and breathing very hard, in his earnestness, Eva alighted, like a bird, on the round of his chair behind him, and peeped over his shoulder.

"O, Uncle Tom! what funny things you *are* making, there!"

"I 'm trying to write to my poor old woman, Miss Eva, and my little chil'en," said Tom, drawing the back of his hand over his eyes; "but some how, I 'm feard I shan't make it out."

"I wish I could help you, Tom! I 've learnt to write some. Last year I could make all the letters, but I 'm afraid I 've forgotten."

So Eva put her little golden head close to his, and the two commenced a grave and anxious discussion, each one equally earnest, and about equally ignorant; and, with a deal of consulting and advising over every word, the composition began, as they both felt very sanguine, to look quite like writing.

"Yes, Uncle Tom, it really begins to look beautiful," said Eva, gazing delightedly on it. "How pleased your wife 'll be, and the poor little children! O, it 's a shame you ever had to go away from them! I mean to ask papa to let you go back, some time."

"Missis said that she would send down money for me, as soon as they could get it together," said Tom. "I 'm 'spectin' she will. Young Mas'r George, he said he 'd come for me; and he gave me this yer dollar as a sign;" and Tom drew from under his clothes the precious dollar.

"O, he 'll certainly come, then!" said Eva. "I 'm so glad!"

"And I wanted to send a letter, you know, to let 'em know whar I was, and tell poor Chloe that I was well off, — cause she felt so drefful, poor soul!"

"I say, Tom!" said St. Clare's voice, coming in the door at this moment.

Tom and Eva both started.

"What 's here?" said St. Clare, coming up and looking at the slate.

"O, it 's Tom's letter. I 'm helping him to write it," said Eva; "is n't it nice?"

"I would n't discourage either of you," said St. Clare, "but I rather think, Tom, you 'd better get me to write your letter for you. I 'll do it, when I come home from my ride."

"It 's very imporant he should write," said Eva, "because his mistress is going to send down money to redeem him, you know, papa; he told me they told him so."

St. Clare thought, in his heart, that this was probably only one of those things which good-natured owners say to their servants, to alleviate their horror of being sold, without any intention of fulfilling the expectation thus excited. But he did not make any audible comment upon it,—only ordered Tom to get the horses out for a ride.

Tom's letter was written in due form for him that evening, and safely lodged in the post-office.

Miss Ophelia still persevered in her labors in the housekeeping line. It was universally agreed, among all the household, from Dinah down to the youngest urchin, that Miss Ophelia was decidedly "curis,"—a term by which a southern servant implies that his or her betters don't exactly suit them.

The higher circle in the family—to wit, Adolph, Jane and Rosa—agreed that she was no lady; ladies never kept working about as she did;—that she had no *air* at all; and they were surprised that she should be any relation of the St. Clares. Even Marie declared that it was absolutely fatiguing to see Cousin Ophelia always so busy. And, in fact, Miss Ophelia's industry was so incessant as to lay some foundation for the complaint. She sewed and stitched away, from daylight till dark, with the energy of one who is pressed on by some immediate urgency; and then, when the light faded, and the work was folded away, with one turn out came the ever-ready knitting-work, and there she was again, going on as briskly as ever. It really was a labor to see her.

XX.

Topsy

One morning, while Miss Ophelia was busy in some of her domestic cares, St. Clare's voice was heard, calling her at the foot of the stairs.

"Come down here, Cousin; I 've something to show you."

"What is it?" said Miss Ophelia, coming down, with her sewing in her hand.

"I 've made a purchase for your department,—see here," said St. Clare; and, with the word, he pulled along a little negro girl, about eight or nine years of age.

She was one of the blackest of her race; and her round, shining eyes, glittering as glass beads, moved with quick and restless glances over everything in the room. Her mouth, half open with astonishment at the wonders of the new Mas'r's parlor, displayed a white and brilliant set of teeth. Her woolly hair was braided in sundry little tails, which stuck out in every direction. The expression of her face was an odd mixture of shrewdness and cunning, over which was oddly drawn, like a kind of veil, an expression of the most doleful gravity and solemnity. She was dressed in a single filthy, ragged garment, made of bagging; and stood with her hands demurely folded before her. Altogether, there was something odd and goblin-like about her appearance,—something, as Miss Ophelia afterwards said, "so heathenish," as to inspire that good lady with utter dismay; and, turning to St. Clare, she said,

"Augustine, what in the world have you brought that thing here for?"

"For you to educate, to be sure, and train in the way she should go.[45] I thought she was rather a funny specimen in the Jim Crow line. Here, Topsy," he added, giving a whistle, as a man would to call the attention of a dog, "give us a song, now, and show us some of your dancing."

The black, glassy eyes glittered with a kind of wicked drollery, and the thing struck up, in a clear shrill voice, an odd negro melody, to which she kept time with her hands and feet, spinning round, clapping her hands, knocking her knees together, in a wild, fantastic sort of time, and producing in her throat all those odd guttural sounds which distinguish the native music of her race; and finally, turning a summerset or two, and giving a prolonged closing note, as odd and unearthly as that of a steam-whistle, she came suddenly down on the carpet, and stood with her hands folded, and a most sanctimonious expression of meekness and solemnity over her face, only broken by the cunning glances which she shot askance from the corners of her eyes.

Miss Ophelia stood silent, perfectly paralyzed with amazement.

St. Clare, like a mischievous fellow as he was, appeared to enjoy her astonishment; and, addressing the child again, said,

"Topsy, this is your new mistress. I'm going to give you up to her; see now that you behave yourself."

"Yes, Mas'r," said Topsy, with sanctimonious gravity, her wicked eyes twinkling as she spoke.

"You're going to be good, Topsy, you understand," said St. Clare.

"O yes, Mas'r," said Topsy, with another twinkle, her hands still devoutly folded.

"Now, Augustine, what upon earth is this for?" said Miss Ophelia. "Your house is so full of these little plagues, now, that a body can't set down their foot without treading on 'em. I get up in the morning, and find one asleep

---

[45]See Proverbs 23:6

behind the door, and see one black head poking out from under the table, one lying on the door-mat,—and they are mopping and mowing and grinning between all the railings, and tumbling over the kitchen floor! What on earth did you want to bring this one for?"

"For you to educate—did n't I tell you? You 're always preaching about educating. I thought I would make you a present of a fresh-caught specimen, and let you try your hand on her, and bring her up in the way she should go."

"*I* don't want her, I am sure,—I have more to do with 'em now than I want to."

"That 's you Christians, all over!—you 'll get up a society, and get some poor missionary to spend all his days among just such heathen. But let me see one of you that would take one into your house with you, and take the labor of their conversion on yourselves! No; when it comes to that, they are dirty and disagreeable, and it 's too much care, and so on."

"Augustine, you know I did n't think of it in that light," said Miss Ophelia, evidently softening. "Well, it might be a real missionary work," said she, looking rather more favorably on the child.

St. Clare had touched the right string. Miss Ophelia's conscientiousness was ever on the alert. "But," she added, "I really did n't see the need of buying this one;—there are enough now, in your house, to take all my time and skill."

"Well, then, Cousin," said St. Clare, drawing her aside, "I ought to beg your pardon for my good-for-nothing speeches. You are so good, after all, that there 's no sense in them. Why, the fact is, this concern belonged to a couple of drunken creatures that keep a low restaurant that I have to pass by every day, and I was tired of hearing her screaming, and them beating and swearing at her. She looked bright and funny, too, as if something might be made of her;—so I bought her, and I 'll give her to you. Try, now, and give her a good orthodox New England bringing up, and see what it 'll make of her. You know I have n't any gift that way; but I 'd like you to try."

"Well, I 'll do what I can," said Miss Ophelia; and she approached her new subject very much as a person might be supposed to approach a black spider, supposing them to have benevolent designs toward it.

"She 's dreadfully dirty, and half naked," she said.

"Well, take her down stairs, and make some of them clean and clothe her up."

Miss Ophelia carried her to the kitchen regions.

"Don't see what Mas'r St. Clare wants of 'nother nigger!" said Dinah, surveying the new arrival with no friendly air. "Won't have her round under *my* feet, *I* know!"

"Pah!" said Rosa and Jane, with supreme disgust; "let her keep out of our way! What in the world Mas'r wanted another of these low niggers for, I can't see!"

"You go long! No more nigger dan you be, Miss Rosa," said Dinah, who felt this last remark a reflection on herself. "You seem to tink yourself white folks. You an't nerry one, black *nor* white. I'd like to be one or turrer."

Miss Ophelia saw that there was nobody in the camp that would undertake to oversee the cleansing and dressing of the new arrival; and so she was forced to do it herself, with some very ungracious and reluctant assistance from Jane.

It is not for ears polite to hear the particulars of the first toilet of a neglected, abused child. In fact, in this world, multitudes must live and die in a state that it would be too great a shock to the nerves of their fellow-mortals even to hear described. Miss Ophelia had a good, strong, practical deal of resolution; and she went through all the disgusting details with heroic thoroughness, though, it must be confessed, with no very gracious air,—for endurance was the utmost to which her principles could bring her. When she saw, on the back and shoulders of the child, great welts and calloused spots, ineffaceable marks of the system under which she had grown up thus far, her heart became pitiful within her.

"See there!" said Jane, pointing to the marks, "don't that show she's a limb? We'll have fine works with her, I reckon. I hate these nigger young uns! so disgusting! I wonder that Mas'r would buy her!"

The "young un" alluded to heard all these comments with the subdued and doleful air which seemed habitual to her, only scanning, with a keen and furtive glance of her flickering eyes, the ornaments which Jane wore in her ears. When arrayed at last in a suit of decent and whole clothing, her hair cropped short to her head, Miss Ophelia, with some satisfaction, said she looked more Christian-like than she did, and in her own mind began to mature some plans for her instruction.

Sitting down before her, she began to question her.

"How old are you, Topsy?"

"Dun no, Missis," said the image, with a grin that showed all her teeth.

"Don't know how old you are? Did n't anybody ever tell you? Who was your mother?"

"Never had none!" said the child, with another grin.

"Never had any mother? What do you mean? Where were you born?"

"Never was born!" persisted Topsy, with another grin, that looked so goblin-like, that, if Miss Ophelia had been at all nervous, she might have fancied that she had got hold of some sooty gnome from the land of Diablerie;[46] but Miss Ophelia was not nervous, but plain and business-like, and she said, with some sternness,

"You must n't answer me in that way, child; I'm not playing with you. Tell me where you were born, and who your father and mother were."

---

[46]Diablerie is witchcraft, wickedness.

"Never was born," reiterated the creature, more emphatically; "never had no father nor mother, nor nothin'. I was raised by a speculator, with lots of others. Old Aunt Sue used to take car on us."

The child was evidently sincere; and Jane, breaking into a short laugh, said,

"Laws, Missis, there's heaps of 'em. Speculators buys 'em up cheap, when they's little, and gets 'em raised for market."

"How long have you lived with your master and mistress?"

"Dun no, Missis."

"Is it a year, or more, or less?"

"Dun no, Missis."

"Laws, Missis, those low negroes,—they can't tell; they don't know anything about time," said Jane; "they don't know what a year is; they don't know their own ages."

"Have you ever heard anything about God, Topsy?"

The child looked bewildered, but grinned as usual.

"Do you know who made you?"

"Nobody, as I knows on," said the child, with a short laugh.

The idea appeared to amuse her considerably; for her eyes twinkled, and she added,

"I spect I grow'd. Don't think nobody never made me."

"Do you know how to sew?" said Miss Ophelia, who thought she would turn her inquiries to something more tangible.

"No, Missis."

"What can you do?—what did you do for your master and mistress?"

"Fetch water, and wash dishes, and rub knives, and wait on folks."

"Were they good to you?"

"Spect they was," said the child, scanning Miss Ophelia cunningly.

Miss Ophelia rose from this encouraging colloquy; St. Clare was leaning over the back of her chair.

"You find virgin soil there, Cousin; put in your own ideas,—you won't find many to pull up."

Miss Ophelia's ideas of education, like all her other ideas, were very set and definite; and of the kind that prevailed in New England a century ago, and which are still preserved in some very retired and unsophisticated parts, where there are no railroads. As nearly as could be expressed, they could be comprised in a very few words: to teach them to mind when they were spoken to; to teach them the catechism, sewing, and reading; and to whip them if they told lies. And though, of course, in the flood of light that is now poured on education, these are left far away in the rear, yet it is an undisputed fact that our grandmothers raised some tolerably fair men and women under this régime, as many of us can remember and testify. At all events, Miss Ophelia knew of nothing else to do; and, therefore, applied her mind to her heathen with the best diligence she could command.

The child was announced and considered in the family as Miss Ophelia's girl; and, as she was looked upon with no gracious eye in the kitchen, Miss Ophelia resolved to confine her sphere of operation and instruction chiefly to her own chamber. With a self-sacrifice which some of our readers will appreciate, she resolved, instead of comfortably making her own bed, sweeping and dusting her own chamber,—which she had hitherto done, in utter scorn of all offers of help from the chambermaid of the establishment,—to condemn herself to the martyrdom of instructing Topsy to perform these operations,—ah, woe the day! Did any of our readers ever do the same, they will appreciate the amount of her self-sacrifice.

Miss Ophelia began with Topsy by taking her into her chamber, the first morning, and solemnly commencing a course of instruction in the art and mystery of bed-making.

Behold, then, Topsy, washed and shorn of all the little braided tails wherein her heart had delighted, arrayed in a clean gown, with well-starched apron, standing reverently before Miss Ophelia, with an expression of solemnity well befitting a funeral.

"Now, Topsy, I'm going to show you just how my bed is to be made. I am very particular about my bed. You must learn exactly how to do it."

"Yes, ma'am," says Topsy, with a deep sigh, and a face of woful earnestness.

"Now, Topsy, look here;—this is the hem of the sheet,—this is the right side of the sheet, and this is the wrong;—will you remember?"

"Yes, ma'am," says Topsy, with another sigh.

"Well, now, the under sheet you must bring over the bolster,—so,—and tuck it clear down under the mattress nice and smooth,—so,—do you see?"

"Yes, ma'am," said Topsy, with profound attention.

"But the upper sheet," said Miss Ophelia, "must be brought down in this way, and tucked under firm and smooth at the foot,—so,—the narrow hem at the foot."

"Yes, ma'am," said Topsy, as before;—but we will add, what Miss Ophelia did not see, that, during the time when the good lady's back was turned, in the zeal of her manipulations, the young disciple had contrived to snatch a pair of gloves and a ribbon, which she had adroitly slipped into her sleeves, and stood with her hands dutifully folded, as before.

"Now, Topsy, let's see *you* do this," said Miss Ophelia, pulling off the clothes, and seating herself.

Topsy, with great gravity and adroitness, went through the exercise completely to Miss Ophelia's satisfaction; smoothing the sheets, patting out every wrinkle, and exhibiting, through the whole process, a gravity and seriousness with which her instructress was greatly edified. By an unlucky slip, however, a fluttering fragment of the ribbon hung out of one of her sleeves, just as she was finishing, and caught Miss Ophelia's attention. Instantly she pounced upon it.

"What's this? You naughty, wicked child,—you've been stealing this?"

The ribbon was pulled out of Topsy's own sleeve, yet she was not in the least disconcerted; she only looked at it with an air of the most surprised and unconscious innocence.

"Laws! why, that ar 's Miss Feely's ribbon, an't it? How could it a got caught in my sleeve?"

"Topsy, you naughty girl, don't you tell me a lie,—you stole that ribbon!"

"Missis, I declar for't, I did n't;—never seed it till dis yer blessed minnit."

"Topsy," said Miss Ophelia, "don't you know it's wicked to tell lies?"

"I never tells no lies, Miss Feely," said Topsy, with virtuous gravity; "it 's jist the truth I 've been a tellin now, and an't nothin else."

"Topsy, I shall have to whip you, if you tell lies so."

"Laws, Missis, if you 's to whip all day, could n't say no other way," said Topsy, beginning to blubber. "I never seed dat ar,—it must a got caught in my sleeve. Miss Feely must have left it on the bed, and it got caught in the clothes, and so got in my sleeve."

Miss Ophelia was so indignant at the barefaced lie, that she caught the child and shook her.

"Don't you tell me that again!"

The shake brought the gloves on to the floor, from the other sleeve.

"There, you!" said Miss Ophelia, "will you tell me now, you did n't steal the ribbon?"

Topsy now confessed to the gloves, but still persisted in denying the ribbon.

"Now, Topsy," said Miss Ophelia, "if you 'll confess all about it, I won't whip you this time." Thus adjured, Topsy confessed to the ribbon and gloves, with woful protestations of penitence.

"Well, now, tell me. I know you must have taken other things since you have been in the house, for I let you run about all day yesterday. Now, tell me if you took anything, and I shan't whip you."

"Laws, Missis! I took Miss Eva's red thing she wars on her neck."

"You did, you naughty child!—Well, what else?"

"I took Rosa's yer-rings,—them red ones."

"Go bring them to me this minute, both of 'em."

"Laws, Missis! I can't,—they's burnt up!"

"Burnt up!—what a story! Go get 'em, or I 'll whip you."

Topsy, with loud protestations, and tears, and groans, declared that she *could* not. "They 's burnt up,—they was."

"What did you burn 'em up for?" said Miss Ophelia.

"Cause I 's wicked,—I is. I 's mighty wicked, any how. I can't help it."

Just at this moment, Eva came innocently into the room, with the identical coral necklace on her neck.

"Why, Eva, where did you get your necklace?" said Miss Ophelia.

"Get it? Why I 've had it on all day," said Eva.

"Did you have it on yesterday?"

"Yes; and what is funny, Aunty, I had it on all night. I forgot to take it off when I went to bed."

Miss Ophelia looked perfectly bewildered; the more so, as Rosa, at that instant, came into the room, with a basket of newly-ironed linen poised on her head, and the coral ear-drops shaking in her ears!

"I 'm sure I can't tell anything what to do with such a child!" she said, in despair. "What in the world did you tell me you took those things for, Topsy?"

"Why, Missis said I must 'fess; and I could n't think of nothin' else to 'fess," said Topsy, rubbing her eyes.

"But, of course, I did n't want you to confess things you did n't do," said Miss Ophelia; "that 's telling a lie, just as much as the other."

"Laws, now, is it?" said Topsy, with an air of innocent wonder.

"La, there an't any such thing as truth in that limb," said Rosa, looking indignantly at Topsy. "If I was Mas'r St. Clare, I 'd whip her till the blood run. I would,—I 'd let her catch it!"

"No, no, Rosa," said Eva, with an air of command, which the child could assume at times; "you must n't talk so, Rosa. I can't bear to hear it."

"La sakes! Miss Eva, you 's so good, you don't know nothing how to get along with niggers. There 's no way but to cut 'em well up, I tell ye."

"Rosa!" said Eva, "hush! Don't you say another word of that sort!" and the eye of the child flashed, and her cheek deepened its color.

Rosa was cowed in a moment.

"Miss Eva has got the St. Clare blood in her, that 's plain. She can speak, for all the world, just like her papa," she said, as she passed out of the room.

Eva stood looking at Topsy.

There stood the two children, representatives of the two extremes of society. The fair, high-bred child, with her golden head, her deep eyes, her spiritual, noble brow, and prince-like movements; and her black, keen, subtle, cringing, yet acute neighbor. They stood the representatives of their races. The Saxon, born of ages of cultivation, command, education, physical and moral eminence; the Afric, born of ages of oppression, submission, ignorance, toil, and vice!

Something, perhaps, of such thoughts struggled through Eva's mind. But a child's thoughts are rather dim, undefined instincts; and in Eva's noble nature many such were yearning and working, for which she had no power of utterance. When Miss Ophelia expatiated on Topsy's naughty, wicked conduct, the child looked perplexed and sorrowful, but said, sweetly,

"Poor Topsy, why need you steal? You 're going to be taken good care of, now. I 'm sure I 'd rather give you anything of mine, than have you steal it."

It was the first word of kindness the child had ever heard in her life; and the sweet tone and manner struck strangely on the wild, rude heart, and a sparkle of something like a tear shone in the keen, round, glittering eye; but it was followed by the short laugh and habitual grin. No! the ear that has never heard anything but abuse is strangely incredulous of anything so heavenly as kindness; and Topsy only thought Eva's speech something funny and inexplicable,—she did not believe it.

But what was to be done with Topsy? Miss Ophelia found the case a puzzler; her rules for bringing up did n't seem to apply. She thought she would take time to think of it; and, by the way of gaining time, and in hopes of some indefinite moral virtues supposed to be inherent in dark closets, Miss Ophelia shut Topsy up in one till she had arranged her ideas further on the subject.

"I don't see," said Miss Ophelia to St. Clare, "how I 'm going to manage that child, without whipping her."

"Well, whip her, then, to your heart's content; I 'll give you full power to do what you like."

"Children always have to be whipped," said Miss Ophelia; "I never heard of bringing them up without."

"O, well, certainly," said St. Clare; "do as you think best. Only I 'll make one suggestion: I 've seen this child whipped with a poker, knocked down with the shovel or tongs, whichever came handiest, &c.; and, seeing that she is used to that style of operation, I think your whippings will have to be pretty energetic, to make much impression."

"What is to be done with her, then?" said Miss Ophelia.

"You have started a serious question," said St. Clare; "I wish you 'd answer it. What is to be done with a human being that can be governed only by the lash,—*that* fails,—it 's a very common state of things down here!"

"I 'm sure I don't know; I never saw such a child as this."

"Such children are very common among us, and such men and women, too. How are they to be governed?" said St. Clare.

"I 'm sure it 's more than I can say," said Miss Ophelia.

"Or I either," said St. Clare. "The horrid cruelties and outrages that once and a while find their way into the papers,—such cases as Prue's, for example,—what do they come from? In many cases, it is a gradual hardening process on both sides,—the owner growing more and more cruel, as the servant more and more callous. Whipping and abuse are like laudanum,[47] you have to double the dose as the sensibilities decline. I saw this very early when I became an owner; and I resolved never to begin, because I did not know when I should stop,—and I resolved, at least, to protect my own moral nature. The consequence is, that my servants act like spoiled children; but I think that better than for us both to be brutalized together. You have talked a great deal about our responsibilities in educating, Cousin. I really wanted you to *try* with one child, who is a specimen of thousands among us."

"It is your system makes such children," said Miss Ophelia.

"I know it; but they are *made*,—they exist,—and what is to be done with them?"

---

[47]Laudanum is an addictive opium-based medicine for relieving pain.

"Well, I can't say I thank you for the experiment. But, then, as it appears to be a duty, I shall persevere and try, and do the best I can," said Miss Ophelia; and Miss Ophelia, after this, did labor, with a commendable degree of zeal and energy, on her new subject. She instituted regular hours and employments for her, and undertook to teach her to read and to sew.

In the former art, the child was quick enough. She learned her letters as if by magic, and was very soon able to read plain reading; but the sewing was a more difficult matter. The creature was lithe as a cat, and as active as a monkey, and the confinement of sewing was her abomination; so she broke her needles, threw them slyly out of windows, or down in chinks of the walls; she tangled, broke, and dirtied her thread, or, with a sly movement, would throw a spool away altogether. Her motions were almost as quick as those of a practised conjurer, and her command of her face quite as great; and though Miss Ophelia could not help feeling that so many accidents could not possibly happen in succession, yet she could not, without a watchfulness which would leave her no time for anything else, detect her.

Topsy was soon a noted character in the establishment. Her talent for every species of drollery, grimace, and mimicry,—for dancing, tumbling, climbing, singing, whistling, imitating every sound that hit her fancy,—seemed inexhaustible. In her play-hours, she invariably had every child in the establishment at her heels, open-mouthed with admiration and wonder,—not excepting Miss Eva, who appeared to be fascinated by her wild diablerie, as a dove is sometimes charmed by a glittering serpent. Miss Ophelia was uneasy that Eva should fancy Topsy's society so much, and implored St. Clare to forbid it.

"Poh! let the child alone," said St. Clare. "Topsy will do her good."

"But so depraved a child,—are you not afraid she will teach her some mischief?"

"She can't teach her mischief; she might teach it to some children, but evil rolls off Eva's mind like dew off a cabbage-leaf,—not a drop sinks in."

"Don't be too sure," said Miss Ophelia. "I know I'd never let a child of mine play with Topsy."

"Well, your children need n't," said St. Clare, "but mine may; if Eva could have been spoiled, it would have been done years ago."

Topsy was at first despised and contemned by the upper servants. They soon found reason to alter their opinion. It was very soon discovered that whoever cast an indignity on Topsy was sure to meet with some inconvenient accident shortly after;—either a pair of ear-rings or some cherished trinket would be missing, or an article of dress would be suddenly found utterly ruined, or the person would stumble accidentally into a pail of hot water, or a libation of dirty slop would unaccountably deluge them from above when in full gala dress;—and on all these occasions, when investigation was made, there was nobody found to stand sponsor for the indignity. Topsy was cited, and had up before all the domestic judicatories, time and again; but always sustained her examinations with most edifying innocence and gravity of appearance. Nobody in the world ever doubted who did the things; but not a scrap of any direct evidence could be found to establish the suppositions, and Miss Ophelia was too just to feel at liberty to proceed to any lengths without it.

The mischiefs done were always so nicely timed, also, as further to shelter the aggressor. Thus, the times for revenge on Rosa and Jane, the two chambermaids, were always chosen in those seasons when (as not unfrequently happened) they were in disgrace with their mistress, when any complaint from them would of course meet with no sympathy. In short, Topsy soon made the household understand the propriety of letting her alone; and she was let alone, accordingly.

Topsy was smart and energetic in all manual operations, learning everything that was taught her with surprising quickness. With a few lessons, she had learned to do the proprieties of Miss Ophelia's chamber in a way with which even that particular lady could find no fault. Mortal hands could not lay spread smoother, adjust pillows more accurately, sweep and dust and arrange more perfectly, than Topsy, when she chose,—but she didn't very often choose. If Miss Ophelia, after three or four days of careful and patient supervision, was so sanguine as to suppose that Topsy had at last fallen into her way, could do without overlooking, and so go off and busy herself about something else, Topsy would hold a perfect carnival of confusion, for some one or two hours. Instead of making the bed, she would amuse herself with pulling off the pillow-cases, butting her woolly head among the pillows, till it would sometimes be grotesquely ornamented with feathers sticking out in various directions; she would climb the posts, and hang head downward from the tops; flourish the sheets and spreads all over the apartment; dress the bolster up in Miss Ophelia's night-clothes, and enact various scenic performances with that,—singing and whistling, and making grimaces at herself in the looking-glass; in short, as Miss Ophelia phrased it, "raising Cain"[48] generally.

On one occasion, Miss Ophelia found Topsy with her very best scarlet India Canton crape[49] shawl wound round her head for a turban, going on with her rehearsals before the glass in great style,—Miss Ophelia having, with carelessness most unheard-of in her, left the key for once in her drawer.

"Topsy!" she would say, when at the end of all patience, "what does make you act so?"

"Dunno, Missis,—I spects cause I's so wicked!"

"I don't know anything what I shall do with you, Topsy."

---

[48]Causing a great commotion, trouble-making. The reference is to the biblical Cain who killed his brother. Genesis 4:1–6.
[49]Crape is a thin fabric with a crinkled surface.

"Law, Missis, you must whip me; my old Missis allers whipped me. I an't used to workin' unless I gets whipped."

"Why, Topsy, I don't want to whip you. You can do well, if you 've a mind to; what is the reason you won't?"

"Laws, Missis, I 's used to whippin'; I spects it 's good for me."

Miss Ophelia tried the recipe, and Topsy invariably made a terrible commotion, screaming, groaning and imploring, though half an hour afterwards, when roosted on some projection of the balcony, and surrounded by a flock of admiring "young uns," she would express the utmost contempt of the whole affair.

"Law, Miss Feely whip!—would n't kill a skeeter, her whippins. Oughter see how old Mas'r made the flesh fly; old Mas'r know'd how!"

Topsy always made great capital of her own sins and enormities, evidently considering them as something peculiarly distinguishing.

"Law, you niggers," she would say to some of her auditors, "does you know you 's all sinners? Well, you is—everybody is. White folks is sinners too,—Miss Feely says so; but I spects niggers is the biggest ones; but lor! ye an't any on ye up to me. I 's so awful wicked there can't nobody do nothin' with me. I used to keep old Missis a swarin' at me half de time. I spects I 's the wickedest critter in the world;" and Topsy would cut a summerset, and come up brisk and shining on to a higher perch, and evidently plume herself on the distinction.

Miss Ophelia busied herself very earnestly on Sundays, teaching Topsy the catechism. Topsy had an uncommon verbal memory, and committed with a fluency that greatly encouraged her instructress.

"What good do you expect it is going to do her?" said St. Clare.

"Why, it always has done children good. It 's what children always have to learn, you know," said Miss Ophelia.

"Understand it or not," said St. Clare.

"O, children never understand it at the time; but, after they are grown up, it 'll come to them."

"Mine hasn't come to me yet," said St. Clare, "though I 'll bear testimony that you put it into me pretty thoroughly when I was a boy."

"Ah, you were always good at learning, Augustine. I used to have great hopes of you," said Miss Ophelia.

"Well, have n't you now?" said St. Clare.

"I wish you were as good as you were when you were a boy, Augustine."

"So do I, that 's a fact, Cousin," said St. Clare. "Well, go ahead and catechize Topsy; may be you 'll make out something yet."

Topsy, who had stood like a black statue during this discussion, with hands decently folded, now, at a signal from Miss Ophelia, went on:

"Our first parents,[50] being left to the freedom of their own will, fell from the state wherein they were created."

---

[50] Adam and Eve

Topsy's eyes twinkled, and she looked inquiringly.

"What is it, Topsy?" said Miss Ophelia.

"Please, Missis, was dat ar state Kintuck?"

"What state, Topsy?"

"Dat state dey fell out of. I used to hear Mas'r tell how we came down from Kintuck."

St. Clare laughed.

"You 'll have to give her a meaning, or she 'll make one," said he. "There seems to be a theory of emigration suggested there."

"O! Augustine, be still," said Miss Ophelia; "how can I do anything, if you will be laughing?"

"Well, I won't disturb the exercises again, on my honor;" and St. Clare took his paper into the parlor, and sat down, till Topsy had finished her recitations. They were all very well, only that now and then she would oddly transpose some important words, and persist in the mistake, in spite of every effort to the contrary; and St. Clare, after all his promises of goodness, took a wicked pleasure in these mistakes, calling Topsy to him whenever he had a mind to amuse himself, and getting her to repeat the offending passages, in spite of Miss Ophelia's remonstrances.

"How do you think I can do anything with the child, if you will go on so, Augustine?" she would say.

"Well, it is too bad,—I won't again; but I do like to hear the droll little image stumble over those big words!"

"But you confirm her in the wrong way."

"What 's the odds? One word is as good as another to her."

"You wanted me to bring her up right; and you ought to remember she is a reasonable creature, and be careful of your influence over her."

"O, dismal! so I ought; but, as Topsy herself says, 'I 's so wicked!'"

In very much this way Topsy's training proceeded, for a year or two,—Miss Ophelia worrying herself, from day to day, with her, as a kind of chronic plague, to whose inflictions she became, in time, as accustomed, as persons sometimes do to the neuralgia[51] or sick head-ache.

St. Clare took the same kind of amusement in the child that a man might in the tricks of a parrot or a pointer. Topsy, whenever her sins brought her into disgrace in other quarters, always took refuge behind his chair; and St. Clare, in one way or other, would make peace for her. From him she got many a stray picayune,[52] which she laid out in nuts and candies, and distributed, with careless generosity, to all the children in the family; for Topsy, to do her justice, was good-natured and liberal, and only spiteful in self-defence.

---

[51]A sharp pain along a nerve.

[52]A picayune is something of little value.

She is fairly introduced into our *corps de ballet*,[53] and will figure, from time to time, in her turn, with other performers.

. . .

XLV.

Concluding Remarks

The writer has often been inquired of, by correspondents from different parts of the country, whether this narrative is a true one; and to these inquiries she will give one general answer.

The separate incidents that compose the narrative are, to a very great extent, authentic, occurring, many of them, either under her own observation, or that of her personal friends. She or her friends have observed characters the counterpart of almost all that are here introduced; and many of the sayings are word for word as heard herself, or reported to her.

The personal appearance of Eliza, the character ascribed to her, are sketches drawn from life. The incorruptible fidelity, piety and honesty, of Uncle Tom, had more than one development, to her personal knowledge. Some of the most deeply tragic and romantic, some of the most terrible incidents, have also their parallel in reality. The incident of the mother's crossing the Ohio river on the ice is a well-known fact. The story of "old Prue," in the second volume, was an incident that fell under the personal observation of a brother of the writer, then collecting-clerk to a large mercantile house, in New Orleans. From the same source was derived the character of the planter Legree. Of him her brother thus wrote, speaking of visiting his plantation, on a collecting tour: "He actually made me feel of his fist, which was like a blacksmith's hammer, or a nodule of iron, telling me that it was 'calloused with knocking down niggers.' When I left the plantation, I drew a long breath, and felt as if I had escaped from an ogre's den."

That the tragical fate of Tom, also, has too many times had its parallel, there are living witnesses, all over our land, to testify. Let it be remembered that in all southern states it is a principle of jurisprudence that no person of colored lineage can testify in a suit against a white, and it will be easy to see that such a case may occur, wherever there is a man whose passions outweigh his interests, and a slave who has manhood or principle enough to resist his will. There is, actually, nothing to protect the slave's life, but the *character* of the master. Facts too shocking to be contemplated occasionally force their way to the public ear, and

---

[53]The *corps de ballet* is the ballet company's ensemble, the regular performers—equivalent, in Stowe's usage, to the cast of characters in a play.

the comment that one often hears made on them is more shocking than the thing itself. It is said, "Very likely such cases may now and then occur, but they are no sample of general practice." If the laws of New England were so arranged that a master could *now and then* torture an apprentice to death, without a possibility of being brought to justice, would it be received with equal composure? Would it be said, "These cases are rare, and no samples of general practice"? This injustice is an *inherent* one in the slave system,—it cannot exist without it.

The public and shameless sale of beautiful mulatto and quadroon girls has acquired a notoriety, from the incidents following the capture of the Pearl. We extract the following from the speech of Hon. Horace Mann,[54] one of the legal counsel for the defendants in that case. He says: "In that company of seventy-six persons, who attempted, in 1848, to escape from the District of Columbia in the schooner Pearl, and whose officers I assisted in defending, there were several young and healthy girls, who had those peculiar attractions of form and feature which connoisseurs prize so highly. Elizabeth Russel was one of them. She immediately fell into the slave-trader's fangs, and was doomed for the New Orleans market. The hearts of those that saw her were touched with pity for her fate. They offered eighteen hundred dollars to redeem her; and some there were who offered to give, that would not have much left after the gift; but the fiend of a slave-trader was inexorable. She was despatched to New Orleans; but, when about half way there, God had mercy on her, and smote her with death. There were two girls named Edmundson in the same company. When about to be sent to the same market, an older sister went to the shambles, to plead with the wretch who owned them, for the love of God, to spare his victims. He bantered her, telling what fine dresses and fine furniture they would have. 'Yes,' she said, 'that may do very well in this life, but what will become of them in the next?' They too were sent to New Orleans; but were afterwards redeemed, at an enormous ransom, and brought back." Is it not plain, from this, that the histories of Emmeline and Cassy may have many counterparts?

Justice, too, obliges the author to state that the fairness of mind and generosity attributed to St. Clare are not without a parallel, as the following anecdote will show. A few years since, a young southern gentleman was in Cincinnati, with a favorite servant, who had been his personal attendant from a boy. The young man took advantage of this opportunity to secure his own freedom, and fled to the protection of a Quaker,[55] who was quite noted in affairs of this kind.

---

[54]Horace Mann (1796–1859) was an American educator. Stowe draws here from Mann's statement at the 1848 trial of Daniel Drayton, a man who attempted to help seventy-six people escape from enslavement.

[55]Also referred to as the Society of Friends, the Quakers practiced a form of Protestant Christianity that emphasized the "Inner Light," or the "Christ within." Although not all members of this religion were opposed to slavery, generally the Quakers were identified with antislavery activity, and included among their numbers many of the most important members of the organized efforts to aid fugitive slaves associated with the Underground Railroad.

The owner was exceedingly indignant. He had always treated the slave with such indulgence, and his confidence in his affection was such, that he believed he must have been practised upon to induce him to revolt from him. He visited the Quaker, in high anger; but, being possessed of uncommon candor and fairness, was soon quieted by his arguments and representations. It was a side of the subject which he never had heard, — never had thought on; and he immediately told the Quaker that, if his slave would, to his own face, say that it was his desire to be free, he would liberate him. An interview was forthwith procured, and Nathan was asked by his young master whether he had ever had any reason to complain of his treatment, in any respect.

"No, Mas'r," said Nathan; "you 've always been good to me."

"Well, then, why do you want to leave me?"

"Mas'r may die, and then who get me? — I 'd rather be a free man."

After some deliberation, the young master replied, "Nathan, in your place, I think I should feel very much so, myself. You are free."

He immediately made him out free papers; deposited a sum of money in the hands of the Quaker, to be judiciously used in assisting him to start in life, and left a very sensible and kind letter of advice to the young man. That letter was for some time in the writer's hands.

The author hopes she had done justice to that nobility, generosity, and humanity, which in many cases characterize individuals at the South. Such instances save us from utter despair of our kind. But, she asks any person, who knows the world, are such characters *common*, anywhere?

For many years of her life, the author avoided all reading upon or allusion to the subject of slavery, considering it too painful to be inquired into, and one which advancing light and civilization would certainly live down. But, since the legislative act of 1850,[56] when she heard, with perfect surprise and consternation, Christian and humane people actually recommending the remanding escaped fugitives into slavery, as a duty binding on good citizens, — when she heard, on all hands, from kind, compassionate and estimable people, in the free states of the North, deliberations and discussions as to what Christian duty could be on this head, — she could only think, These men and Christians cannot know what slavery is; if they did, such a question could never be open for discussion. And from this arose a desire to exhibit it in a *living dramatic reality*. She has endeavored to show it fairly, in its best and its worst phases. In its *best* aspect, she has, perhaps, been successful; but, oh! who shall say what yet remains untold in that valley and shadow of death, that lies on the other side?

---

[56]Stowe here refers to the Fugitive Slave Law, part of the Compromise of 1850, which was a restatement and radical extension of the previously existing fugitive slave law. States had before attempted to resist, by state law, the capturing of fugitive slaves within their boundaries; the new law was designed to control these attempts at the federal level.

To you, generous, noble-minded men and women, of the South,—you, whose virtue, and magnanimity, and purity of character, are the greater for the severer trial it has encountered,—to you is her appeal. Have you not, in your own secret souls, in your own private conversings, felt that there are woes and evils, in this accursed system, far beyond what are here shadowed, or can be shadowed? Can it be otherwise? Is *man* ever a creature to be trusted with wholly irresponsible power? And does not the slave system, by denying the slave all legal right of testimony, make every individual owner an irresponsible despot? Can anybody fail to make the inference what the practical result will be? If there is, as we admit, a public sentiment among you, men of honor, justice and humanity, is there not also another kind of public sentiment among the ruffian, the brutal and debased? And cannot the ruffian, the brutal, the debased, by slave law, own just as many slaves as the best and purest? Are the honorable, the just, the high-minded and compassionate, the majority anywhere in this world?

The slave-trade is now, by American law, considered as piracy. But a slave-trade, as systematic as ever was carried on on the coast of Africa, is an inevitable attendant and result of American slavery. And its heart-break and its horrors, *can* they be told?

The writer has given only a faint shadow, a dim picture, of the anguish and despair that are, at this very moment, riving thousands of hearts, shattering thousands of families, and driving a helpless and sensitive race to frenzy and despair. There are those living who know the mothers whom this accursed traffic has driven to the murder of their children; and themselves seeking in death a shelter from woes more dreaded than death. Nothing of tragedy can be written, can be spoken, can be conceived, that equals the frightful reality of scenes daily and hourly acting on our shores, beneath the shadow of American law, and the shadow of the cross of Christ.

And now, men and women of America, is this a thing to be trifled with, apologized for, and passed over in silence? Farmers of Massachusetts, of New Hampshire, of Vermont, of Connecticut, who read this book by the blaze of your winter-evening fire,—strong-hearted, generous sailors and shipowners of Maine,—is this a thing for you to countenance and encourage? Brave and generous men of New York, farmers of rich and joyous Ohio, and ye of the wide prairie states,—answer, is this a thing for you to protect and countenance? And you, mothers of America,—you, who have learned, by the cradles of your own children, to love and feel for all mankind,—by the sacred love you bear your child; by your joy in his beautiful, spotless infancy; by the motherly pity and tenderness with which you guide his growing years; by the anxieties of his education; by the prayers you breathe for his soul's eternal good;—I beseech you, pity the mother who has all your affections, and not one legal right to protect, guide, or educate, the child of her bosom! By the sick hour of your child; by those dying eyes, which you can never forget; by those last cries, that wrung your heart when you could neither help nor save; by the desolation of that empty cradle, that silent nursery,—I beseech you, pity those mothers that are constantly made childless by the American slave-trade! And say, mothers of America, is this a thing to be defended, sympathized with, passed over in silence?

Do you say that the people of the free states have nothing to do with it, and can do nothing? Would to God this were true! But it is not true. The people of the free states have defended, encouraged, and participated; and are more guilty for it, before God, than the South, in that they have *not* the apology of education or custom.

If the mothers of the free states had all felt as they should, in times past, the sons of the free states would not have been the holders, and, proverbially, the hardest masters of slaves; the sons of the free states would not have connived at the extension of slavery, in our national body; the sons of the free states would not, as they do, trade the souls and bodies of men as an equivalent to money, in their mercantile dealings. There are multitudes of slaves temporarily owned, and sold again, by merchants in northern cities; and shall the whole guilt or obloquy of slavery fall only on the South?

Northern men, northern mothers, northern Christians, have something more to do than denounce their brethren at the South; they have to look to the evil among themselves.

But, what can any individual do? Of that, every individual can judge. There is one thing that every individual can do,—they can see to it that *they feel right.* An atmosphere of sympathetic influence encircles every human being; and the man or woman who *feels* strongly, healthily and justly, on the great interests of humanity, is a constant benefactor to the human race. See, then, to your sympathies in this matter! Are they in harmony with the sympathies of Christ? or are they swayed and perverted by the sophistries of worldly policy?

Christian men and women of the North! still further,—you have another power; you can *pray*! Do you believe in prayer? or has it become an indistinct apostolic tradition? You pray for the heathen abroad; pray also for the heathen at home. And pray for those distressed Christians whose whole chance of religious improvement is an accident of trade and sale; from whom any adherence to the morals of Christianity is, in many cases, an impossibility, unless they have given them, from above, the courage and grace of martyrdom.

But, still more. On the shores of our free states are emerging the poor, shattered, broken remnants of families,—men and women, escaped, by miraculous providences, from the surges of slavery,—feeble in knowledge, and, in many cases, infirm in moral constitution, from a system which confounds and confuses every principle of Christianity and morality. They come to seek a refuge among you; they come to seek education, knowledge, Christianity.

What do you owe to these poor unfortunates, oh Christians? Does not every American Christian owe to the African race some effort at reparation for the wrongs that the American nation has brought upon them? Shall the doors of churches and school-houses be shut upon them? Shall states arise and shake them out? Shall the church of Christ hear in silence the taunt that is thrown at them, and shrink away from the helpless hand that they stretch out; and, by her silence, encourage the cruelty that would chase them from our borders? If it must be so, it will be a mournful spectacle. If it must be so, the country will have reason to tremble, when it remembers that the fate of nations is in the hands of One who is very pitiful, and of tender compassion.

Do you say, "We don't want them here; let them go to Africa?"

That the providence of God has provided a refuge in Africa, is, indeed, a great and noticeable fact; but that is no reason why the church of Christ should throw off that responsibility to this outcast race which her profession demands of her.

To fill up Liberia[57] with an ignorant, inexperienced, half-barbarized race, just escaped from the chains of slavery, would be only to prolong, for ages, the period of struggle and conflict which attends the inception of new enterprises. Let the church of the north receive these poor sufferers in the spirit of Christ; receive them to the educating advantages of Christian republican society and schools, until they have attained to somewhat of a moral and intellectual maturity, and then assist them in their passage to those shores, where they may put in practice the lessons they have learned in America.

There is a body of men at the north, comparatively small, who have been doing this; and, as the result, this country has already seen examples of men, formerly slaves, who have rapidly acquired property, reputation, and education. Talent has been developed, which, considering the circumstances, is certainly remarkable; and, for moral traits of honesty, kindness, tenderness of feeling,—for heroic efforts and self-denials, endured for the ransom of brethren and friends yet in slavery,—they have been remarkable to a degree that, considering the influence under which they were born, is surprising.

The writer has lived, for many years, on the frontier-line of slave states, and has had great opportunities of observation among those who formerly were slaves. They have been in her family as servants; and, in default of any other school to receive them, she has, in many cases, had them instructed in a family school, with her own children. She has also the testimony of missionaries, among the fugitives in Canada, in coincidence with her own

---

[57]Liberia was founded by the American Colonization Society (ACS) in 1821 as the destination for relocated African Americans. It was the mission of the ACS to transport emancipated and free African Americans to Africa. While some abolitionists supported the ACS in its early years, most came to oppose the organization, inspired especially by the arguments of black abolitionists. Stowe's approval of Liberia in both the plot and concluding remarks of *Uncle Tom's Cabin* was vigorously denounced by various prominent African Americans.

experience; and her deductions, with regard to the capabilities of the race, are encouraging in the highest degree.

The first desire of the emancipated slave, generally, is for *education*. There is nothing that they are not willing to give or do to have their children instructed; and, so far as the writer has observed herself, or taken the testimony of teachers among them, they are remarkably intelligent and quick to learn. The results of schools, founded for them by benevolent individuals in Cincinnati, fully establish this.[58]

The author gives the following statement of facts, on the authority of Professor C. E. Stowe,[59] then of Lane Seminary, Ohio, with regard to emancipated slaves, now resident in Cincinnati; given to show the capability of the race, even without any very particular assistance or encouragement.

The initial letters alone are given. They are all residents of Cincinnati.

"B———. Furniture maker; twenty years in the city; worth ten thousand dollars, all his own earnings; a Baptist.

"C———. Full black; stolen from Africa; sold in New Orleans; been free fifteen years; paid for himself six hundred dollars; a farmer; owns several farms in Indiana; Presbyterian; probably worth fifteen or twenty thousand dollars, all earned by himself.

"K———. Full black; dealer in real estate; worth thirty thousand dollars; about forty years old; free six years; paid eighteen hundred dollars for his family; member of the Baptist church; received a legacy from his master, which he has taken good care of, and increased.

"G———. Full black; coal dealer; about thirty years old; worth eighteen thousand dollars; paid for himself twice, being once defrauded to the amount of sixteen hundred dollars; made all his money by his own efforts—much of it while a slave, hiring his time of his master, and doing business for himself; a fine, gentlemanly fellow.

"W———. Three-fourths black; barber and waiter; from Kentucky; nineteen years free; paid for self and family over three thousand dollars; deacon in the Baptist church.

"G.D———. Three-fourths black; white-washer; from Kentucky; nine years free; paid fifteen hundred dollars for self and family; recently died, aged sixty; worth six thousand dollars."

Professor Stowe says, "With all these, except G———, I have been, for some years, personally acquainted, and make my statements from my own knowledge."

---

[58]A school associated with Lane Seminary was organized in 1834 for fugitives in Cincinnati, and the Reverend Hiram Gilmore opened a high school in 1844.

[59]Calvin Ellis Stowe (1802–1886) was Harriet Beecher Stowe's husband. He joined the faculty of Lane Theological Seminary in 1833.

The writer well remembers an aged colored woman, who was employed as a washerwoman in her father's family. The daughter of this woman married a slave. She was a remarkably active and capable young woman, and, by her industry and thrift, and the most persevering self-denial, raised nine hundred dollars for her husband's freedom, which she paid, as she raised it, into the hands of his master. She yet wanted a hundred dollars of the price, when he died. She never recovered any of the money.

These are but a few facts, among multitudes which might be adduced, to show the self-denial, energy, patience, and honesty, which the slave has exhibited in a state of freedom.

And let it be remembered that these individuals have thus bravely succeeded in conquering for themselves comparative wealth and social position, in the face of every disadvantage and discouragement. The colored man, by the law of Ohio, cannot be a voter, and, till within a few years, was even denied the right of testimony in legal suits with the white. Nor are these instances confined to the State of Ohio. In all states of the Union we see men, but yesterday burst from the shackles of slavery, who, by a self-educating force, which cannot be too much admired, have risen to highly respectable stations in society. Pennington, among clergymen, Douglass and Ward, among editors, are very well known instances.[60]

If this persecuted race, with every discouragement and disadvantage, have done thus much, how much more they might do, if the Christian church would act towards them in the spirit of her Lord!

This is an age of the world when nations are trembling and convulsed. A mighty influence is abroad, surging and heaving the world, as with an earthquake. And is America safe? Every nation that carries in its bosom great and unredressed injustice has in it the elements of this last convulsion.

For what is this mighty influence thus rousing in all nations and languages those groanings that cannot be uttered, for man's freedom and equality?

O, Church of Christ, read the signs of the times! Is not this power the spirit of HIM whose kingdom is yet to come, and whose will to be done on earth as it is in heaven?

But who may abide the day of his appearing? "for that day shall burn as an oven: and he shall appear as a swift witness against those that oppress the hireling in his wages, the widow and the fatherless, and that *turn aside the stranger in his right:* and he shall break in pieces the oppressor."[61]

---

[60]J. W. C. Pennington (1807–1870) was born in slavery in Maryland. Following his escape in 1828, he became a minister, lecturer, and writer. Frederick Douglass (c. 1817–1895) was probably the most prominent and influential African-American leader of his time. Born in slavery in Maryland, Douglass became an antislavery lecturer, writer, and newspaper editor. Samuel Ringgold Ward (c. 1817–1866) was born in slavery and was known as a powerful lecturer in addition to being an influential writer and editor.

[61]See Malachi 4:1

Are not these dread words for a nation bearing in her bosom so mighty an injustice? Christians! every time that you pray that the kingdom of Christ may come, can you forget that prophecy associates, in dread fellowship, the *day of vengeance* with the year of his redeemed?

A day of grace is yet held out to us. Both North and South have been guilty before God; and the *Christian church* has a heavy account to answer. Not by combining together, to protect injustice and cruelty, and making a common capital of sin, is this Union to be saved, — but by repentance, justice and mercy; for, not surer is the eternal law by which the millstone sinks in the ocean, than that stronger law, by which injustice and cruelty shall bring on nations the wrath of Almighty God!

FREDERICK DOUGLASS
[1818–1895]

One of the most prolific and influential writers of the nineteenth century is known to most readers today for a single, slim book: Narrative of the Life of Frederick Douglass, An American Slave, Written by Himself *(1845). There's good reason to remember this book in particular, for it is considered by many to be the classic example of the genre of writing commonly called "slave narratives," and it remains an eloquent, wise, and compelling commentary on slavery and the struggle for freedom—a book from which readers still have much to learn these many years later. But today's recognition of Douglass's power as a writer should not be limited to his first book, however compelling, for throughout his life Douglass remained devoted to the conviction that the written word was a powerful weapon in the cause of social justice, and that literature could change the world. In three autobiographies, a novella ("The Heroic Slave"), newspaper writings (for his papers* The North Star *and Frederick Douglass' Paper), and published orations (among many others, "What to the Slave Is the Fourth of July?"), Douglass demonstrated this faith throughout his long public career as the most celebrated African-American leader of the nineteenth century, and as one of the most influential men in American history.*

Much of Douglass's writing career can be understood as an attempt to promote his own life as a representative story of African-American life in the nineteenth century, and then to meet the responsibilities that follow from that role. In part, this challenge led Douglass back to autobiographical writing throughout his career—including his 1845 Narrative, My Bondage and My Freedom, *published in 1855, and* Life and Times of Frederick Douglass, *published in 1881 and expanded in 1892. Douglass recognized the importance of this genre of writing to African Americans, for their experience, and the perspectives and understanding shaped by that experience, were largely either unrepresented or misrepresented in the publications of the day. "My part," Douglass wrote in the last of the autobiographies, "has been to tell the story of the slave. The story of the master never wanted for narrators. The masters, to tell their story, had at call all the talent and genius that wealth could command. They have had their day in court. Literature, theology, philosophy, law, and learning have come willingly to their service, and, if condemned, they have not been condemned unheard." Marshaling the forces of literature, Douglass was determined that others would have their day in court as well, and in his newspaper writing, fiction, and orations he brought theology, philosophy, law, and learning to the antislavery movement, to the women's rights movement, and broadly to the cause of educational, social, and occupational opportunity for African Americans.*

Douglass was enslaved at birth in Talbot County, Maryland, in February 1818, and years later would speak of himself, with considerable justice, as a "self-made man," the topic of one of his most popular lectures. His mother, Harriet Bailey, was enslaved; his father was a white man whose identity Douglass could never determine with certainty. A turning point in Douglass's life came when he was sent to Baltimore in 1826 to be a house servant for Sophia and Hugh Auld. Initially kind, Sophia Auld began to teach the young Douglass to read, but both her kindness and the lessons soon came to a halt. Convinced of the importance of that which was denied to him, Douglass continued the lessons on his own, sometimes recruiting the help of young white boys in the city. He was sent back to his rural plantation in 1833, but was sent back to Baltimore in 1836 following his unsuccessful attempt to escape. Finally, in 1838, and with the help of a free black woman in Baltimore, Anna Murray, Douglass escaped by posing as a sailor and taking a train to New York City. Anna followed shortly after that, and she and Douglass married and settled in New Bedford, Massachusetts. Douglass, who had heard of abolitionists while enslaved, began reading William Lloyd Garrison's antislavery newspaper the Liberator *in 1839. Within a few years Douglass joined his own voice to the movement, and his power as a speaker was so great that he was quickly invited, after his initial speech in 1841, to become a lecturing agent for the Massachusetts Anti-Slavery Society. From 1841 to 1845 he traveled the antislavery lecture circuit, gaining recognition and prominence within the movement, speaking so powerfully and eloquently that some audiences doubted that he could have been born a slave.*

In part to put such doubts to rest, Douglass wrote his Narrative of the Life of Frederick Douglass, an American Slave, Written by Himself, *a book instantly recognized in its own time as a singular achievement and celebrated ever since as a classic of American literary history. Published by the American Anti-Slavery Society of Boston, the* Narrative *sold close to five thousand copies in its first four months, and nearly thirty thousand copies in the United States and Great Britain by 1850. The 1845 American edition was followed by a Dutch translation in 1846 and a French translation in 1848. In the* Narrative, *Douglass tells the story of coming of age under the system of slavery, learning to read, and struggling to realize his developing dreams of freedom. Many episodes in the* Narrative *presented readers with horrors and struggles they would expect to hear, with eloquent testament to the ideal of liberty. As Douglass writes in one of the* Narrative's *best-known statements, "You have seen how a man was made a slave; you shall see how a slave was made a man." But the* Narrative *is notable as well for what Douglass chooses not to relate—the details of the story of his escape, for example, and the personal story of his relationship with Anna. The* Narrative *is a strategic story, denying readers certain intimacies of his life, and specific information about his means of escape from slavery. The* Narrative *is a critique of slavery, one designed to enlist support; and it was a sufficiently sharp critique that Douglass added an Appendix to defend his representation of white slaveholding religion, drawing a sharp distinction "between the Christianity of this land, and the Christianity of Christ."*

The Narrative *succeeded in establishing Douglass's credentials as one who had experienced slavery firsthand—to the point that, for personal safety, Douglass was forced to leave the country. The narrative of enslavement could too easily become the tool of Douglass's reenslavement, for he was a fugitive under American law. From 1845 to 1847 Douglass worked in Great Britain for the antislavery movement by giving lectures in England, Ireland, and Scotland. His efforts inspired significant support for his cause and for his leadership, and when he returned to the United States (following the indignity of having to purchase, with the assistance of white supporters, his own liberty), he returned with funds to start his own weekly newspaper, the* North Star. *Douglass established the new antislavery paper (which heightened developing tensions with William Lloyd Garrison, editor of the* Liberator) *at his new home, Rochester, New York, in December 1847, proclaiming its guiding philosophy in its masthead: "Right is of no Sex—Truth is of no Color—God is the Father of us all, and we are all Brethren." In 1851, the* North Star *would become* Frederick Douglass' Paper, *and in 1858 Douglass initiated a monthly publication as well,* Douglass' Monthly. *In all of these periodicals Douglass reprinted articles from other papers, and enlisted black and white abolitionists as contributors—but necessarily, filled the paper with his own writing.*

Some of Douglass' most influential work of this period followed his conviction that "the people want to do what is best," but that "they must be shown that to do right is best." In 1853, Douglass wrote "The Heroic Slave," a fictionalized novella of the true story of Madison Washington, leader of the successful mutiny on the slave ship Creole *in 1841. Douglass begins the narrative by associating Washington with the white founding fathers and heroes of the American Revolution—but Douglass notes that while the story of white revolutionary heroism is amply documented, Washington's story can only be pieced together, and he focuses much of the story on the experiences, the partial understanding and the occasional resolve, of a white character, Mr. Listwell, whose ability to listen well to Washington's experiences converts him to the antislavery movement and inspires him to act on his convictions.*

Douglass's hesitations about the sincerity of white antislavery efforts became increasingly a subject of his writing, and was suggested dramatically in his 1855 autobiography, My Bondage and My Freedom. *Whereas the 1845* Narrative *included a preface by white abolitionist William Lloyd Garrison,* My Bondage and My Freedom *begins with a preface from black abolitionist James McCune Smith, one of the preeminent African-American scholars of his time and an established critic of Garrison's methods. Douglass draws from the earlier autobiography, but his portrayal of slavery is more harsh, and his consideration of it as a political and cultural system is more detailed than in the 1845* Narrative. *Moreover, Douglass extends his story to a glimpse into racial prejudice in the North and into the antislavery movement itself. In many of his newspaper editorials, Douglass was even more frank about life in the "free" North—asserting, for example, in an 1850 article that "properly speaking,* prejudice against color *does not exist in this country. The feeling (or whatever it is) which we call* prejudice *is no less than a* murderous, hell-born hatred *of every virtue which may adorn the character of a black man." Much of Douglass's writing during this period was devoted to the full range of African-American experience, and to the various aspects of a cultural system that supported and encouraged the restriction of African-American opportunity and the misrepresentation of black identity.*

Douglass's frustrations are clear in one of his most famous speeches from this period, "What to the Slave Is the Fourth of July?" On July 5, 1852, Douglass responded to an invitation to speak in Rochester, New York, by asking his audience, "Do you mean, citizens, to mock me, by asking me to speak to-day?" Douglass begins his speech by reviewing, with admiration, the great events of the American Revolution so ceremoniously celebrated on the Fourth of July, but he argues that the ideals of the American Revolution have been violated and the national founders dishonored by subsequent events, for rather than follow through on their devotion to liberty they had instead abandoned it to the system of slavery. Douglass accordingly asks and answers what is, for him, the question of the day: "What, to the American slave, is your Fourth of July? I answer: a day that reveals to him, more than all other days in the year, the gross injustice and cruelty to which he is the constant victim." The force of Douglass's comments, though, is only increased by his expressed admiration for the ideals that drove the American Revolution. Indeed, through his most trying times as a prominent critic of slavery and racism, Douglass remained a staunch friend to those white Americans who had similarly devoted themselves to the cause. Throughout his career, in fact, Douglass held onto his remarkable faith that things could and would change, and that Americans could come to view themselves differently and embrace a community based on the belief that "a diverse origin does not disprove a common nature, nor does it disprove a united destiny. The essential characteristics of humanity are everywhere the same."

As the Civil War approached, Douglass's convictions were both challenged and seemingly vindicated. He was sufficiently militant in his resistance to things as they were that he consulted with the white abolitionist John Brown before Brown's raid at Harpers Ferry, though Douglass did not have the faith in Brown's plan to join the raid himself. His association with Brown was sufficiently incriminating, however, to force Douglass to leave the country briefly after Brown was captured. But with the arrival of the Civil War in 1861, Douglass believed that the nation was finally in a position to confront the sins of the past, and he was influential in finally convincing Abraham Lincoln to recruit African Americans for the Union army and in guiding the recruitment efforts. After the war, Douglass tried to convince President Andrew Johnson to guide the nation toward African-American rights.

In the years that followed, Douglass's leadership was broadly acknowledged, if often frustrated and limited. He held various public offices, including United States Marshal of the District of Columbia (1877–81), Recorder of Deeds for the District of Columbia (1881–86), president of the Freedman's Bureau Bank, consul to Haiti and chargé d'affaires for the Dominican Republic (1889–91). When he returned to autobiography in his 1881 publication, Life and Times of Frederick Douglass, *and when he expanded that final story of his life in 1892, he could write of his belief, after the Civil War, that his life's work had been completed—but he had to write as well of the great work that remained in education, civil rights, and economic opportunity. Telling the story of his life remained the great work of his life, as he looked in his own experience for evidence that African Americans would be recognized as free and equal citizens in a nation that had learned to finally embrace its own professed ideals. As he states toward the end of* Life and Times, *"it will be seen in these pages that I have lived several lives in one: first, the life of slavery; secondly, the life of a fugitive from slavery; thirdly, the life of comparative freedom; fourthly, the life of conflict and battle; and fifthly, the life of victory, if not complete, at least assured." That his story remains important, but still unfinished, is evident in the many biographies and poems devoted to him by various American writers, black and white, who recognize the importance of understanding the first four stories if Americans are to complete the fifth.*

John Ernest
University of New Hampshire

For Further Reading

Primary Works

Narrative of the Life of Frederick Douglass, an American Slave, Written by Himself (1845); What to the Slave Is the Fourth of July? An Address Delivered in Rochester, New York, on 5 July 1852 (1852); The Heroic Slave (1853); My Bondage and My Freedom (1855); Life and Times of Frederick Douglass (1881,

1892); *Introduction, The Reason Why the Colored American Is Not in the World Columbian Exposition* (1893); *The Lessons of the Hour* (1894); *Life and Writings of Frederick Douglass,* ed. Philip S. Foner. 5 vols. New York: International, 1950–75; *The Frederick Douglass Papers,* ed. John W. Blassingame. 5 vols. New Haven: Yale University Press, 1979–.

Biography

Blight, David W., *Frederick Douglass' Civil War* (Baton Rouge: Louisiana State University Press, 1989). Chesnutt, Charles Waddell, *Frederick Douglass* (London: K. Paul, Trench, Trübner & Co., 1899). Huggins, Nathan Irvin, *Slave and Citizen: The Life of Frederick Douglass* (Boston: Little, Brown, 1980). Martin, Waldo E., *The Mind of Frederick Douglass,* (Chapel Hill: University of North Carolina Press, 1982). McFeely, William S., *Frederick Douglass* (New York: W.W. Norton, 1991). Preston, Dickson, J., *Young Frederick Douglass: The Maryland Years* (Baltimore: Johns Hopkins University Press, 1980). Quarles, Benjamin, *Frederick Douglass* (Washington, D.C.: Associated Publishers, 1948). Washington, Booker T., *Frederick Douglass* (New York: Haskell House, 1968).

Secondary Works

Andrews, William L., ed., *Critical Essays on Frederick Douglass* (Boston: G.K. Hall, 1991). Andrews, William L., *To Tell a Free Story: The First Century of Afro-American Autobiography, 1760–1865* (Urbana: University of Illinois Press, 1986). Baker, Houston A., Jr., *Blues, Ideology, and Afro-American Literature* (Chicago: University of Chicago Press, 1984). Butterfield, Stephen, *Black Autobiography in America,* (Amherst: University of Massachusetts Press, 1974). Davis, Charles T., and Henry Louis Gates, Jr., eds., *The Slave's Narrative* (New York: Oxford University Press, 1985). Ernest, John, *Resistance and Reformation in Nineteenth-Century African-American Literature: Brown, Wilson, Jacobs, Delany, Douglass, and Harper* (Jackson: University Press of Mississippi, 1995). Fisch, Audrey, *American Slaves in Victorian England: Abolitionist Politics in Popular Literature and Culture* (Cambridge: Cambridge University Press, 2000). Foster, Frances Smith, *Witnessing Slavery: The Development of Ante-bellum Slave Narratives,* 1979. 2nd ed. (Madison: University of Wisconsin Press, 1994). Gates, Henry Louis, Jr., ed., *Black Literature & Literary Theory* (New York: Routledge, 1984). Gates, Henry Louis, Jr., *Figures in Black: Words, Signs, and the "Racial" Self* (New York: Oxford University Press, 1987). Hall, Jim, ed., *Approaches to Teaching The Narrative of the Life of Frederick Douglass* (New York: The Modern Language Association of America, 1999). Howard-Pittney, David, *The Afro-American Jeremiad: Appeals for Justice in America* (Philadelphia: Temple University Press, 1990). Levine, Robert S., *Martin Delany, Frederick Douglass, and the Politics of Representative Identity* (Chapel Hill: The University of North Carolina Press, 1997). Lott, Tommy L., ed., *Subjugation & Bondage: Critical Essays on Slavery and Social Philosophy* (Lanham: Rowman & Littlefield, 1998). Rice, Alan J., and Martin Crawford, eds., *Liberating Sojourn:*

Frederick Douglass & Transatlantic Reform (Athens: The University of Georgia Press, 1999). Rogers, William B., *"We Are All Together Now": Frederick Douglass, William Lloyd Garrison, and the Prophetic Tradition* (New York: Garland, 1995). Sale, Maggie Montesinos, *The Slumbering Volcano: American Slave Ship Revolts and the Production of Rebellious Masculinity* (Durham: Duke University Press, 1997). Sartwell, Crispin, *Act Like You Know: African-American Autobiography and White Identity* (Chicago: The University of Chicago Press, 1998). Smith, Valerie, *Self-Discovery and Authority in Afro-American Narrative* (Cambridge: Harvard University Press, 1991). Starling, Marion Wilson, *The Slave Narrative: Its Place in American History* (Washington, D.C.: Howard University Press, 1988). Stuckey, Sterling, *Going Through the Storm: The Influence of African American Art in History* (New York: Oxford University Press, 1994). Sundquist, Eric J., ed., *Frederick Douglass: New Literary and Historical Essays* (Cambridge: Cambridge University Press, 1990). Sundquist, Eric J., *To Wake the Nations: Race in the Making of American Literature* (Cambridge, Mass: Belknap Press of Harvard University Press, 1993). Wald, Priscilla, *Constituting Americans: Cultural Anxiety and Narrative Form* (Durham: Duke University Press, 1995). Wood, Marcus, *Blind Memory: Visual Representations of Slavery in England and America, 1780–1865* (New York: Routledge, 2000).

Narrative of the Life of Frederick Douglass, an American Slave,* Preface and Chapter I

FREDERICK DOUGLASS

Preface

In the month of August, 1841, I attended an anti-slavery convention in Nantucket, at which it was my happiness to become acquainted with FREDERICK DOUGLASS, the writer of the following Narrative. He was a stranger to nearly every member of that body; but, having recently made his escape from the southern prisonhouse of bondage, and feeling his curiosity excited to ascertain the principles and measures of the abolitionists,—of whom he had heard a somewhat vague description while he was a slave,—he was induced to give his attendance, on the occasion alluded to, though at that time a resident in New Bedford.

Fortunate, most fortunate occurrence!—fortunate for the millions of his manacled brethren, yet panting for deliverance from their awful thraldom!—fortunate for the cause of negro emancipation, and of universal liberty!—fortunate for the land of his birth, which he has already done so much to save and bless!—fortunate for a large circle of friends and acquaintances, whose sympathy and affection he has strongly secured by the many sufferings he has endured, by his virtuous traits of character, by his ever-abiding remembrance of those who are in bonds, as being bound with them!—fortunate for the multitudes, in various parts of our republic, whose minds he has enlightened on the subject of slavery, and who have been melted to tears by his pathos, or roused to virtuous indignation by his stirring eloquence against the enslavers of men!—fortunate for himself, as it at once brought him into the field of public usefulness, "gave the world assurance of a man,"[1] quickened the slumbering energies of his soul, and consecrated him to the great work of breaking the rod of the oppressor, and letting the oppressed go free!

I shall never forget his first speech at the convention—the extraordinary emotion it excited in my own mind—the powerful impression it created upon a crowded auditory, completely taken by surprise—the applause which fol-

---

*The best-known of Douglass's autobiographies was first published by the American Anti-Slavery Society of Boston in 1845. This text is based on the 1847 edition.
[1]From William Shakespeare, *Hamlet*, act III, scene 4, line 62.

lowed from the beginning to the end of his felicitous remarks. I think I never hated slavery so intensely as at that moment; certainly, my perception of the enormous outrage which is inflicted by it, on the godlike nature of its victims, was rendered far more clear than ever. There stood one, in physical proportion and stature commanding and exact—in intellect richly endowed—in natural eloquence a prodigy—in soul manifestly "created but a little lower than the angels"[2]—yet a slave, ay, a fugitive slave,—trembling for his safety, hardly daring to believe that on the American soil, a single white person could be found who would befriend him at all hazards, for the love of God and humanity! Capable of high attainments as an intellectual and moral being—needing nothing but a comparatively small amount of cultivation to make him an ornament to society and a blessing to his race—by the law of the land, by the voice of the people, by the terms of the slave code, he was only a piece of property, a beast of burden, a chattel personal, nevertheless!

A beloved friend from New Bedford[3] prevailed on MR. DOUGLASS to address the convention: He came forward to the platform with a hesitancy and embarrassment, necessarily the attendants of a sensitive mind in such a novel position. After apologizing for his ignorance, and reminding the audience that slavery was a poor school for the human intellect and heart, he proceeded to narrate some of the facts in his own history as a slave, and in the course of his speech gave utterance to many noble thoughts and thrilling reflections. As soon as he had taken his seat, filled with hope and admiration, I rose, and declared that PATRICK HENRY,[4] of revolutionary fame, never made a speech more eloquent in the cause of liberty, than the one we had just listened to from the lips of that hunted fugitive. So I believed at that time—such is my belief now. I reminded the audience of the peril which surrounded this self-emancipated young man at the North,—even in Massachusetts, on the soil of the Pilgrim Fathers, among the descendants of revolutionary sires; and I appealed to them, whether they would ever allow him to be carried back into slavery,—law or no law, constitution or no constitution. The response was unanimous and in thundertones—"NO!" "Will you succor and protect him as a brother-man—a resident of the old Bay State."[5] "YES!" shouted the whole mass, with an energy so startling, that the ruthless tyrants south of Mason and Dixon's line might almost have heard the mighty burst of feeling, and recognized it as the pledge of an invincible determination, on the part of those who gave it, never to betray him that wanders, but to hide the outcast, and firmly to abide the consequences.

---

[2]Psalms 8:5

[3]William C. Coffin (1816–?), of New Bedford, Massachusetts, was a white Quaker and abolitionist who served as recording secretary of the Bristol County Anti-Slavery Society.

[4]Patrick Henry (1736–1799) presented his famous "liberty or death" speech to the Virginia House of Delegates on March 23, 1775. The speech, important in early national American history, was often referred to in African-American writing before the Civil War.

[5]Massachusetts

It was at once deeply impressed upon my mind, that, if Mr. DOUGLASS could be persuaded to consecrate his time and talents to the promotion of the anti-slavery enterprise, a powerful impetus would be given to it, and a stunning blow at the same time inflicted on northern prejudice against a colored complexion. I therefore endeavored to instill hope and courage into his mind, in order that he might dare to engage in a vocation so anomalous and responsible for a person in his situation; and I was seconded in this effort by warm-hearted friends, especially by the late General Agent of the Massachusetts Anti-Slavery Society, Mr. JOHN A. COLLINS,[6] whose judgment in this instance entirely coincided with my own. At first, he could give no encouragement; with unfeigned diffidence, he expressed his conviction that he was not adequate to the performance of so great a task; the path marked out was wholly an untrodden one; he was sincerely apprehensive that he should do more harm than good. After much deliberation, however, he consented to make a trial; and ever since that period, he has acted as a lecturing agent, under the auspices either of the American or the Massachusetts Anti-Slavery Society. In labors he has been most abundant; and his success in combating prejudice, in gaining proselytes, in agitating the public mind, has far surpassed the most sanguine expectations that were raised at the commencement of his brilliant career. He has borne himself with gentleness and meekness, yet with true manliness of character. As a public speaker, he excels in pathos, wit, comparison, imitation, strength of reasoning, and fluency of language. There is in him that union of head and heart, which is indispensable to an enlightenment of the heads and a winning of the hearts of others. May his strength continue to be equal to his day! May he continue to "grow in grace, and in the knowledge of God,"[7] that he may be increasingly serviceable in the cause of bleeding humanity, whether at home or abroad!

It is certainly a very remarkable fact, that one of the most efficient advocates of the slave population, now before the public, is a fugitive slave, in the person of FREDERICK DOUGLASS; and that the free colored population of the United States are as ably represented by one of their own number, in the person of CHARLES LENOX REMOND,[8] whose eloquent appeals have extorted the highest applause of multitudes on both sides of the Atlantic. Let the calumniators of the colored race despise themselves for their baseness and illiberality of spirit, and henceforth cease to talk of the natural inferiority of those who require nothing but time and opportunity to attain to the highest point of human excellence.

---

[6]John A. Collins (1810–1879) was, as Douglass states, at this time a general agent of the Massachusetts Anti-Slavery Society.

[7]See Peter 3: 17–18.

[8]Charles Lenox Remond (1810–1873) was a black abolitionist, born to free parents in Massachusetts, well known for his powerful lectures. Remond had lectured in England and Ireland after attending the World's Anti-Slavery Convention in London in 1840.

It may, perhaps, be fairly questioned, whether any other portion of the population of the earth could have endured the privations, sufferings and horrors of slavery, without having become more degraded in the scale of humanity than the slaves of African descent. Nothing has been left undone to cripple their intellects, darken their minds, debase their moral nature, obliterate all traces of their relationship to mankind; and yet how wonderfully they have sustained the mighty load of a most frightful bondage, under which they have been groaning for centuries! To illustrate the effect of slavery on the white man,—to show that he has no powers of endurance, in such a condition, superior to those of his black brother,—DANIEL O'CONNELL,[9] the distinguished advocate of universal emancipation, and the mightiest champion of prostrate but not conquered Ireland, relates the following anecdote in a speech delivered by him in the Conciliation Hall, Dublin, before the Loyal National Repeal Association,[10] March 31, 1845. "No matter," said Mr. O'CONNELL, "under what specious term it may disguise itself, slavery is still hideous. *It has a natural, an inevitable tendency to brutalize every noble faculty of man.* An American sailor, who was cast away on the shore of Africa, where he was kept in slavery for three years, was at the expiration of that period, found to be imbruted and stultified—he had lost all reasoning power; and having forgotten his native language, could only utter some savage gibberish between Arabic and English, which nobody could understand, and which even he himself found difficulty in pronouncing. So much for the humanizing influence of THE DOMESTIC INSTITUTION!" Admitting this to have been an extraordinary case of mental deterioration, it proves at least that the white slave can sink as low in the scale of humanity as the black one.

Mr. DOUGLASS has very properly chosen to write his own Narrative, in his own style, and according to the best of his ability, rather than to employ some one else. It is, therefore, entirely his own production; and, considering how long and dark was the career he had to run as a slave,—how few have been his opportunities to improve his mind since he broke his iron fetters,—it is, in my judgment, highly creditable to his head and heart. He who can peruse it without a tearful eye, a heaving breast, an afflicted spirit,—without being filled with an unutterable abhorrence of slavery and all its abettors, and animated with a determination to seek the immediate overthrow of that execrable system,—without trembling for the fate of this country in the hands of a righteous God,[11] who is ever on the side of the oppressed, and whose arm is

---

[9]Daniel O'Connell (1775–1847) was an Irish Catholic political leader and abolitionist well known in the United States.

[10]The Loyal National Repeal Association was formed in 1840 under the leadership of Daniel O'Connell. The Association advocated for the restoration of a separate Irish parliament.

[11]In his reflections on the character of the new nation in *Notes on the State of Virginia*, Thomas Jefferson famously worried about the moral consequences of the nation's reliance on the system of slavery. Jefferson's statement—"I tremble for my country when I reflect that God is just"—appeared frequently in antislavery publications.

not shortened that it cannot save,[12] —must have a flinty heart, and be qualified to act the part of a trafficker "in slaves and the souls of men."[13] I am confident that it is essentially true in all its statements; that nothing has been set down in malice, nothing exaggerated, nothing drawn from the imagination; that it comes short of the reality, rather than overstates a single fact in regard to SLAVERY AS IT IS. The experience of FREDERICK DOUGLASS, as a slave, was not a peculiar one; his lot was not especially a hard one; his case may be regarded as a very fair specimen of the treatment of slaves in Maryland, in which State it is conceded that they are better fed and less cruelly treated than in Georgia, Alabama, or Louisiana. Many have suffered incomparably more, while very few on the plantations have suffered less, than himself. Yet how deplorable was his situation! what terrible chastisements were inflicted upon his person! what still more shocking outrages were perpetrated upon his mind! with all his noble powers and sublime aspirations, how like a brute was he treated, even by those professing to have the same mind in them that was in Christ Jesus! to what dreadful liabilities was he continually subjected! how destitute of friendly counsel and aid, even in his greatest extremities! how heavy was the midnight of woe which shrouded in blackness the last ray of hope, and filled the future with terror and gloom! what longings after freedom took possession of his breast, and how his misery augmented, in proportion as he grew reflective and intelligent,—thus demonstrating that a happy slave is an extinct man! how he thought, reasoned, felt, under the lash of the driver, with the chains upon his limbs! what perils he encountered in his endeavors to escape from his horrible doom! and how signal have been his deliverance and preservation in the midst of a nation of pitiless enemies!

This Narrative contains many affecting incidents, many passages of great eloquence and power; but I think the most thrilling one of them all is the description DOUGLASS gives of his feelings, as he stood soliloquizing respecting his fate, and the chances of his one day being a freeman, on the banks of the Chesapeake Bay—viewing the receding vessels as they flew with their white wings before the breeze, and apostrophizing them as animated by the living spirit of freedom. Who can read that passage, and be insensible to its pathos and sublimity? Compressed into it is a whole Alexandrian library[14] of thought, feeling, and sentiment—all that can, all that need be urged, in the form of expostulation, entreaty, rebuke, against that crime of crimes,—making man the property of his fellow-man! O, how accursed is that system, which entombs the godlike mind of man, defaces the divine image, reduces those who by creation were crowned with glory and honor to a level with four-footed beasts, and exalts the dealer in human flesh above all that is called God! Why should its existence be

---

[12]See Isaiah, 50:2.
[13]See Revelations 18:11–13.
[14]The Alexandrian library in Egypt was said to have contained well over half a million books.

prolonged one hour? Is it not evil, only evil, and that continually? What does its presence imply but the absence of all fear of God, all regard for man, on the part of the people of the United States! Heaven speed its eternal overthrow!

So profoundly ignorant of the nature of slavery are many persons, that they are stubbornly incredulous whenever they read or listen to any recital of the cruelties which are daily inflicted on its victims. They do not deny that the slaves are held as property; but that terrible fact seems to convey to their minds no idea of injustice, exposure to outrage, or savage barbarity. Tell them of cruel scourgings, of mutilations and brandings, of scenes of pollution and blood, of the banishment of all light and knowledge, and they affect to be greatly indignant at such enormous exaggerations, such wholesale misstatements, such abominable libels on the character of the southern planters! As if all these direful outrages were not the natural results of slavery! As if it were less cruel to reduce a human being to the condition of a thing, than to give him a severe flagellation, or to deprive him of necessary food and clothing! As if whips, chains, thumb-screws, paddles, bloodhounds, overseers, drivers, patrols, were not all indispensable to keep the slaves down, and to give protection to their ruthless oppressors! As if, when the marriage institution is abolished, concubinage, adultery, and incest, must not necessary abound; when all the rights of humanity are annihilated, any barrier remains to protect the victim from the fury of the spoiler; when absolute power is assumed over life and liberty, it will not be wielded with destructive sway! Skeptics of this character abound in society. In some few instances, their incredulity arises from a want of reflection; but, generally, it indicates a hatred of the light, a desire to shield slavery from the assaults of its foes, a contempt of the colored race, whether bond or free. Such will try to discredit the shocking tales of slaveholding cruelty which are recorded in this truthful Narrative, but they will labor in vain. Mr. DOUGLASS has frankly disclosed the place of his birth, the names of those who claimed ownership in his body and soul, and the names also of those who committed the crimes which he has alleged against them. His statements, therefore, may easily be disproved, if they are untrue.

In the course of his Narrative, he relates two instances of murderous cruelty,—in one of which a planter deliberately shot a slave belonging to a neighboring plantation, who had unintentionally gotten within his lordly domain in quest of fish; and in the other, an overseer blew out the brains of a slave who had fled to a stream of water to escape a bloody scourging. Mr. DOUGLASS states that in neither of these instances was any thing done by way of legal arrest or judicial investigation. The Baltimore American, of March 17, 1845, relates a similar case of atrocity, perpetrated with similar impunity—as follows:—
"*Shooting a Slave.*—We learn, upon the authority of a letter from Charles county, Maryland, received by a gentleman of this city, that a young man, named Matthews, a nephew of General Matthews, and whose father, it is believed, holds an office at Washington, killed one of the slaves upon his father's

farm by shooting him. The letter states that young Matthews had been left in charge of the farm; that he gave an order to the servant, which was disobeyed, when he proceeded to the house, *obtained a gun, and, returning, shot the servant.* He immediately, the letter continues, fled to his father's residence, where he still remains unmolested."—Let it never be forgotten, that no slaveholder or overseer can be convicted of any outrage perpetrated on the person of a slave, however diabolical it may be, on the testimony of colored witnesses, whether bond or free. By the slave code, they are adjudged to be as incompetent to testify against a white man, as though they were indeed a part of the brute creation. Hence, there is no legal protection in fact, whatever there may be in form, for the slave population; and any amount of cruelty may be inflicted on them with impunity. Is it possible for the human mind to conceive of a more horrible state of society?

The effect of a religious profession on the conduct of southern masters is vividly described in the following Narrative, and shown to be any thing but salutary. In the nature of the case, it must be in the highest degree pernicious. The testimony of Mr. DOUGLASS, on this point, is sustained by a cloud of witnesses,[15] whose veracity is unimpeachable. "A slaveholder's profession of Christianity is a palpable imposture. He is a felon of the highest grade. He is a man-stealer. It is of no importance what you put in the other scale."

Reader! are you with the man-stealers in sympathy and purpose, or on the side of their down-trodden victims? If with the former, then are you the foe of God and man. If with the latter, what are you prepared to do and dare in their behalf? Be faithful, be vigilant, be untiring in your efforts to break every yoke, and let the oppressed go free. Come what may—cost what it may—inscribe on the banner which you unfurl to the breeze, as your religious and political motto—"NO COMPROMISE WITH SLAVER! NO UNION WITH SLAVEHOLDERS!"

WM. LLOYD GARRISON[16]

Boston, *May* 1, 1845.

Letter from Wendell Phillips, Esq.[17]

Boston, *April* 22, 1845.

My Dear Friend:

You remember the old fable of "The Man and the Lion," where the lion complained that he should not be so misrepresented "when the lions wrote history."

---

[15]Paul 12:1

[16]William Lloyd Garrison (1805–1879) was the most prominent and influential of the white abolitionists. He established the antislavery newspaper *The Liberator* in 1831.

[17]Wendell Phillips (1811–1884), an important leader in the American Anti-Slavery Society, was a white reformer known for his oratorical talent and his devotion to various reform movements.

I am glad the time has come when the "lions write history." We have been left long enough to gather the character of slavery from the involuntary evidence of the masters. One might, indeed, rest sufficiently satisfied with what, it is evident, must be, in general, the results of such a relation, without seeking farther to find whether they have followed in every instance. Indeed, those who stare at the half-peck of corn a week, and love to count the lashes on the slave's back, are seldom the "stuff" out of which reformers and abolitionists are to be made. I remember that, in 1838, many were waiting for the results of the West India experiment,[18] before they could come into our ranks. Those "results" have come long ago; but, alas! few of that number have come with them, as converts. A man must be disposed to judge of emancipation by other tests than whether it has increased the produce of sugar,—and to have slavery for other reasons than because it starves men and whips women,—before he is ready to lay the first stone of his anti-slavery life.

I was glad to learn, in your story, how early the most neglected of God's children waken to a sense of their rights, and of the injustice done them. Experience is a keen teacher; and long before you had mastered your A B C, or knew where the "white sails" of the Chesapeake were bound, you began, I see, to gauge the wretchedness of the slave, not by his hunger and want, not by his lashes and toil, but by the cruel and blighting death which gathers over his soul.

In connection with this, there is one circumstance which makes your recollections peculiarly valuable, and renders your early insight the more remarkable. You come from that part of the country where we are told slavery appears with its fairest features. Let us hear, then, what it is at its best estate—gaze on its bright side, if it has one; and then imagination may task her powers to add dark lines to the picture, as she travels southward to that (for the colored man) Valley of the Shadow of Death, where the Mississippi sweeps along.

Again, we have known you long, and can put the most entire confidence in your truth, candor, and sincerity. Every one who has heard you speak has felt, and, I am confident, every one who reads your book will feel, persuaded that you give them a fair specimen of the whole truth. No one-sided portrait,—no wholesale complaints,—but a strict justice done, whenever individual kindliness has neutralized, for a moment, the deadly system with which it was strangely allied. You have been with us, too, some years, and can fairly compare the twilight of rights, which your race enjoy at the North, with that "noon of night" under which they labor south of Mason and Dixon's line. Tell us whether, after all, the half-free colored man of Massachusetts is worse off than the pampered slave of the rice swamps!

In reading your life, no one can say that we have unfairly picked out some rare specimens of cruelty. We know that the bitter drops, which even you

---

[18]Under the Abolition Act of August 28, 1833, slaves in the British West Indies were emancipated (and slaveholders were compensated for their loss of "property") effective August 1, 1834.

have drained from the cup, are no incidental aggravations, no individual ills, but such as must mingle always and necessarily in the lot of every slave. They are the essential ingredients, not the occasional results, of the system.

After all, I shall read your book with trembling for you. Some years ago, when you were beginning to tell me your real name and birthplace, you may remember I stopped you, and preferred to remain ignorant of all. With the exception of a vague description, so I continued, till the other day, when you read me your memoirs. I hardly knew, at the time, whether to thank you or not for the sight of them, when I reflected that it was still dangerous, in Massachusetts, for honest men to tell their names! They say the fathers, in 1776, signed the Declaration of Independence with the halter about their necks. You, too, publish your declaration of freedom with danger compassing you around. In all the broad lands which the Constitution of the United States overshadows, there is no single spot,—however narrow or desolate,—where a fugitive slave can plant himself and say, "I am safe." The whole armory of Northern Law has no shield for you. I am free to say that, in your place, I should throw the MS. into the fire.

You, perhaps, may tell your story in safety, endeared as you are to so many warm hearts by rare gifts, and a still rare devotion of them to the service of others. But it will be owing only to your labors, and the fearless efforts of those who, trampling the laws and Constitution of the country under their feet, are determined that they will "hide the outcast," [19] and that their hearts shall be, spite of the law, an asylum for the oppressed, if, some time or other, the humblest may stand in our streets, and bear witness in safety against the cruelties of which he has been the victim.

Yet it is sad to think, that these very throbbing hearts which welcome your story, and form your best safeguard in telling it, are all beating contrary to the "statute in such case made and provided." Go on, my dear friend, till you, and those who, like you, have been saved, so as by fire, from the dark prisonhouse, shall stereotype these free, illegal pulses into statutes; and New England, cutting loose from a blood-stained Union, shall glory in being the house of refuge for the oppressed;—till we no longer merely "*hide* the outcast," or make a merit of standing idly by while he is hunted in our midst; but, consecrating anew the soil of the Pilgrims as an asylum for the oppressed, proclaim our *welcome* to the slave so loudly, that the tones shall reach every hut in the Carolinas, and make the broken-hearted bondman leap up at the thought of old Massachusetts.

God speed the day!

Till then, and ever,
Yours truly,
WENDELL PHILLIPS

---

[19]Isaiah 16:3

Chapter I

I was born in Tuckahoe, near Hillsborough, and about twelve miles from Easton, in Talbot county, Maryland. I have no accurate knowledge of my age, never having seen any authentic record containing it. By far the larger part of the slaves know as little of their ages as horses know of theirs, and it is the wish of most masters within my knowledge to keep their slaves thus ignorant. I do not remember to have ever met a slave who could tell of his birthday. They seldom come nearer to it than planting-time, harvest-time, cherry-time, spring-time, or fall-time. A want of information concerning my own was a source of unhappiness to me even during childhood. The white children could tell their ages. I could not tell why I ought to be deprived of the same privilege. I was not allowed to make any inquiries of my master concerning it. He deemed all such inquiries on the part of a slave improper and impertinent, and evidence of a restless spirit. The nearest estimate I can give makes me now between twenty-seven and twenty-eight years of age. I come to this, from hearing my master say, some time during 1835, I was about seventeen years old.

My mother was named Harriet Bailey. She was the daughter of Isaac and Betsey Bailey, both colored, and quite dark. My mother was of a darker complexion than either my grandmother or grandfather.

My father was a white man. He was admitted to be such by all I ever heard speak of my parentage. The opinion was also whispered that my master was my father; but of the correctness of this opinion, I know nothing; the means of knowing was withheld from me. My mother and I were separated when I was but an infant—before I knew her as my mother. It is a common custom, in the part of Maryland from which I ran away, to part children from their mothers at a very early age. Frequently, before the child has reached its twelfth month, its mother is taken from it, and hired out on some farm a considerable distance off, and the child is placed under the care of an old woman, too old for field labor. For what this separation is done, I do not know, unless it be to hinder the development of the child's affection toward its mother, and to blunt and destroy the natural affection of the mother for the child. This is the inevitable result.

I never saw my mother, to know her as such, more than four or five times in my life; and each of these times was very short in duration, and at night. She was hired by a Mr. Stewart, who lived about twelve miles from my home. She made her journeys to see me in the night, travelling the whole distance on foot, after the performance of her day's work. She was a field hand, and a whipping is the penalty of not being in the field at sunrise, unless a slave has special permission from his or her master to the contrary—a permission which they seldom get, and one that gives to him that gives it the proud name of being a kind master. I do not recollect of ever seeing my mother by the light of day. She was with me in the night. She would lie down with me, and get me to sleep, but long before I waked she was gone. Very little communication ever took place between us. Death soon ended what little we could have while she lived, and with it her hardships and suffering. She died when I was about seven years old, on one of my master's farms, near Lee's Mill. I was not allowed to be present during her illness, at her death, or burial. She was gone long before I knew anything about it. Never having enjoyed, to any considerable extent, her soothing presence, her tender and watchful care, I received the tidings of her death with much the same emotions I should have probably felt at the death of a stranger.

Called thus suddenly away, she left me without the slightest intimation of who my father was. The whisper that my master was my father, may or may not be true; and, true or false, it is of but little consequence to my purpose whilst the fact remains, in all its glaring odiousness, that slaveholders have ordained, and by law established, that the children of slave women shall in all cases follow the condition of their mothers; and this is done too obviously to administer to their own lusts, and make a gratification of their wicked desires profitable as well as pleasurable; for by this cunning arrangement, the slaveholder, in cases not a few, sustains to his slaves the double relation of master and father.

I know of such cases; and it is worthy of remark that such slaves invariably suffer greater hardships, and have more to contend with, than others. They are, in the first place, a constant offence to their mistress. She is ever disposed to find fault with them; they can seldom do anything to please her; she is never better pleased than when she sees them under the lash, especially when she suspects her husband of showing to his mulatto children favors which he withholds from his black slaves. The master is frequently compelled to sell this class of his slaves, out of deference to the feelings of his white wife; and, cruel as the deed may strike any one to be, for a man to sell his own children to human flesh-mongers, it is often the dictate of humanity for him to do so; for, unless he does this, he must not only whip them himself, but must stand by and see one white son tie up his brother, of but few shades darker complexion than himself, and ply the gory lash to his naked back; and if he lisp one word of disapproval, it is set down to his parental partiality, and only makes a bad matter worse, both for himself and the slave whom he would protect and defend.

Every year brings with it multitudes of this class of slaves. It was doubtless in consequence of a knowledge of this fact, that one great statesman of the south predicted the downfall of slavery by the inevitable laws of population. Whether this prophecy is ever fulfilled or not, it is nevertheless plain that a very different-looking class of people are springing up at the south, and are now held in slavery, from those originally brought to this country from Africa; and if their increase will do no other good, it will do away the force of the argument, that God cursed Ham, and therefore American slavery is right.[20] If the lineal descendants of Ham are alone to be scripturally enslaved, it is certain that slavery at the south must soon become unscriptural; for thousands are ushered into the world, annually, who, like myself, owe their existence to white fathers, and those fathers most frequently their own masters.

I have had two masters. My first master's name was Anthony. I do not remember his first name. He was generally called Captain Anthony—a title which, I presume, he acquired by sailing a craft on the Chesapeake Bay. He was not considered a rich slaveholder. He owned two or three farms, and about thirty slaves. His farms and slaves were under the care of an overseer. The overseer's name was Plummer. Mr. Plummer was a miserable drunkard, a profane swearer, and a savage monster. He always went armed with a cowskin[21] and a heavy cudgel. I have known him to cut and slash the women's heads so horribly, that even master would be enraged at his cruelty, and would threaten to whip him if he did not mind himself. Master, however, was not a humane slaveholder. It required extraordinary barbarity on the part of an overseer to affect him. He was a cruel man, hardened by a long life of slaveholding. He would at times seem to take great pleasure in whipping a slave. I have often been awakened at the dawn of day by the most heartrending shrieks of an old aunt of mine, whom he used to tie up to a joist, and whip upon her naked back till she was literally covered with blood. No words, no tears, no prayers, from his gory victim, seemed to move his iron heart from its bloody purpose. The louder she screamed, the harder he whipped; and where the blood ran fastest, there he whipped longest. He would whip her to make her scream, and whip her to make her hush; and not until overcome by fatigue, would he cease to swing the blood-clotted cowskin. I remember the first time I ever witnessed this horrible exhibition. I was quite a child, but I well remember it. I never shall forget it whilst I remember any thing. It was the first of a long series of such outrages, of which I was doomed to be a witness and a participant. It struck me with awful force. It was the bloodstained gate, the entrance to the hell of slavery, through which I was about to pass. It was a most terrible spectacle. I wish I could commit to paper the feelings with which I beheld it.

This occurence took place very soon after I went to live with my old master, and under the following circumstances. Aunt Hester went out one night,—where or for what I do not know,—and happened to be absent when my master desired her presence. He had ordered her not to go out evenings,

---

[20]See Genesis 9:20–27. Noah's curse on Ham's son Canaan was used as justification for the enslavement of those of African heritage. Canaan's curse was misattributed to Ham sometime during the Middle Ages, which helped to set the stage for later racist interpretations of the Bible.
[21]A whip made of cowhide.

and warned her that she must never let him catch her in company with a young man, who was paying attention to her belonging to Colonel Lloyd. The young man's named was Ned Roberts, generally called Lloyd's Ned. Why master was so careful of her, may be safely left to conjecture. She was a woman of noble form, and of graceful proportions, having very few equals, and fewer superiors, in personal appearance, among the colored or white women of our neighborhood.

Aunt Hester had not only disobeyed his orders in going out, but had been found in company with Lloyd's Ned; which circumstance, I found, from what he said while whipping her, was the chief offence. Had he been a man of pure morals himself, he might have been thought interested in protecting the innocence of my aunt; but those who knew him will not suspect him of any such virtue. Before he commenced whipping Aunt Hester, he took her into the kitchen, and stripped her from neck to waist, leaving her neck, shoulders, and back, entirely naked. He then told her to cross her hands, calling her at the same time a d—d b—h. After crossing her hands, he tied them with a strong rope, and led her to a stool under a large hook in the joist, put in for the purpose. He made her get upon the stool, and tied her hands to the hook. She now stood fair for his infernal purpose. Her arms were stretched up at their full length, so that she stood upon the ends of her toes. He then said to her, "Now, you d—d b—h, I'll learn you how to disobey my orders!" and after rolling up his sleeves, he commenced to lay on the heavy cowskin, and soon the warm, red blood (amid heart-rending shrieks from her, and horrid oaths from him) came dripping to the floor. I was so terrified and horror-stricken at the sight, that I hid myself in a closet, and dared not venture out till long after the bloody transaction was over. I expected it would be my turn next. It was all new to me. I had never seen any thing like it before. I had always lived with my grandmother on the outskirts of the plantation, where she was put to raise the children of the younger women. I had therefore been, until now, out of the way of the bloody scenes that often occurred on the plantation.

[1847]

My Name

SANDRA CISNEROS

In English my name means hope. In Spanish it means too many letters. It means sadness, it means waiting. It is like the number nine. A muddy color. It is the Mexican records my father plays on Sunday mornings when he is shaving, songs like sobbing.

It was my great-grandmother's name and now it is mine. She was a horse woman too, born like me in the Chinese year of the horse—which is supposed to be bad luck if you're born female—but I think this is a Chinese lie because the Chinese, like the Mexicans, don't like their women strong.

My great-grandmother. I would've liked to have known her, a wild horse of a woman, so wild she wouldn't marry. Until my great-grandfather threw a sack over her head and carried her off. Just like that, as if she were a fancy chandelier. That's the way he did it.

And the story goes she never forgave him. She looked out the window her whole life, the way so many women sit their sadness on an elbow. I wonder if she made the best with what she got or was she sorry because she couldn't be all the things she wanted to be. Esperanza. I have inherited her name, but I don't want to inherit her place by the window.

At school they say my name funny as if the syllables were made out of tin and hurt the roof of your mouth. But in Spanish my name is made out of a softer some-thing, like silver, not quite as thick as sister's name—Magdalena—which is uglier than mine. Magdalena who at least can come home and become Nenny. But I am always Esperanza.

I would like to baptize myself under a new name, a name more like the real me, the one nobody sees. Espe-ranza as Lisandra or Maritza or Zeze the X. Yes. Something like Zeze the X will do.

Reprinted from *The House on Mango Street* (1989), by permission of Susan Bergholz Literary Services.

How to Mark a Book

MORTIMER J. ADLER

It is ironic that Mortimer Adler, the father of the Great Books Program and promoter of Aristotle and the classics, was a high school dropout. He did attend Columbia University, but he did not receive his BA because he refused to take a required swimming test. Adler did, however, eventually receive a PhD, become an editor for the Encyclopedia Britannica, *and write dozens of books on philosophy and education, including* How to Read a Book: The Art of Getting a Liberal Education *(1940), and* The Great Ideas: A Syntopicon of Great Books of the Western World *(1952).*

For Mortimer Adler, reading the great books does not mean buying expensive, leather-bound volumes to display behind glass doors. Reading means consuming, as you consume a steak, to "get it into your bloodstream." In "How to Mark a Book," Adler proposes a radical method for reading the classics. "Marking up a book," he claims, "is not an act of mutilation but of love. Read his essay and see if you agree with his method of paying "your respects to the author."

You know you have to read "between the lines" to get the most out of anything. I want to persuade you to do something equally important in the course of your reading. I want to persuade you to "write between the lines." Unless you do, you are not likely to do the most efficient kind of reading.

I contend, quite bluntly, that marking up a book is not an act of mutilation but of love.

You shouldn't mark up a book which isn't yours. Librarians (or your friends) who lend you books expect you to keep them clean, and you should. If you decide that I am right about the usefulness of marking books, you will have to buy them. Most of the world's great books are available today, in reprint editions, at less than a dollar.

Reprinted from *Saturday Review* (1940), Philip Adler.

There are two ways in which one can own a book. The first is the property right you establish by paying for it, just as you pay for clothes and furniture. But this act of purchase is only the prelude to possession. Full ownership comes only when you have made it a part of yourself, and the best way to make yourself a part of it is by writing in it. An illustration may make the point clear. You buy a beefsteak and transfer it from the butcher's icebox to your own. But you do not own the beefsteak in the most important sense until you consume it and get it into your bloodstream. I am arguing that books, too, must be absorbed in your bloodstream to do you any good.

Confusion about what it means to own a book leads people to a false reverence for paper, binding, and type—a respect for the physical thing—the craft of the printer rather than the genius of the author. They forget that it is possible for a man to acquire the idea, to possess the beauty, which a great book contains, without staking his claim by pasting his bookplate inside the cover. Having a fine library doesn't prove that its owner has a mind enriched by books; it proves nothing more than that he, his father, or his wife, was rich enough to buy them.

There are three kinds of book owners. The first has all the standard sets and best-sellers—unread, untouched. (This deluded individual owns woodpulp and ink, not books.) The second has a great many books—a few of them read through, most of them dipped into, but all of them as clean and shiny as the day they were bought. (This person would probably like to make books his own, but is restrained by a false respect for their physical appearance.) The third has a few books or many—every one of them dog-eared and dilapidated, shaken and loosened by continual use, marked and scribbled in from front to back. (This man owns books.)

Is it false respect, you may ask, to preserve intact and unblemished a beautifully printed book, an elegantly bound edition? Of course not. I'd no more scribble all over a first edition of "Paradise Lost" than I'd give my baby a set of crayons and an original Rembrandt! I wouldn't mark up a painting or a statue. Its soul, so to speak, is inseparable from its body. And the beauty of a rare edition or of a richly manufactured volume is like that of a painting or a statue.

But the soul of a book can be separated from its body. A book is more like the score of a piece of music than it is like a painting. No great musician confuses a symphony with the printed sheets of music. Arturo Toscanini reveres Brahms, but Toscanini's score of the C-minor Symphony is so thoroughly marked up that no one but the maestro himself can read it. The reason why a great conductor makes notations on his musical scores—marks them up again and again each time he returns to study them—is the reason why you should mark your books. If your respect for magnificent binding or typography gets in the way, buy yourself a cheap edition and pay your respects to the author.

Why is marking up a book indispensable to reading? First, it keeps you awake. (And I don't mean merely conscious; I mean wide awake.) In the second place, reading, if it is active, is thinking, and thinking tends to express itself in words, spoken or written. The marked book is usually the thought-through book. Finally, writing helps you remember the thoughts you had, or the thoughts the author expressed. Let me develop these three points.

If reading is to accomplish anything more than passing time, it must be active. You can't let your eyes glide across the lines of a book and come up with an understanding of what you have read. Now an ordinary piece of light fiction, like, say, "Gone with the Wind," doesn't require the most active kind of reading. The books you read for pleasure can be read in a state of relaxation, and nothing is lost. But a great book, rich in ideas and beauty, a book that raises and tries to answer great fundamental questions, demands the most active reading of which you are capable. You don't absorb the ideas of John Dewey the way you absorb the crooning of Mr. Vallee. You have to reach for them. That you cannot do while you're asleep.

If, when you've finished reading a book, the pages are filled with your notes, you know that you read actively. The most famous active reader of great books I know is President Hutchins, of the University of Chicago. He also has the hardest schedule of business activities of any man I know. He invariably reads with a pencil, and sometimes, when he picks up a book and pencil in the evening, he finds himself, instead of making intelligent notes, drawing what he calls "caviar factories" on the margins. When that happens, he puts the book down. He knows he's too tired to read, and he's just wasting time.

But, you may ask, why is writing necessary? Well, the physical act of writing, with your own hand, brings words and sentences more sharply before your mind and preserves them better in your memory. To set down your reaction to important words and sentences you have read, and the questions they have raised in your mind, is to preserve those reactions and sharpen those questions.

Even if you wrote on a scratch pad, and threw the paper away when you had finished writing, your grasp of the book would be surer. But you don't have to throw the paper away. The margins (top and bottom, as well as side), the end-papers, the very space between the lines, are all available. They aren't sacred. And, best of all, your marks and notes become an integral part of the book and stay there forever. You can pick up the book the following week or year, and there are all your points of agreement, disagreement, doubt, and inquiry. It's like resuming an interrupted conversation with the advantage of being able to pick up where you left off.

And that is exactly what reading a book should be: a conversation between you and the author. Presumably he knows more about the subject than you do; naturally, you'll have the proper humility as you approach him.

But don't let anybody tell you that a reader is supposed to be solely on the receiving end. Understanding is a two-way operation; learning doesn't consist in being an empty receptacle. The learner has to question himself and question the teacher. He even has to argue with the teacher, once he understands what the teacher is saying. And marking a book is literally an expression of your differences, or agreements of opinion, with the author.

There are all kinds of devices for marking a book intelligently and fruitfully. Here's the way I do it:

1. Underlining: of major points, of important or forceful statements.
2, Vertical lines at the margin: to emphasize a statement already underlined.
3. Star, asterisk, or other doo-dad at the margin: to be used sparingly, to emphasize the ten or twenty most important statements in the book. (You may want to fold the bottom corner of each page on which you use such marks. It won't hurt the sturdy paper on which most modern books are printed, and you will be able to take the book off the shelf at any time and, by opening it at the folded-corner page, refresh your recollection of the book.)
4. Numbers in the margin: to indicate the sequence of points the author makes in developing a single argument.
5. Numbers of other pages in the margin: to indicate where else in the book the author made points relevant to the point marked; to tie up the ideas in a book, which, though they may be separated by many pages, belong together.
6. Circling of key words or phrases.
7. Writing in the margin, or at the top or bottom of the page, for the sake of: recording questions (and perhaps answers) which a passage raised in your mind; reducing a complicated discussion to a simple statement; recording the sequence of major points right through the books. I use the end-papers at the back of the book to make a personal index of the author's points in the order of their appearance.

The front end-papers are, to me, the most important. Some people reserve them for a fancy bookplate. I reserve them for fancy thinking. After I have finished reading the book and making my personal index on the back end-papers, I turn to the front and try to outline the book, not page by page, or point by point (I've already done that at the back), but as an integrated structure, with a basic unity and an order of parts. This outline is, to me, the measure of my understanding of the work.

If you're a die-hard anti-book-marker, you may object that the margins, the space between the lines, and the end-papers don't give you room enough. All right. How about using a scratch pad slightly smaller than the page-size of the book—so that the edges of the sheets won't protrude? Make your index, outlines, and even your notes on the pad, and then insert these sheets permanently inside the front and back covers of the book.

Or, you may say that this business of marking books is going to slow up your reading. It probably will. That's one of the reasons for doing it. Most of us have been taken in by the notion that speed of reading is a measure of our intelligence. There is no such thing as the right speed for intelligent reading. Some things should be read quickly and effortlessly, and some should be read slowly and even laboriously. The sign of intelligence in reading is the ability to read different things differently according to their worth. In the case of good books, the point is not to see how many of them you can get through, but rather how many can get through you—how many you can make your own. A few friends are better than a thousand acquaintances. If this be your aim, as it should be, you will not be impatient if it takes more time and effort to read a great book than it does a newspaper.

You may have one final objection to marking books. You can't lend them to your friends because nobody else can read them without being distracted by your notes. Furthermore, you won't want to lend them because a marked copy is a kind of intellectual diary, and lending it is almost like giving your mind away.

If your friend wishes to read your "Plutarch's Lives," "Shakespeare," or "The Federalist Papers," tell him gently but firmly, to buy a copy. You will lend him your car or your coat—but your books are as much a part of you as your head or your heart.

The *Chicago Defender* Sends a Man to Little Rock

GWENDOLYN BROOKS

In Little Rock the people bear
Babes, and comb and part their hair
And watch the want ads, put repair
To roof and latch. While wheat toast burns
A woman waters multiferns.   5

Time upholds or overturns
The many, tight, and small concerns.

In Little Rock the people sing
Sunday hymns like anything,
Through Sunday pomp and polishing.   10

And after testament and tunes,
Some soften Sunday afternoons
With lemon tea and Lorna Doones.

I forecast
And I believe   15
Come Christmas Little Rock will cleave
To Christmas tree and trifle, weave,
From laugh and tinsel, texture fast.

In Little Rock is baseball; Barcarolle.
That hotness in July . . . the uniformed figures raw and implacable   20
And not intellectual,
Batting the hotness or clawing the suffering dust.
The Open Air Concert, on the special twilight green . . .

Reprinted from *The Essential Gwendolyn Brooks* (2005), Penguin Putnam, Inc.

When Beethoven is brutal or whispers to lady-like air.
Blanket-sitters are solemn, as Johann troubles to lean   25
To tell them what to mean . . .

There is love, too, in Little Rock. Soft women softly
Opening themselves in kindness,

Or, pitying one's blindness,
Awaiting one's pleasure   30
In azure
Glory with anguished rose at the root . . .
To wash away old semi-discomfitures.
They re-teach purple and unsullen blue.
The wispy soils go. And uncertain   35
Half-havings have they clarified to sures.

In Little Rock they know
Not answering the telephone is a way of rejecting life,
That it is our business to be bothered, is our business
To cherish bores or boredom, be polite   40
To lies and love and many-faceted fuzziness.

I scratch my head, massage the hate-I-had.
I blink across my prim and pencilled pad.
The saga I was sent for is not down.
Because there is a puzzle in this town.   45
The biggest News I do not dare
Telegraph to the Editor's chair:
"They are like people everywhere."

The angry Editor would reply
In hundred harryings of Why.   50

And true, they are hurling spittle, rock,
Garbage and fruit in Little Rock.
And I saw coiling storm a-writhe
On bright madonnas. And a scythe
Of men harassing brownish girls.   55
(The bows and barrettes in the curls
And braids declined away from joy.)

I saw a bleeding brownish boy. . . .

The lariat lynch-wish I deplored.

The loveliest lynchee was our Lord.   60

[Fall, 1957]

MALCOLM X
(EL-HAJJ MALIK EL-SHABAZZ)
[1925–1965]

In February 1965, Malcolm X, former minister of the Nation of Islam, died at the age of thirty-nine from gunshots fired at him while he spoke in Harlem. His commanding presence and compelling message had an enormous influence on American political life and African-American political thought. His The Autobiography of Malcolm X (written with the help of Alex Haley) has become one of the most important autobiographies of the twentieth century. Throughout Malcolm X's too-short public life, he incited controversy for his stark and combative critique of racial politics in the United States. His numerous speeches and interviews simultaneously indicted white American racism and black acquiescence to integration. He made his 1964 Ballot or the Bullet speech when many African Americans had grown impatient with the nonviolent philosophy of the postwar civil rights movement. Malcolm X's call for black self-defense "by any means necessary" occurred just as black neighborhoods throughout America erupted in rebellions. His influence ranged from shaping the post-1965 Black Power movement to the phenomenal growth of traditional Islam in black communities.

Born in Omaha, Nebraska, on May 19, 1925, Malcolm X began life as Malcolm Little. The fourth of eight children, his father, Reverend Earl Little, was a Baptist minister and a committed member of the Universal Negro Improvement Association (UNIA); Malcolm's mother, Louise Little, had emigrated from the West Indies. Earl Little challenged segregation at every opportunity, inciting the ire of whites around him. In response to this radicalism, the rapidly expanding Ku Klux Klan burned the family's home. Not long after they moved to Lansing, Michigan, Earl Little was found beaten and crushed on the trolley car tracks. For some time, Louise Little struggled to feed and care for her children, but poverty and her depression made it impossible. She entered a mental asylum and the children were permanently placed in foster care.

Though assigned to a detention home in Mason, Michigan, and destined to enter reform school, Malcolm remained in the care of the woman who ran the home. One of the few blacks in the small town, Malcolm attended the local *school, where his teachers refused to recognize that his significant intellectual abilities might help him go on to college and a profession. When a teacher asked him what he wanted to do for a career, Malcolm responded: "A lawyer." The teacher encouraged him to "be realistic about being a nigger" and instead aspire for a life more "practical" for African Americans' perceived "abilities." Why not become a carpenter, the teacher inquired. By the time Malcolm finished eighth grade, he begged his much older half-sister Ella to let him move to Boston. She consented and Malcolm began the first of his many transformations.*

Malcolm quickly changed from what he called a Midwestern "hick" with kinky, reddish hair and a green suit, into a criminal wearing a zoot suit and conked hair. He stayed in Boston briefly, but soon moved to Harlem where he became "Detroit Red," or "Big Red." He participated in petty crime, hustled for a brothel, took drugs cocaine and hash, and became a numbers runner. Increased scrutiny by the local police prompted his return to Boston where he organized an interracial burglary gang that included two white young women from Beacon Hill. They eventually got caught and Malcolm faced the possibility of a two-year sentence. Instead, he received an eight- to ten-year sentence, apparently for keeping company with white women. Not quite twenty-one, Malcolm had yet to start shaving.

During the six-and-a half years Malcolm spent in prison, he began his second and most critical transformation: from criminal to follower of the Honorable Elijah Muhammad and the Lost-Found Nation of Islam. Though he initially began his stay in prison as a recalcitrant and verbally aggressive young man—his rants earned him the nickname "Satan"—he soon came under the influence of his siblings. Malcolm's brother, Philbert, began to write him letters filled with information about the Nation of Islam, claiming that it was "the natural religion for the black man." Malcolm's brothers and sisters in Detroit and Chicago became members and they urged him to do the same. Malcolm rejected this first effort, but he soon changed his mind when another brother suggested that refusing to eat pork and not smoking cigarettes might help him get out of prison.

At first pragmatic in his decision to join the Nation of Islam, Malcolm quickly became a devoted convert. Through visits and twice-daily letters from his siblings, Malcolm began to learn about and eventually accept the teachings of Elijah Muhammad. He learned to pray and he received instruction in the Nation of Islam by mail, first from his siblings, then from Elijah Muhammad. He quickly came to accept Elijah Muhammad's central organizing principle that posited white people were the devil. Despite the narrow theology of the Nation of Islam, Malcolm also significantly expanded his intellectual world. He read voraciously and learned Latin; he copied words out of the dictionary and became obsessed with words. His stringent adherence to the principles of the Nation of Islam, along with his rigorous intellectual development, turned him into a model prisoner. Released in 1952, Malcolm donned a cheap suit and headed for Detroit under the watchful care of his siblings. Now renamed Malcolm X, he formally met the Honorable Elijah Muhammad.

Within five years, Malcolm X rapidly moved from organizing in Detroit to becoming one of the most important ministers in the Nation of Islam. In a period of months after his release from prison, he became the assistant minister in Detroit and then minister in Boston and Philadelphia, where he organized the eleventh and twelfth temples of Islam. By 1954 he had become minister of Mosque No. 7 in Harlem, one of the most important positions in the Lost-Found Nation. By 1957, white New York became aware of Mosque No. 7 and Minister Malcolm X. When police in Harlem severely beat Hinton Johnson, Malcolm X simultaneously demonstrated the Nation of Islam's ability to prevent a riot and the organization's growing importance to black America.

His actions and a short-lived column in Harlem's Amsterdam News *increased his temple's membership and provided him national exposure. Noted scholar C. Eric Lincoln, then a divinity student at Boston University, became acquainted with Malcolm X. First a dissertation and then a book, Lincoln's* Black Muslims in America *coined the name Black Muslims and was the first book about the Nation of Islam. A television documentary and requests for Malcolm to speak at colleges and universities provided exposure to Elijah Muhammad and the Nation of Islam. While Malcolm enjoyed the attention, he was portrayed as a man who proselytized hate toward white people. This narrow depiction of the Nation of Islam's philosophy, along with the increased media attention of Malcolm X, exacerbated his growing tension with Elijah Muhammad that would eventually lead to the rupture in their relationship. Despite his controversial verbal attacks on the racism of white America, Malcolm X remained essential to the growth and financial stability of the Nation of Islam until 1963, however. When President John F. Kennedy was assassinated late that year, Malcolm remarked publicly, that "America's climate of hate had been responsible for the President's death." Long angered over what he perceived as undue attention toward Malcolm, Elijah Muhammad silenced him. Malcolm X quickly assessed that he would eventually be ousted from the Nation of Islam.*

Malcolm X spent the last year of his life challenging his spiritual and political beliefs. He withdrew his association with the Nation of Islam in March 1964, beginning his final transformation to El-Hajj Malik El-Shabazz. With financial help from his oldest sister, Ella, Malcolm went on a pilgrimage to Mecca in April 1964. His twelve days in Mecca helped him understand, finally, that Islam did not belong to black people alone, but instead was a religion grounded in the belief of peace and the unity of all human beings. He could no longer ascribe to the central belief in the Nation of Islam that all white people were devils. He changed his name, reflecting his new status as a member of the Sunni Muslims, the largest single sect in Islam. He then spent weeks traveling through Africa. On February 21, 1965, just three months after a second trip to Africa, Malcolm X was assassinated as he rose to speak in a hall in Harlem.

The speeches, interviews, and conversations from the last year of his life demonstrate the flux in his political thought. At the center of his thought was the firm conviction that African Americans had the right "by any means necessary" to create a world where they would be recognized as human beings. Ten days after he declared his severance from the Nation of Islam, Malcolm began to deliver "The Ballot or the Bullet" speech. His first effort was in Harlem; over the next month, he delivered the speech in Chester, Pennsylvania, Boston, Cleveland, and Detroit. His speech at the Congress of Racial Equality (CORE) rally in Cleveland, Ohio, provided the published transcription of the now famous talk. Malcolm shared the podium with the well-known writer Louis Lomax. In this version of "The Ballot or the Bullet," delivered on April 3, 1964, at Corey Methodist Church, Malcolm X advocated the necessity of an independent black politics; he also acknowledged that black people needed to defend their interests, though he did call for armed revolution.

Kimberley L. Phillips
The College of William and Mary

For Further Reading

Primary Works

The Autobiography of Malcolm X, with Alex Haley, (New York: Grove Press, 1965); *Malcolm X Speaks: Selected Speeches and Statements* (New York: Grove Weidenfeld, 1990).

Secondary Works

Breitman, George. *The Last Year of Malcolm X*, third edition (New York: Pathfinder Press, 1991); Goldman, Peter, *The Death and Life of Malcolm X*, second edition (Urbana: University of Illinois Press, 1979); Lincoln, C. Eric, *The Black Muslims in America* (Boston: Beacon Press, 1961).

The Ballot or the Bullet

MALCOLM X (EL-HAJJ MALIK EL-SHABAZZ)

Mr. Moderator, Brother Lomax, brothers and sisters, friends and enemies: I just can't believe everyone in here is a friend and I don't want to leave anybody out. The question tonight, as I understand it, is "The Negro Revolt, and Where Do We Go From Here?" or "What Next?"[1] In my little humble way of understanding it, it points toward either the ballot or the bullet.

Before we try and explain what is meant by the ballot or the bullet, I would like to clarify something concerning myself. I'm still a Muslim, my religion is still Islam. That's my personal belief. Just as Adam Clayton Powell is a Christian minister who heads the Abyssinian Baptist Church in New York, but at the same time takes part in the political struggles to try and bring about rights to the black people in this country,[2] and Dr. Martin Luther King is a Christian minister down in Atlanta, Georgia, who heads another organization fighting for the civil rights of black people in this country; and Rev. Galamison, I guess you've heard of him, is another Christian minister in New York who has been deeply involved in the school boycotts to eliminate segregated education; well, I myself am a minister, not a Christian minister, but a Muslim minister; and I believe in action on all fronts by whatever means necessary.

Although I'm still a Muslim, I'm not here tonight to discuss my religion. I'm not here to try and change your religion. I'm not here to argue or discuss anything that we differ about, because it's time for us to submerge our differences and realize that it is best for us to first see that we have the same problem, a common problem—a problem that will make you catch hell whether you're a Baptist, or a Methodist, or a Muslim, or a nationalist. Whether you're educated or illiterate, whether you live on the boulevard or

---

[1]Louis Lomax, a journalist and long-time friend of Malcolm X, spoke before him. In these opening sentences, Malcolm X referred to a phrase (and title of a book published in 1967) used by Reverend Martin Luther King, Jr. and the subtitle of Lomax's 1962 *The Negro Revolt*.

[2]A minister of one of the most prominent churches in Harlem, Adam Clayton Powell, Jr., who represented Harlem in the U.S. House of Representatives (1944–70), became the first elected African American from the Northeast.

in the alley, you're going to catch hell just like I am. We're all in the same boat and we all are going to catch the same hell from the same man. He just happens to be a white man. All of us have suffered here, in this country, political oppression at the hands of the white man, economic exploitation at the hands of the white man, and social degradation at the hands of the white man.

Now in speaking like this, it doesn't mean that we're anti-white, but it does mean we're anti-exploitation, we're anti-degradation, we're anti-oppression. And if the white man doesn't want us to be anti-him, let him stop oppressing and exploiting and degrading us. Whether we are Christians or Muslims or nationalists or agnostics or atheists, we must first learn to forget our differences. If we have differences, let us differ in the closet; when we come out in front, let us not have anything to argue about until we get finished arguing with the man. If the late President Kennedy could get together with Khrushchev[3] and exchange some wheat, we certainly have more in common with each other than Kennedy and Khrushchev had with each other.

If we don't do something real soon, I think you'll have to agree that we're going to be forced either to use the ballot or the bullet. It's one or the other in 1964. It isn't that time is running out—time has run out! 1964 threatens to be the most explosive year America has ever witnessed. The most explosive year. Why? It's also a political year. It's the year when all of the white politicians will be back in the so-called Negro community jiving you and me for some votes. The year when all of the white political crooks will be right back in your and my community with their false promises, building up our hopes for a letdown, with their trickery and their treachery, with their false promises which they don't intend to keep. As they nourish these dissatisfactions, it can only lead to one thing, an explosion; and now we have the type of black man on the scene in America today—I'm sorry, Brother Lomax—who just doesn't intend to turn the other cheek any longer.

Don't let anybody tell you anything about the odds are against you. If they draft you, they send you to Korea and make you face 800 million Chinese. If you can be brave over there, you can be brave right here. These odds aren't as great as those odds. And if you fight here, you will at least know what you're fighting for.

I'm not a politician, not even a student of politics; in fact, I'm not a student of much of anything. I'm not a Democrat, I'm not a Republican, and I don't even consider myself an American. If you and I were Americans, there'd be no problems. Those Hunkies that just got off the boat, they're already Americans; Polacks are already Americans; the Italian refugees are

---

[3]Nikita Krushchev served as Premier of the Soviet Union from 1958–64.

already Americans. Everything that came out of Europe, every blue-eyed thing, is already an American. And as long as you and I have been over here, we aren't Americans yet.

Well, I am one who doesn't believe in deluding myself. I'm not going to sit at your table and watch you eat, with nothing on my plate, and call myself a diner. Sitting at the table doesn't make you a diner, unless you eat some of what's on that plate.[4] Being here in America doesn't make you an American. Being born here in America doesn't make you an American. Why, if birth made you American, you wouldn't need any legislation, you wouldn't need any amendments to the Constitution, you wouldn't be faced with civil-rights filibustering in Washington, D.C., right now. They don't have to pass civil-rights legislation to make a Polack an American.

No, I'm not an American. I'm one of the 22 million black people who are the victims of Americanism. One of the 22 million black people who are the victims of democracy, nothing but disguised hypocrisy. So, I'm not standing here speaking to you as an American, or a patriot, or a flag-saluter, or a flag-waver—no, not I. I'm speaking as a victim of this American system. And I see America through the eyes of the victim. I don't see any American dream; I see an American nightmare.

These 22 million victims are waking up. Their eyes are coming open. They're beginning to see what they used to only look at. They're becoming politically mature. They are realizing that there are new political trends from coast to coast. As they see these new political trends, it's possible for them to see that every time there's an election the races are so close that they have to have a recount. They had to recount in Massachusetts to see who was going to be governor, it was so close. It was the same way in Rhode Island, in Minnesota, and in many other parts of the country. And the same with Kennedy and Nixon when they ran for president. It was so close they had to count all over again. Well, what does this mean? It means that when white people are evenly divided, and black people have a bloc of votes of their own, it is left up to them to determine who's going to sit in the White House and who's going to be in the dog house.[5]

It was the black man's vote that put the present administration in Washington, D.C. Your vote, your dumb vote, your ignorant vote, your wasted vote put in an administration in Washington, D.C., that has seen fit to pass every kind of legislation imaginable, saving you until last, then filibustering

---

[4]Malcolm X referred to the sit-ins at segregated lunch counters undertaken by college students in the Student Non-Violent Coordinating Committee (SNCC).

[5]After John F. Kennedy called Coretta Scott King in 1960 when her husband Reverend Martin Luther King, Jr. had been jailed for protesting segregation in Atlanta, urban black voters in the North helped him narrowly defeat Richard Nixon for the presidency of the United States.

on top of that.[6] And your and my leaders have the audacity to run around clapping their hands and talk about how much progress we're making. And what a good president we have. If he wasn't good in Texas, he sure can't be good in Washington, D.C. Because Texas is a lynch state. It is in the same breath as Mississippi, no different; only they lynch you in Texas with a Texas accent and lynch you in Mississippi with a Mississippi accent. And these Negro leaders have the audacity to go and have some coffee in the White House with a Texan, a Southern cracker—that's all he is—and then come out and tell you and me that he's going to be better for us because, since he's from the South, he knows how to deal with the Southerners. What kind of logic is that? Let Eastland be president, he's from the South too.[7] He should be better able to deal with them than Johnson.

In this present administration they have in the House of Representatives 257 Democrats to only 177 Republicans. They control two-thirds of the House vote. Why can't they pass something that will help you and me? In the Senate, there are 67 senators who are of the Democratic Party. Only 33 of them are Republicans. Why, the Democrats have got the government sewed up, and you're the one who sewed it up for them. And what have they given you for it? Four years in office, and just now getting around to some civil-rights legislation. Just now, after everything else is gone, out of the way, they're going to sit down now and play with you all summer long—the same old giant con game that they call filibuster. All those are in cahoots together. Don't you ever think they're not in cahoots together, for the man that is heading the civil-rights filibuster is a man from Georgia named Richard Russell.[8] When Johnson became president, the first man he asked for when he got back to Washington, D.C., was "Dicky"—that's how tight they are. That's his boy, that's his pal, that's his buddy. But they're playing that old con game. One of them makes believe he's for you, and he's got it fixed where the other one is so tight against you, he never has to keep his promise.

So it's time in 1964 to wake up. And when you see them coming up with that kind of conspiracy, let them know your eyes are open. And let them know you got something else that's wide open too. It's got to be the ballot or the bullet. The ballot or the bullet. If you're afraid to use an expression like that, you should get on out of the country, you should get back in the cotton

---

[6]Anxious about Southern voters, President Kennedy did not propose major civil rights legislation until late in his term. Some Southern congressional leaders, such as Mississippi Senator James Eastland (who organized the segregationist organization the White Citizen's Council), ardently opposed civil rights legislation by filibustering.

[7]A former senator from Texas, Lyndon Johnson became president after Kennedy's assassination. He did not support civil rights until faced with the murders of civil rights activists; Johnson then became a strong supporter of legislation, pushing the 1964 Civil Rights Act.

[8]Senator Richard Russell from Georgia led the filibuster effort against civil rights legislation.

patch, you should get back in the alley. They get all the Negro vote, and after they get it, the Negro gets nothing in return. All they did when they got to Washington was give a few big Negroes big jobs. Those big Negroes didn't need big jobs, they already had jobs. That's camouflage, that's trickery, that's treachery, window-dressing. I'm not trying to knock out the Democrats for the Republicans, we'll get to them in a minute. But it is true—you put the Democrats first and the Democrats put you last.

Look at it the way it is. What alibis do they use, since they control Congress and the Senate? What alibi do they use when you and I ask, "Well, when are you going to keep your promise?" They blame the Dixiecrats. What is a Dixiecrat? A Democrat. A Dixiecrat is nothing but a Democrat in disguise. The titular head of the Democrats is also the head of the Dixiecrats, because the Dixiecrats are a part of the Democratic Party. The Democrats have never kicked the Dixiecrats out of the party. The Dixiecrats bolted themselves once, but the Democrats didn't put them out. Imagine, these low-down Southern segregationists put the Northern Democrats down. But the Northern Democrats have never put the Dixiecrats down. No, look at that thing the way it is.[9] They have got a con game going on, a political con game, and you and I are in the middle. It's time for you and me to wake up and start looking at it like it is, and trying to understand it like it is; and then we can deal with it like it is.

The Dixiecrats in Washington, D.C., control the key committees that run the government. The only reason the Dixiecrats control these committees is because they have seniority. The only reason they have seniority is because they come from states where Negroes can't vote. This is not even a government that's based on democracy. It is not a government that is made up of representatives of the people. Half of the people in the South can't even vote. Eastland is not even supposed to be in Washington. Half of the senators and congressmen who occupy these key positions in Washington, D.C., are there illegally, are there unconstitutionally.

I was in Washington, D.C., a week ago Thursday, when they were debating whether or not they should let the bill come onto the floor. And in the back of the room where the Senate meets, there's a huge map of the United States, and on that map it shows the location of Negroes throughout the country. And it shows that the Southern section of the country, the states that are most heavily concentrated with Negroes, are the ones that have senators and congressmen

---

[9]Southern Democrats in favor of a segregated South became known as Dixiecrats. Angered by President Harry S. Truman's civil rights initiatives and the 1948 Democratic Party platform, Southern Democrats bolted the party and formed a splinter group to nominate then Democratic governor of South Carolina, Strom Thurmond, for president. Many of these Democrats, including Thurmond, later joined the Republican Party. Few Northern Democrats openly criticized Southern Democrats' anti–civil rights position.

standing up filibustering and doing all other kinds of trickery to keep the Negro from being able to vote. This is pitiful. But it's not pitiful for us any longer; it's actually pitiful for the white man, because soon now, as the Negro awakens a little more and sees the vise that he's in, sees the bag that he's in, sees the real game that he's in, then the Negro's going to develop a new tactic.

These senators and congressmen actually violate the constitutional amendments that guarantee the people of that particular state or county the right to vote. And the Constitution itself has within it the machinery to expel any representative from a state where the voting rights of the people are violated. You don't even need new legislation. Any person in Congress right now, who is there from a state or a district where the voting rights of the people are violated, that particular person should be expelled from Congress. And when you expel him, you've removed one of the obstacles in the path of any real meaningful legislation in this country. In fact, when you expel them, you don't need new legislation, because they will be replaced by black representatives from counties and districts where the black man is in the majority, not in the minority.

If the black man in these Southern states had his full voting rights, the key Dixiecrats in Washington, D.C., which means the key Democrats in Washington, D.C., would lose their seats. The Democratic Party itself would lose its power. It would cease to be powerful as a party. When you see the amount of power that would be lost by the Democratic Party if it were to lose the Dixiecrat wing, or branch, or element, you can see where it's against the interests of the Democrats to give voting rights to Negroes in states where the Democrats have been in complete power and authority ever since the Civil War. You just can't belong to that party without analyzing it.

I say again, I'm not anti-Democrat, I'm not anti-Republican, I'm not anti-anything. I'm just questioning their sincerity, and some of the strategy that they've been using on our people by promising them promises that they don't intend to keep. When you keep the Democrats in power, you're keeping the Dixiecrats in power. I doubt that my good Brother Lomax will deny that. A vote for a Democrat is a vote for a Dixiecrat. That's why, in 1964, it's time now for you and me to become more politically mature and realize what the ballot is for; what we're supposed to get when we cast a ballot; and that if we don't cast a ballot, it's going to end up in a situation where we're going to have to cast a bullet. It's either a ballot or a bullet.

In the North, they do it a different way. They have a system that's known as gerrymandering, whatever that means. It means when Negroes become too heavily concentrated in a certain area, and begin to gain too much political power, the white man comes along and changes the district lines. You may say, "Why do you keep saying white man?" Because it's the white man who does it. I haven't ever seen any Negro changing any lines. They don't let him get near the line. It's the white man who does this. And usually, it's the white man who grins at you the most, and pats you on the back, and is supposed to be your friend. He may be friendly, but he's not your friend.

So, what I'm trying to impress upon you, in essence, is this: You and I in America are faced not with a segregationist conspiracy, we're faced with a government conspiracy. Everyone who's filibustering is a senator—that's the government. Everyone who's finagling in Washington, D.C., is a congressman—that's the government. You don't have anybody putting blocks in your path but people who are a part of the government. The same government that you go abroad to fight for and die for is the government that is in a conspiracy to deprive you of your voting rights, deprive you of your economic opportunities, deprive you of decent housing, deprive you of decent education. You don't need to go to the employer alone, it is the government itself, the government of America, that is responsible for the oppression and exploitation and degradation of black people in this country. And you should drop it in their lap. This government has failed the Negro. This so-called democracy has failed the Negro. And all these white liberals have definitely failed the Negro.

So, where do we go from here? First, we need some friends. We need some new allies. The entire civil-rights struggle needs a new interpretation, a broader interpretation. We need to look at this civil-rights thing from another angle—from the inside as well as from the outside. To those of us whose philosophy is black nationalism, the only way you can get involved in the civil-rights struggle is give it a new interpretation. That old interpretation excluded us. It kept us out. So, we're giving a new interpretation to the civil-rights struggle, an interpretation that will enable us to come into it, take part in it. And these handkerchief-heads who have been dillydallying and pussyfooting and compromising—we don't intend to let them pussyfoot and dillydally and compromise any longer.

How can you thank a man for giving you what's already yours? How then can you thank him for giving you only part of what's already yours? You haven't even made progress, if what's being given to you, you should have had already. That's not progress. And I love my Brother Lomax, the way he pointed out we're right back where we were in 1954. We're not even as far up as we were in 1954. We're behind where we were in 1954. There's more segregation now than there was in 1954. There's more racial animosity, more racial hatred, more racial violence today in 1964, than there was in 1954. Where is the progress?

And now you're facing a situation where the young Negro's coming up. They don't want to hear that "turn-the-other-cheek" stuff, no. In Jacksonville, those were teenagers, they were throwing Molotov cocktails.[10]

---

[10]A Molotov cocktail, first used during World War I, is an improvised explosive made from gasoline, sand, and soap suds.

Negroes have never done that before. But it shows you there's a new deal coming in. There's new thinking coming in. There's new strategy coming in. It'll be Molotov cocktails this month, hand grenades next month, and something else next month. It'll be ballots, or it'll be bullets. It'll be liberty, or it will be death. The only difference about this kind of death—it'll be reciprocal. You know what is meant by "reciprocal"? That's one of Brother Lomax's words, I stole it from him. I don't usually deal with those big words because I don't usually deal with big people. I deal with small people. I find you can get a whole lot of small people and whip hell out of a whole lot of big people. They haven't got anything to lose, and they've got everything to gain. And they'll let you know in a minute: "It takes two to tango; when I go, you go."

The black nationalists, those whose philosophy is black nationalism, in bringing about this new interpretation of the entire meaning of civil rights, look upon it as meaning, as Brother Lomax has pointed out, equality of opportunity. Well, we're justified in seeking civil rights, if it means equality of opportunity, because all we're doing there is trying to collect for our investment. Our mothers and fathers invested sweat and blood. Three hundred and ten years we worked in this country without a dime in return—I mean without a *dime* in return. You let the white man walk around here talking about how rich this country is, but you never stop to think how it got rich so quick. It got rich because you made it rich.

You take the people who are in this audience right now. They're poor, we're all poor as individuals. Our weekly salary individually amounts to hardly anything. But if you take the salary of everyone in here collectively it'll fill up a whole lot of baskets. It's a lot of wealth. If you can collect the wages of just these people right here for a year, you'll be rich—richer than rich. When you look at it like that, think how rich Uncle Sam had to become, not with this handful, but millions of black people. Your and my mother and father, who didn't work an eight-hour shift, but worked from "can't see" in the morning until "can't see" at night, and worked for nothing, making the white man rich, making Uncle Sam rich.

This is our investment. This is our contribution—our blood. Not only did we give of our free labor, we gave of our blood. Every time he had a call to arms, we were the first ones in uniform. We died on every battlefield the white man had. We have made a greater sacrifice than anybody who's standing up in America today. We have made a greater contribution and have collected less. Civil rights, for those of us whose philosophy is black nationalism, means: "Give it to us now. Don't wait for next year. Give it to us yesterday, and that's not fast enough."

I might stop right here to point out one thing. Whenever you're going after something that belongs to you, anyone who's depriving you of the right to have it is a criminal. Understand that. Whenever you are going after something that is yours, you are within your legal rights to lay claim to it. And anyone who puts forth any effort to deprive you of that which is yours, is breaking the law, is a criminal. And this was pointed out by the Supreme Court decision. It outlawed segregation.[11] Which means segregation is against the law. Which means a segregationist is breaking the law. A segregationist is a criminal. You can't label him as anything other than that. And when you demonstrate against segregation, the law is on your side. The Supreme Court is on your side.

Now, who is it that opposes you in carrying out the law? The police department itself. With police dogs and clubs. Whenever you demonstrate against segregation, whether it is segregated education, segregated housing, or anything else, the law is on your side, and anyone who stands in the way is not the law any longer. They are breaking the law, they are not representatives of the law. Any time you demonstrate against segregation and a man has the audacity to put a police dog on you, kill that dog, kill him, I'm telling you, kill that dog. I say it, if they put me in jail tomorrow, kill—that—dog. Then you'll put a stop to it. Now, if these white people in here don't want to see that kind of action, get down and tell the mayor to tell the police department to pull the dogs in. That's all you have to do. If you don't do it, someone else will.

If you don't take this kind of stand, your little children will grow up and look at you and think "shame." If you don't take an uncompromising stand—I don't mean go out and get violent; but at the same time you should never be nonviolent unless you run into some nonviolence. I'm nonviolent with those who are nonviolent with me. But when you drop that violence on me, then you've made me go insane, and I'm not responsible for what I do. And that's the way every Negro should get. Any time you know you're within the law, within your legal rights, within your moral rights, in accord with justice, then die for what you believe in. But don't die alone. Let your dying be reciprocal. This is what is meant by equality. What's good for the goose is good for the gander.

When we begin to get in this area, we need new friends, we need new allies. We need to expand the civil-rights struggle to a higher level—to the level of human rights. Whenever you are in a civil-rights struggle, whether you know it or not, you are confining yourself to the jurisdiction of Uncle Sam. No one from the outside world can speak out in your behalf as long as your struggle is a civil-rights struggle. Civil rights comes within the domestic affairs of this country. All of our African brothers and our Asian brothers and our Latin-American brothers cannot open their mouths and interfere in

---

[11]Between the 1930s and 1961, various Supreme Court decisions (including the 1954 *Brown v. Topeka*) prohibited segregation in housing, primary elections, public education, and transportation.

the domestic affairs of the United States. And as long as it's civil rights, this comes under the jurisdiction of Uncle Sam.

But the United Nations has what's known as the charter of human rights, it has a committee that deals in human rights. You may wonder why all of the atrocities that have been committed in Africa and in Hungary and in Asia and in Latin America are brought before the UN, and the Negro problem is never brought before the UN. This is part of the conspiracy. This old, tricky, blue-eyed liberal who is supposed to be your and my friend, supposed to be in our corner, supposed to be subsidizing our struggle, and supposed to be acting in the capacity of an adviser, never tells you anything about human rights. They keep you wrapped up in civil rights. And you spend so much time barking up the civil-rights tree, you don't even know there's a human-rights tree on the same floor.

When you expand the civil-rights struggle to the level of human rights, you can then take the case of the black man in this country before the nations in the UN. You can take it before the General Assembly. You can take Uncle Sam before a world court. But the only level you can do it on is the level of human rights. Civil rights keeps you under his restrictions, under his jurisdiction. Civil rights keeps you in his pocket. Civil rights means you're asking Uncle Sam to treat you right. Human rights are something you were born with. Human rights are your God-given rights. Human rights are the rights that are recognized by all nations of this earth. And any time any one violates your human rights, you can take them to the world court. Uncle Sam's hands are dripping with blood, dripping with the blood of the black man in this country. He's the earth's number-one hypocrite. He has the audacity—yes, he has—imagine him posing as the leader of the free world. The free world!—and you over here singing "We Shall Overcome." Expand the civil-rights struggle to the level of human rights, take it into the United Nations, where our African brothers can throw their weight on our side, where our Asian brothers can throw their weight on our side, where our Latin-American brothers can throw their weight on our side, and where 800 million Chinamen are sitting there waiting to throw their weight on our side.

Let the world know how bloody his hands are. Let the world know the hypocrisy that's practiced over here. Let it be the ballot or the bullet. Let him know that it must be the ballot or the bullet.

When you take our case to Washington, D.C., you're taking it to the criminal who's responsible; it's like running from the wolf to the fox. They're all in cahoots together. They all work political chicanery and make you look like a chump before the eyes of the world. Here you are walking around in America, getting ready to be drafted and sent abroad, like a tin soldier, and when you get over there, people ask you what are you fighting for, and you have to stick your tongue in your cheek. No, take Uncle Sam to court, take him before the world.

By ballot I only mean freedom. Don't you know—I disagree with Lomax on this issue—that the ballot is more important than the dollar? Can I prove it? Yes. Look in the UN. There are poor nations in the UN; yet those poor nations can get together with their voting power and keep the rich nations from making a move. They have one nation—one vote, everyone has an equal vote. And when those brothers from Asia, and Africa and the darker parts of this earth get together, their voting power is sufficient to hold Sam in check. Or Russia in check. Or some other section of the earth in check. So, the ballot is most important.

Right now, in this country, if you and I, 22 million African-Americans—that's what we are—Africans who are in America. You're nothing but Africans. Nothing but Africans. In fact, you'd get farther calling yourself African instead of Negro. Africans don't catch hell. You're the only one catching hell. They don't have to pass civil-rights bills for Africans. An African can go anywhere he wants right now. All you've got to do is tie your head up. That's right, go anywhere you want. Just stop being a Negro. Change your name to Hoogagagooba. That'll show you how silly the white man is. You're dealing with a silly man. A friend of mine who's very dark put a turban on his head and went into a restaurant in Atlanta before they called themselves desegregated. He went into a white restaurant, he sat down, they served him, and he said, "What would happen if a Negro came in here?" And there he's sitting, black as night, but because he had his head wrapped up the waitress looked back at him and says, "Why, there wouldn't no nigger dare come in here."

So, you're dealing with a man whose bias and prejudice are making him lose his mind, his intelligence, every day. He's frightened. He looks around and sees what's taking place on this earth, and he sees that the pendulum of time is swinging in your direction. The dark people are waking up. They're losing their fear of the white man. No place where he's fighting right now is he winning. Everywhere he's fighting, he's fighting someone your and my complexion. And they're beating him. He can't win any more. He's won his last battle. He failed to win the Korean War. He couldn't win it. He had to sign a truce. That's a loss. Any time Uncle Sam, with all his machinery for warfare, is held to a draw by some rice-eaters, he's lost the battle. He had to sign a truce. America's not supposed to sign a truce. She's supposed to be bad. But she's not bad any more. She's bad as long as she can use her hydrogen bomb, but she can't use hers for fear Russia might use hers. Russia can't use hers, for fear that Sam might use his. So, both of them are weaponless. They can't use the weapon because each's weapon nullifies the other's. So the only place where action can take place is on the ground. And the white man can't win another war fighting on the ground. Those days are over. The black man knows it, the brown man knows it, the red man knows it, and the yellow man knows it. So they engage him in guerrilla warfare. That's not his style. You've got to have heart to be a guerrilla warrior, and he hasn't got any heart. I'm telling you now.

I just want to give you a little briefing on guerrilla warfare because, before you know it, before you know it—It takes heart to be a guerrilla warrior because you're on your own. In conventional warfare you have tanks and a whole lot of other people with you to back you up, planes over your head and all that kind of stuff. But a guerrilla is on his own. All you have is a rifle, some sneakers and a bowl of rice, and that's all you need—and a lot of heart. The Japanese on some of those islands in the Pacific, when the American soldiers landed, one Japanese sometimes could hold the whole army off. He'd just wait until the sun went down, and when the sun went down they were all equal. He would take his little blade and slip from bush to bush, and from American to American. The white soldiers couldn't cope with that. Whenever you see a white soldier that fought in the Pacific, he has the shakes, he has a nervous condition, because they scared him to death.

The same thing happened to the French up in French Indochina.[12] People who just a few years previously were rice farmers got together and ran the heavily-mechanized French army out of Indochina. You don't need it—modern warfare today won't work. This is the day of the guerrilla. They did the same thing in Algeria. Algerians, who were nothing but Bedouins, took a rifle and sneaked off to the hills, and de Gaulle and all of his highfalutin' war machinery couldn't defeat those guerrillas.[13] Nowhere on this earth does the white man win in a guerrilla warfare. It's not his speed. Just as guerrilla warfare is prevailing in Asia and in parts of Africa and in parts of Latin America, you've got to be mighty naive, or you've got to play the black man cheap, if you don't think some day he's going to wake up and find that it's got to be the ballot or the bullet.

I would like to say, in closing, a few things concerning the Muslim Mosque, Inc., which we established recently in New York City. It's true we're Muslims and our religion is Islam, but we don't mix our religion with our politics and our economics and our social and civil activities—not any more. We keep our religion in our mosque. After our religious services are over, then as Muslims we become involved in political action, economic action and social and civic action. We become involved with anybody, anywhere, any time and in any manner that's designed to eliminate the evils, the political, economic and social evils that are afflicting the people of our community.

---

[12]French Indochina, now Vietnam, Cambodia, and Laos, was a colony of France until the 1954 Geneva Conference ended its war with Vietnamese nationalists. The United States then became involved.

[13]Charles de Gaulle (1890–1970) was president during the Algerian struggle to gain independence from France.

The political philosophy of black nationalism means that the black man should control the politics and the politicians in his own community; no more. The black man in the black community has to be re-educated into the science of politics so he will know what politics is supposed to bring him in return. Don't be throwing out any ballots. A ballot is like a bullet. You don't throw your ballots until you see a target, and if that target is not within your reach, keep your ballot in your pocket. The political philosophy of black nationalism is being taught in the Christian church. It's being taught in the NAACP. It's being taught in CORE meetings. It's being taught in SNCC meetings.[14] It's being taught in Muslim meetings. It's being taught where nothing but atheists and agnostics come together. It's being taught everywhere. Black people are fed up with the dillydallying, pussyfooting, compromising approach that we've been using toward getting our freedom. We want freedom *now*, but we're not going to get it saying "We Shall Overcome." We've got to fight until we overcome.

The economic philosophy of black nationalism is pure and simple. It only means that we should control the economy of our community. Why should white people be running all the stores in our community? Why should white people be running the banks of our community? Why should the economy of our community be in the hands of the white man? Why? If a black man can't move his store into a white community, you tell me why a white man should move his store into a black community. The philosophy of black nationalism involves a re-education program in the black community in regards to economics. Our people have to be made to see that any time you take your dollar out of your community and spend it in a community where you don't live, the community where you live will get poorer and poorer, and the community where you spend your money will get richer and richer. Then you wonder why where you live is always a ghetto or a slum area. And where you and I are concerned, not only do we lose it when we spend it out of the community, but the white man has got all our stores in the community tied up; so that though we spend it in the community, at sundown the man who runs the store takes it over across town somewhere. He's got us in a vise.

So the economic philosophy of black nationalism means in every church, in every civic organization, in every fraternal order, it's time now for our people to become conscious of the importance of controlling the economy of our community. If we own the stores, if we operate the businesses, if we try and establish some industry in our own community, then we're developing to the position where we are creating employment for our own kind. Once

---

[14]The National Association for the Advancement of Colored People (NAACP), the Congress of Racial Equality (CORE), and the Student Nonviolent Coordinating Committee (SNCC) advocated nonviolence, while acknowledging some principles of black nationalism.

you gain control of the economy of your own community, then you don't have to picket and boycott and beg some cracker downtown for a job in his business.

The social philosophy of black nationalism only means that we have to get together and remove the evils, the vices, alcoholism, drug addiction, and other evils that are destroying the moral fiber of our community. We ourselves have to lift the level of our community, the standard of our community to a higher level, make our own society beautiful so that we will be satisfied in our own social circles and won't be running around here trying to knock our way into a social circle where we're not wanted.

So I say, in spreading a gospel such as black nationalism, it is not designed to make the black man re-evaluate the white man—you know him already—but to make the black man re-evaluate himself. Don't change the white man's mind—you can't change his mind, and that whole thing about appealing to the moral conscience of America—America's conscience is bankrupt. She lost all conscience a long time ago. Uncle Sam has no conscience. They don't know what morals are. They don't try and eliminate an evil because it's evil, or because it's illegal, or because it's immoral; they eliminate it only when it threatens their existence. So you're wasting your time appealing to the moral conscience of a bankrupt man like Uncle Sam. If he had a conscience, he'd straighten this thing out with no more pressure being put upon him. So it is not necessary to change the white man's mind. We have to change our own mind. You can't change his mind about us. We've got to change our own minds about each other. We have to see each other with new eyes. We have to see each other as brothers and sisters. We have to come together with warmth so we can develop unity and harmony that's necessary to get this problem solved ourselves. How can we do this? How can we avoid jealousy? How can we avoid the suspicion and the divisions that exist in the community? I'll tell you how.

I have watched how Billy Graham comes into a city, spreading what he calls the gospel of Christ, which is only white nationalism.[15] That's what he is. Billy Graham is a white nationalist; I'm a black nationalist. But since it's the natural tendency for leaders to be jealous and look upon a powerful figure like Graham with suspicion and envy, how is it possible for him to come into a city and get all the cooperation of the church leaders? Don't think because they're church leaders that they don't have weaknesses that make them envious and jealous—no, everybody's got it. It's not an accident that when they want to choose a cardinal [as Pope] over there in Rome, they get in a closet so you can't hear them cussing and fighting and carrying on.

---

[15]Billy Graham, a popular Christian evangelist, began to desegregate his audiences in the 1950s, but he did not publicly endorse desegregation efforts until 1965.

Billy Graham comes in preaching the gospel of Christ, he evangelizes the gospel, he stirs everybody up, but he never tries to start a church. If he came in trying to start a church, all the churches would be against him. So, he just comes in talking about Christ and tells everybody who gets Christ to go to any church where Christ is; and in this way the church cooperates with him. So we're going to take a page from his book.

Our gospel is black nationalism. We're not trying to threaten the existence of any organization, but we're spreading the gospel of black nationalism. Anywhere there's a church that is also preaching and practicing the gospel of black nationalism, join that church. If the NAACP is preaching and practicing the gospel of black nationalism, join the NAACP. If CORE is spreading and practicing the gospel of black nationalism, join CORE. Join any organization that has a gospel that's for the uplift of the black man. And when you get into it and see them pussyfooting or compromising, pull out of it because that's not black nationalism. We'll find another one.

And in this manner, the organizations will increase in number and in quantity and in quality, and by August, it is then our intention to have a black nationalist convention which will consist of delegates from all over the country who are interested in the political, economic and social philosophy of black nationalism. After these delegates convene, we will hold a seminar, we will hold discussions, we will listen to everyone. We want to hear new ideas and new solutions and new answers. And at that time, if we see fit then to form a black nationalist party, we'll form a black nationalist party. If it's necessary to form a black nationalist army, we'll form a black nationalist army. It'll be the ballot or the bullet. It'll be liberty or it'll be death.

It's time for you and me to stop sitting in this country, letting some cracker senators, Northern crackers and Southern crackers, sit there in Washington, D.C., and come to a conclusion in their mind that you and I are supposed to have civil rights. There's no white man going to tell me anything about *my* rights. Brothers and sisters, always remember, if it doesn't take senators and congressmen and presidential proclamations to give freedom to the white man, it is not necessary for legislation or proclamation or Supreme Court decisions to give freedom to the black man. You let that white man know, if this is a country of freedom, let it be a country of freedom; and if it's not a country of freedom, change it.

We will work with anybody, anywhere, at any time, who is genuinely interested in tackling the problem head-on, nonviolently as long as the enemy is nonviolent, but violent when the enemy gets violent. We'll work with you on the voter-registration drive, we'll work with you on rent strikes, we'll work with you on school boycotts—I don't believe in any kind of integration; I'm not even worried about it because I know you're not going to get it anyway; you're not going to get it because you're afraid to die; you've got to be ready to die if you try and force yourself on the white man, because he'll get just as violent as those crackers in Mississippi, right here in Cleveland. But we will still work with you on the school boycotts because we're against a segregated school system. A segregated school system produces children who, when they graduate, graduate with crippled minds. But this does not mean that a school is segregated because it's all black. A segregated school means a school that is controlled by people who have no real interest in it whatsoever.

Let me explain what I mean. A segregated district or community is a community in which people live, but outsiders control the politics and the economy of that community. They never refer to the white section as a segregated community. It's the all-Negro section that's a segregated community. Why? The white man controls his own school, his own bank, his own economy, his own politics, his own everything, his own community—but he also controls yours. When you're under someone else's control, you're segregated. They'll always give you the lowest or the worst that there is to offer, but it doesn't mean you're segregated just because you have your own. You've got to *control* your own. Just like the white man has control of his, you need to control yours.

You know the best way to get rid of segregation? The white man is more afraid of separation than he is of integration. Segregation means that he puts you away from him, but not far enough for you to be out of his jurisdiction; separation means you're gone. And the white man will integrate faster than he'll let you separate. So we will work with you against the segregated school system because it's criminal, because it is absolutely destructive, in every way imaginable, to the minds of the children who have to be exposed to that type of crippling education.

Last but not least, I must say this concerning the great controversy over rifles and shotguns. The only thing that I've ever said is that in areas where the government has proven itself either unwilling or unable to defend the lives and the property of Negroes, it's time for Negroes to defend themselves. Article number two of the constitutional amendments provides you and me the right to own a rifle or a shotgun. It is constitutionally legal to own a shotgun or a rifle. This doesn't mean you're going to get a rifle and form battalions and go out looking for white folks, although you'd be within your rights—I mean, you'd be justified; but that would be illegal and we don't do anything illegal.[16] If the white man doesn't want the black man buying rifles and shotguns, then let the government do its job. That's all. And

---

[16]Although known for his incendiary remarks, Malcolm X made vague and cautious comments about armed violence. He never carried a gun during these years nor did he advocate that others should do so. He did seek legal advice about the right of individuals to carry guns in the United States.

don't let the white man come to you and ask you what you think about what Malcolm says—why, you old Uncle Tom. He would never ask you if he thought you were going to say, "Amen!" No, he is making a Tom out of you.

So, this doesn't mean forming rifle clubs and going out looking for people, but it is time, in 1964, if you are a man, to let that man know. If he's not going to do his job in running the government and providing you and me with the protection that our taxes are supposed to be for, since he spends all those billions for his defense budget, he certainly can't begrudge you and me spending $12 or $15 for a single-shot, or double-action. I hope you understand. Don't go out shooting people, but any time, brothers and sisters, and especially the men in this audience—some of you wearing Congressional Medals of Honor, with shoulders this wide, chests this big, muscles that big—any time you and I sit around and read where they bomb a church and murder in cold blood, not some grownups, but four little girls while they were praying to the same god the white man taught them to pray to, and you and I see the government go down and can't find who did it.[17]

Why, this man—he can find Eichmann hiding down in Argentina somewhere.[18] Let two or three American soldiers, who are minding somebody else's business way over in South Vietnam, get killed, and he'll send battleships, sticking his nose in their business. He wanted to send troops down to Cuba and make them have what he calls free elections—this old cracker who doesn't have free elections in his own country. No, if you never see me another time in your life, if I die in the morning, I'll die saying one thing: the ballot or the bullet, the ballot or the bullet.

If a Negro in 1964 has to sit around and wait for some cracker senator to filibuster when it comes to the rights of black people, why, you and I should hang our heads in shame. You talk about a march on Washington in 1963, you haven't seen anything. There's some more going down in '64. And this time they're not going like they went last year. They're not going singing "We Shall Overcome." They're not going with white friends. They're not going with placards already painted for them. They're not going with round-trip tickets. They're going with one-way tickets.

And if they don't want that non-violent army going down there, tell them to bring the filibuster to a halt. The black nationalists aren't going to wait. Lyndon B. Johnson is the head of the Democratic Party. If he's for civil

---

[17]On September 17, 1963, four young African-American girls died when their church in Birmingham, Alabama, exploded from a bomb planted by the Ku Klux Klan. After the bombings, the FBI claimed they could not track down the people who bombed the church; one man was finally convicted of the crime on May 1, 2001.

[18]High-ranking Nazi official Adolph Eichmann, who had organized the massacre of Jews in Germany and Austria, fled to Argentina where he was found in 1960 by the FBI and Israeli officials.

rights, let him go into the Senate next week and declares himself. Let him go in there right now and declare himself. Let him go in there and denounce the Southern branch of his party. Let him go in there right now and take a moral stand—right now, not later. Tell him, don't wait until election time. If he waits too long, brothers and sisters, he will be responsible for letting a condition develop in this country which will create a climate that will bring seeds up out of the ground with vegetation on the end of them looking like something these people never dreamed of. In 1964, it's the ballot or the bullet. Thank you.

[1964]

REVEREND MARTIN LUTHER KING, JR.
[1929–1968]

Reverend Martin Luther King, Jr.'s considerable spiritual and oratorical abilities helped galvanize millions of people to protest against legal segregation in the United States. In numerous speeches, interviews, and writings, King interlaced the long tradition of American and African-American political dissent with an African-American Christian faith in and practice of nonviolent action against injustice. In the years before his assassination in 1968, King spoke out against the war in Vietnam and economic injustice against the poor of all races and ethnicities. His efforts received international recognition, including the 1964 Nobel Peace Prize. In 1968, Reverend King was assassinated while appealing for better work conditions for Memphis sanitation workers. Since his death, many have called him a prophet of peace, justice, freedom, and democracy. A statue of Reverend King now sits above the entrance to Westminster Abbey in England.

Born on January 15, 1929, into a prominent black middle class family in Atlanta, Georgia, Martin Luther King, Jr. came of age when legalized segregation had been in place for nearly half a century. King's maternal great-grandfather, grandfather, and his father were all black Baptist preachers. King's father, Reverend Martin Luther King, Sr., was a pastor at Ebenezer Baptist Church. Between 1935 and 1944, King attended David T. Howard Elementary School, Atlanta University Laboratory School, and Booker T. Washington High School. He did not finish high school, opting instead to take a special examination that allowed him to enter Morehouse College at the age of fifteen. Over the next four years, King came in contact with many of the most important liberal and spiritual leaders of the time, including Dr. Benjamin Mays, then president of Morehouse College. In 1947, King's father ordained him as a minister and then licensed him to preach at Ebenezer Baptist Church.

After King graduated from Morehouse at the age of nineteen, he continued his education. He first enrolled in Crozer Theological Seminary in Chester, Pennsylvania, then part of the Northern Baptist Association. After he obtained a bachelor's degree in divinity in 1951, King entered the doctoral program at Boston University School of Theology. While in Boston, he met and soon married Coretta Scott, a graduate student at the New England Conservatory of Music. In 1954, Reverend King accepted the position as pastor of Dexter

Avenue Baptist Church in Montgomery, Alabama, one year before he com-pleted his graduate work.

Later that same year, the landmark Supreme Court case, Brown v. Topeka, made public school segregation illegal. Despite the 1954 Supreme Court case that called for desegregation in public schools, schools and the federal govern-ment made little, if any, effort to do so; de facto and de jure segregation remained firmly intact in other areas of American life. Frustrated by the lim-ited federal and state response to the court's mandate, African Americans turned to boycotts and public protests, forms of dissent long used against racial discrimination. This time, however, these protests became more widespread and the participants encountered violent attacks; many African Americans faced economic intimidation and reprisals. Nonetheless, many persevered and the efforts spread to communities throughout the South. In Montgomery, Alabama, an African-American women's organization, whose members included Rosa Parks and JoAnn Gibson Robinson, decided to protest the city's bus segregation. On December 1, 1955, Rosa Parks was arrested for refusing to give up her seat to a white man. Other members of the women's organiza-tion quickly organized a bus boycott. Seeking a minister who could lead the community, but did not have ties to the local white political structure, the community turned to the new minister of Dexter Avenue Baptist Church.

During the 381 days of the bus boycott, Reverend King emerged as a powerful and eloquent speaker who wove together an African-American Christian vision of a beloved community with an American political belief in the right to full citi-zenship. King added to these ideas by fitting the nonviolent forms of protest used by Mahatama Gandhi in India to the needs of African-American protest. Rev-erend King called for a disciplined and loving approach to end discrimination through nonviolent but purposeful marches, sit-ins, and boycotts. Reverend King's challenging call to end injustice and oppression through nonviolent protest was quickly embraced by many African Americans. Other Americans, too, be-gan to support this revolution in U.S. social and political life. This increasingly interracial effort sparked a violent and organized backlash from people commit-ted to maintaining segregation. This new approach to confront racial discrimina-tion along with the frequent violent—and often murderous—efforts to maintain segregation shaped the civil rights movement for the next decade.

Though many other African Americans emerged to plan and lead the civil rights movement, Reverend King's charismatic personality and his eloquent ability to convey the moral and political reasons for ending segregation made him the most recognizable leader. Jailed in 1963 in Birmingham for partici-pating in a boycott against the city's segregation laws and local police brutal-ity, Reverend King wrote his now famous "Letter from Birmingham City Jail," articulating the moral imperative to defy unjust laws. Part theology, part political critique, King swayed a nation still skeptical of the movement's goals and tactics. He always recognized, however, that the movement he led depended on the courage of many. When he won the Nobel Peace Prize in 1964, he noted that he accepted "this award in behalf of a civil rights movement." Over the next years, King and others in the civil rights movement pushed for and ultimately won federal support for legislation that overturned discriminatory laws based on race in housing, voting, employment, transportation, and social services. His criticism of the war in Vietnam and economic discrimination claimed his attention during the last four years of his life. Reverend King was assassinated on April 4, 1968.

Over the course of his short public life, Reverend King left a variety of writing, including books, essays, sermons, and speeches. His "I Have a Dream" speech has become one of the most recognized speeches in American history; it has become one of the most significant orations of the twentieth century. The keynote speaker at the March on Washington, Reverend King delivered the speech in front of the Lincoln Memorial on August 28, 1963. He abandoned the text that he had written and instead gave an extemporaneous speech that masterfully articulated his hope in Americans' ability to create a "beloved community"; he also criticized American society for its failure to extend its democratic promise to all of its citizens. He nonetheless imagined that black and white Americans, together, would bring forth "a bright day of justice." Nearly a quarter of a million people attended the march, first conceived more than twenty years earlier by the labor activist A. Philip Randolph. Broadcast on television, millions more heard the speech in their living rooms. Thirty years after its delivery, the speech is a reminder that ordinary individuals can make extraordinary efforts to bring peace to the world.

Kimberly L. Phillips
The College of William and Mary

For Further Reading

Primary Works

Stride Toward Freedom: The Montgomery Story (New York: Harper and Row, 1958); *Where Do We Go from Here: Chaos or Community* (New York: Harper and Row, 1967); *Why We Can't Wait* (New York: Harper and Row, 1963).

Secondary Works

Fairclough, Adam. *To Redeem the Soul of America: The Southern Christian Leadership Conference and Martin Luther King, Jr.* (Athens, Ga.: University of Georgia Press, 1987); King, Coretta Scott. *My Life with Martin Luther King, Jr.* (New York: Rinehart and Winston, Inc., 1969); Lewis, David L. *King: A Critical Biography* (Baltimore: Penguin Books, Inc., 1970); Washington, James M., ed. *A Testament of Hope: The Essential Writings and Speeches of Martin Luther King, Jr.* (San Francisco: HarperSanFrancisco, 1986).

The Drum Major Instinct

DR. MARTIN LUTHER KING, JR.

This morning I would like to use as a subject from which to preach: "The Drum Major Instinct." "The Drum Major Instinct." And our text for the morning is taken from a very familiar passage in the tenth chapter as recorded by Saint Mark. Beginning with the thirty-fifth verse of that chapter, we read these words: "And James and John, the sons of Zebedee, came unto him saying, 'Master, we would that thou shouldest do for us whatsoever we shall desire.' And he said unto them, 'What would ye that I should do for you?' And they said unto him, 'Grant unto us that we may sit, one on thy right hand, and the other on thy left hand, in thy glory.' But Jesus said unto them, 'Ye know not what ye ask: Can ye drink of the cup that I drink of? and be baptized with the baptism that I am baptized with?' And they said unto him, 'We can.' And Jesus said unto them, 'Ye shall indeed drink of the cup that I drink of, and with the baptism that I am baptized withal shall ye be baptized: but to sit on my right hand and on my left hand is not mine to give; but it shall be given to them for whom it is prepared.'" And then Jesus goes on toward the end of that passage to say, "But so shall it not be among you: but whosoever will be great among you, shall be your servant: and whosoever of you will be the chiefest, shall be servant of all."

The setting is clear. James and John are making a specific request of the master. They had dreamed, as most of the Hebrews dreamed, of a coming king of Israel who would set Jerusalem free and establish his kingdom on Mount Zion, and in righteousness rule the world. And they thought of Jesus as this kind of king. And they were thinking of that day when Jesus would reign supreme as this new king of Israel. And they were saying, "Now when you establish your kingdom, let one of us sit on the right hand and the other on the left hand of your throne."

Now very quickly, we would automatically condemn James and John, and we would say they were selfish. Why would they make such a selfish request? But before we condemn them too quickly, let us look calmly and

Reprinted from *Testament of Hope: Essential Writings of Martin Luther King Jr.* (1986), by permission of the Copyright Clearance Center, Inc. Copyright © 1986 by Harper and Row.

honestly at ourselves, and we will discover that we too have those same basic desires for recognition, for importance. That same desire for attention, that same desire to be first. Of course, the other disciples got mad with James and John, and you could understand why, but we must understand that we have some of the same James and John qualities. And there is deep down within all of us an instinct. It's a kind of drum major instinct—a desire to be out front, a desire to lead the parade, a desire to be first. And it is something that runs the whole gamut of life.

And so before we condemn them, let us see that we all have the drum major instinct. We all want to be important, to surpass others, to achieve distinction, to lead the parade. Alfred Adler, the great psychoanalyst, contends that this is the dominant impulse. Sigmund Freud used to contend that sex was the dominant impulse, and Adler came with a new argument saying that this quest for recognition, this desire for attention, this desire for distinction is the basic impulse, the basic drive of human life, this drum major instinct.

And you know, we begin early to ask life to put us first. Our first cry as a baby was a bid for attention. And all through childhood the drum major impulse or instinct is a major obsession. Children ask life to grant them first place. They are a little bundle of ego. And they have innately the drum major impulse or the drum major instinct.

Now in adult life, we still have it, and we really never get by it. We like to do something good. And you know, we like to be praised for it. Now if you don't believe that, you just go on living life, and you will discover very soon that you like to be praised. Everybody likes it, as a matter of fact. And somehow this warm glow we feel when we are praised or when our name is in print is something of the vitamin A to our ego. Nobody is unhappy when they are praised, even if they know they don't deserve it and even if they don't believe it. The only unhappy people about praise is when that praise is going too much toward somebody else. *(That's right)* But everybody likes to be praised because of this real drum major instinct.

Now the presence of the drum major instinct is why so many people are "joiners." You know, there are some people who just join everything. And it's really a quest for attention and recognition and importance. And they get names that give them that impression. So you get your groups, and they become the "Grand Patron," and the little fellow who is henpecked at home needs a chance to be the "Most Worthy of the Most Worthy" of something. It is the drum major impulse and longing that runs the gamut of human life. And so we see it everywhere, this quest for recognition. And we join things, overjoin really, that we think that we will find that recognition in.

Now the presence of this instinct explains why we are so often taken by advertisers. You know, those gentlemen of massive verbal persuasion. And they have a way of saying things to you that kind of gets you into buying. In order to be a man of distinction, you must drink this whiskey. In order to make your neighbors envious, you must drive this type of car. *(Make it plain)* In order to be lovely to love you must wear this kind of lipstick or this kind of perfume. And you know, before you know it, you're just buying that stuff. *(Yes)* That's the way the advertisers do it.

I got a letter the other day, and it was a new magazine coming out. And it opened up, "Dear Dr. King: As you know, you are on many mailing lists. And you are categorized as highly intelligent, progressive, a lover of the arts and the sciences, and I know you will want to read what I have to say." Of course I did. After you said all of that and explained me so exactly, of course I wanted to read it. *[laughter]*

But very seriously, it goes through life; the drum major instinct is real. *(Yes)* And you know what else it causes to happen? It often causes us to live above our means. *(Make it plain)* It's nothing but the drum major instinct. Do you ever see people buy cars that they can't even begin to buy in terms of their income? *(Amen) [laughter]* You've seen people riding around in Cadillacs and Chryslers who don't earn enough to have a good T-Model Ford. *(Make it plain)* But it feeds a repressed ego.

You know, economists tell us that your automobile should not cost more than half of your annual income. So if you make an income of five thousand dollars, your car shouldn't cost more than about twenty-five hundred. That's just good economics. And if it's a family of two, and both members of the family make ten thousand dollars, they would have to make out with one car. That would be good economics, although it's often inconvenient. But so often, haven't you seen people making five thousand dollars a year and driving a car that costs six thousand? And they wonder why their ends never meet. *[laughter]* That's a fact.

Now the economists also say that your house shouldn't cost—if you're buying a house, it shouldn't cost more than twice your income. That's based on the economy and how you would make ends meet. So, if you have an income of five thousand dollars, it's kind of difficult in this society. But say it's a family with an income of ten thousand dollars, the house shouldn't cost much more than twenty thousand. Well, I've seen folk making ten thousand dollars, living in a forty- and fifty-thousand-dollar house. And you know they just barely make it. They get a check every month somewhere, and they owe all of that out before it comes in. Never have anything to put away for rainy days.

But now the problem is, it is the drum major instinct. And you know, you see people over and over again with the drum major instinct taking them over. And they just live their lives trying to outdo the Joneses. *(Amen)* They got to get this coat because this particular coat is a little better and a little better-looking than Mary's coat. And I got to drive this car because it's something about this car that makes my car a little better than my neighbor's car. *(Amen)* I know a man who used to live in a thirty-five-thousand-dollar house. And other people started building thirty-five-thousand-dollar houses, so he built a seventy-five-thousand-dollar house. And then somebody else built a seventy-five-thousand-dollar house, and he built a hundred-thousand-dollar house. And I don't know where he's going to end up if he's going to live his life trying to keep up with the Joneses.

There comes a time that the drum major instinct can become destructive. *(Make it plain)* And that's where I want to move now. I want to move to the point of saying that if this instinct is not harnessed, it becomes a very dangerous, pernicious instinct. For instance, if it isn't harnessed, it causes one's personality to become distorted. I guess that's the most damaging aspect of it: what it does to the personality. If it isn't harnessed, you will end up day in and day out trying to deal with your ego problem by boasting. Have you ever heard people that—you know, and I'm sure you've met them—that really become sickening because they just sit up all the time talking about themselves. *(Amen)* And they just boast and boast and boast, and that's the person who has not harnessed the drum major instinct.

And then it does other things to the personality. It causes you to lie about who you know sometimes. *(Amen, Make it plain)* There are some people who are influence peddlers. And in their attempt to deal with the drum major instinct, they have to try to identify with the so-called big-name people. *(Yeah, Make it plain)* And if you're not careful, they will make you think they know somebody that they don't really know. *(Amen)* They know them well, they sip tea with them, and they this-and-that. That happens to people.

And the other thing is that it causes one to engage ultimately in activities that are merely used to get attention. Criminologists tell us that some people are driven to crime because of this drum major instinct. They don't feel that they are getting enough attention through the normal channels of social behavior, and so they turn to anti-social behavior in order to get attention, in order to feel important. *(Yeah)* And so they get that gun, and before they know it they robbed a bank in a quest for recognition, in a quest for importance.

And then the final great tragedy of the distorted personality is the fact that when one fails to harness this instinct, *(Glory to God)* he ends up trying to push others down in order to push himself up. *(Amen)* And whenever you do that, you engage in some of the most vicious activities. You will spread evil, vicious, lying gossip on people, because you are trying to pull them down in order to push yourself up. *(Make it plain)* And the great issue of life is to harness the drum major instinct.

Now the other problem is, when you don't harness the drum major instinct—this uncontrolled aspect of it—is that it leads to snobbish exclusivism. It leads to snobbish exclusivism. *(Make it plain)* And you know, this is the danger of social clubs and fraternities—I'm in a fraternity; I'm in two or three—for sororities and all of these, I'm not talking against them. I'm saying it's the danger. The danger is that they can become forces of classism and exclusivism where somehow you get a degree of satisfaction because you are in something exclusive. And that's fulfilling something, you know—that I'm in this fraternity, and it's the best fraternity in the world, and everybody can't get in this fraternity. So it ends up, you know, a very exclusive kind of thing.

And you know, that can happen with the church; I know churches get in that bind sometimes. *(Amen, Make it plain)* I've been to churches, you know, and they say, "We have so many doctors, and so many school teachers, and so many lawyers, and so many businessmen in our church." And that's fine, because doctors need to go to church, and lawyers, and businessmen, teachers—they ought to be in church. But they say that—even the preacher sometimes will go all through that—they say that as if the other people don't count. *(Amen)*

And the church is the one place where a doctor ought to forget that he's a doctor. The church is the one place where a Ph.D. ought to forget that he's a Ph.D. *(Yes)* The church is the one place that the school teacher ought to forget the degree she has behind her name. The church is the one place where the lawyer ought to forget that he's a lawyer. And any church that violates the "whosoever will, let him come" doctrine is a dead, cold church, *(Yes)* and nothing but a little social club with a thin veneer of religiosity.

When the church is true to its nature, *(Whoo)* it says, "Whosoever will, let him come." *(Yes)* And it does not supposed to satisfy the perverted uses of the drum major instinct. It's the one place where everybody should be the same, standing before a common master and savior. *(Yes, sir)* And a recognition grows out of this—that all men are brothers because they are children *(Yes)* of a common father.

The drum major instinct can lead to exclusivism in one's thinking and can lead one to feel that because he has some training, he's a little better than that person who doesn't have it. Or because he has some economic security, that he's a little better than that person who doesn't have it. And that's the uncontrolled, perverted use of the drum major instinct.

Now the other thing is, that it leads to tragic—and we've seen it happen so often—tragic race prejudice. Many who have written about this problem—Lillian Smith used to say it beautifully in some of her books. And she would say it to the point of getting men and women to see the source of the problem. Do you know that a lot of the race problem grows out of the drum major instinct? A need that some people have to feel superior. A need that some people have to feel that they are first, and to feel that their white skin ordained them to be first. *(Make it plain, today, 'cause I'm against it, so help me God)* And they have said over and over again in ways that we see with our own eyes. In fact, not too long ago, a man down in Mississippi said that God was a charter member of the White Citizens Council. And so God being the charter member means that everybody who's in that has a kind of divinity, a kind of superiority. And think of what has happened in history as a result of this perverted use of the drum major instinct. It has led to the most tragic prejudice, the most tragic expressions of man's inhumanity to man.

The other day I was saying, I always try to do a little converting when I'm in jail. And when we were in jail in Birmingham the other day, the white wardens and all enjoyed coming around the cell to talk about the race problem. And they were showing us where we were so wrong demonstrating. And they were showing us where segregation was so right. And they were showing us where intermarriage was so wrong. So I would get to preaching, and we would get to talking—calmly, because they wanted to talk about it. And then we got down one day to the point—that was the second or third day—to talk about where they lived, and how much they were earning. And when those brothers told me what they were earning, I said, "Now, you know what? You ought to be marching with us. *[laughter]* You're just as poor as Negroes." And I said, "You are put in the position of supporting your oppressor, because through prejudice and blindness, you fail to see that the same forces that oppress Negroes in American society oppress poor white people. *(Yes)* And all you are living on is the satisfaction of your skin being white, and the drum major instinct of thinking that you are somebody big because you are white. And you're so poor you can't send your children to school. You ought to be out here marching with every one of us every time we have a march."

Now that's a fact. That the poor white has been put into this position, where through blindness and prejudice, *(Make it plain)* he is forced to support his oppressors. And the only thing he has going for him is the false feeling that he's superior because his skin is white—and can't hardly eat and make his ends meet week in and week out. *(Amen)*

And not only does this thing go into the racial struggle, it goes into the struggle between nations. And I would submit to you this morning that what is wrong in the world today is that the nations of the world are engaged in a bitter, colossal contest for supremacy. And if something doesn't happen to stop this trend, I'm sorely afraid that we won't be here to talk about Jesus Christ and about God and about brotherhood too many more years. *(Yeah)* If somebody doesn't bring an end to this suicidal thrust that we see in the world today, none of us are going to be around, because somebody's going to make the mistake through our senseless blunderings of dropping a nuclear bomb somewhere. And then another one is going to drop. And don't let anybody fool you, this can happen within a matter of seconds. *(Amen)* They have twenty-megaton bombs in Russia right now that can destroy a city as big as New York in three seconds, with everybody wiped away, and every building. And we can do the same thing to Russia and China.

But this is why we are drifting. And we are drifting there because nations are caught up with the drum major instinct. "I must be first." "I must be supreme." "Our nation must rule the world." *(Preach it)* And I am sad to say that the nation in which we live is the supreme culprit. And I'm going to continue to say it to America, because I love this country too much to see the drift that it has taken.

God didn't call America to do what she's doing in the world now. *(Preach it, preach it)* God didn't call America to engage in a senseless, unjust war as the war in Vietnam. And we are criminals in that war. We've committed more war crimes almost than any nation in the world, and I'm going to continue to say it. And we won't stop it because of our pride and our arrogance as a nation.

But God has a way of even putting nations in their place. *(Amen)* The God that I worship has a way of saying, "Don't play with me." *(Yes)* He has a way of saying, as the God of the Old Testament used to say to the Hebrews, "Don't play with me, Israel. Don't play with me, Babylon. *(Yes)* Be still and know that I'm God. And if you don't stop your reckless course, I'll rise up and break the backbone of your power." *(Yes)* And that can happen to America. (Yes) Every now and then I go back and read Gibbons' Decline and Fall of the Roman Empire. And when I come and look at America, I say to myself, the parallels are frightening. And we have perverted the drum major instinct.

But let me rush on to my conclusion, because I want you to see what Jesus was really saying. What was the answer that Jesus gave these men? It's very interesting. One would have thought that Jesus would have condemned them. One would have thought that Jesus would have said, "You are out of your place. You are selfish. Why would you raise such a question?"

But that isn't what Jesus did; he did something altogether different. He said in substance, "Oh, I see, you want to be first. You want to be great. You want to be important. You want to be significant. Well, you ought to be. If you're going to be my disciple, you must be." But he reordered priorities. And he said, "Yes, don't give up this instinct. It's a good instinct if you use it right. (Yes) It's a good instinct if you don't distort it and pervert it. Don't give it up. Keep feeling the need for being important. Keep feeling the need for being first. But I want you to be first in love. *(Amen)* I want you to be first in moral excellence. I want you to be first in generosity. That is what I want you to do."

And he transformed the situation by giving a new definition of greatness. And you know how he said it? He said, "Now brethren, I can't give you greatness. And really, I can't make you first." This is what Jesus said to James and John. "You must earn it. True greatness comes not by favoritism, but by fitness. And the right hand and the left are not mine to give, they belong to those who are prepared." *(Amen)*

And so Jesus gave us a new norm of greatness. If you want to be important—wonderful. If you want to be recognized—wonderful. If you want to be great—wonderful. But recognize that he who is greatest among you shall be your servant. *(Amen)* That's a new definition of greatness.

And this morning, the thing that I like about it: by giving that definition of greatness, it means that everybody can be great, *(Everybody)* because everybody can serve. *(Amen)* You don't have to have a college degree to serve. *(All right)* You don't have to make your subject and your verb agree to serve. You don't have to know about Plato and Aristotle to serve. You don't have to know Einstein's theory of relativity to serve. You don't have to know the second theory of thermodynamics in physics to serve. *(Amen)* You only need a heart full of grace, (Yes, sir, Amen) a soul generated by love. *(Yes)* And you can be that servant.

I know a man—and I just want to talk about him a minute, and maybe you will discover who I'm talking about as I go down the way *(Yeah)* because he was a great one. And he just went about serving. He was born in an obscure village, *(Yes, sir)* the child of a poor peasant woman. And then he grew up in still another obscure village, where he worked as a carpenter until he was thirty years old. *(Amen)* Then for three years, he just got on his feet, and he was an itinerant preacher. And he went about doing some things. He didn't have much. He never wrote a book. He never held an office. He never had a family. *(Yes)* He never owned a house. He never went to college. He never visited a big city. He never went two hundred miles from where he was born. He did none of the usual things that the world would associate with greatness. He had no credentials but himself.

He was only thirty-three when the tide of public opinion turned against him. They called him a rabble-rouser. They called him a troublemaker. They said he was an agitator. *(Glory to God)* He practiced civil disobedience; he broke injunctions. And so he was turned over to his enemies and went through the mockery of a trial. And the irony of it all is that his friends turned him over to them. *(Amen)* One of his closest friends denied him. Another of his friends turned him over to his enemies. And while he was dying, the people who killed him gambled for his clothing, the only possession that he had in the world. *(Lord help him)* When he was dead he was buried in a borrowed tomb, through the pity of a friend.

Nineteen centuries have come and gone and today he stands as the most influential figure that ever entered human history. All of the armies that ever marched, all the navies that ever sailed, all the parliaments that ever sat, and all the kings that ever reigned put together *(Yes)* have not affected the life of man on this earth *(Amen)* as much as that one solitary life. His name may be a familiar one. *(Jesus)* But today I can hear them talking about him. Every now and then somebody says, "He's King of Kings." *(Yes)* And again I can hear somebody saying, "He's Lord of Lords." Somewhere else I can hear somebody saying, "In Christ there is no East nor West." *(Yes)* And then they go on and talk about, "In Him there's no North and South, but one great Fellowship of Love throughout the whole wide world." He didn't have any-thing. *(Amen)* He just went around serving and doing good.

This morning, you can be on his right hand and his left hand if you serve. *(Amen)* It's the only way in.

Every now and then I guess we all think realistically *(Yes, sir)* about that day when we will be victimized with what is life's final common denomina-tor—that something that we call death. We all think about it. And every now and then I think about my own death and I think about my own funeral. And I don't think of it in a morbid sense. And every now and then I ask myself, "What is it that I would want said?" And I leave the word to you this morning.

If any of you are around when I have to meet my day, I don't want a long funeral. And if you get somebody to deliver the eulogy, tell them not to talk too long. *(Yes)* And every now and then I wonder what I want them to say. Tell them not to mention that I have a Nobel Peace Prize—that isn't impor-tant. Tell them not to mention that I have three or four hundred other awards—that's not important. Tell them not to mention where I went to school. *(Yes)*

I'd like somebody to mention that day that Martin Luther King, Jr., tried to give his life serving others. *(Yes)*

I'd like for somebody to say that day that Martin Luther King, Jr., tried to love somebody.

I want you to say that day that I tried to be right on the war question. *(Amen)*

I want you to be able to say that day that I did try to feed the hungry. *(Yes)*

And I want you to be able to say that day that I did try in my life to clothe those who were naked. *(Yes)*

I want you to say on that day that I did try in my life to visit those who were in prison. *(Lord)*

I want you to say that I tried to love and serve humanity. *(Yes)*

Yes, if you want to say that I was a drum major, say that I was a drum major for justice. *(Amen)* Say that I was a drum major for peace. *(Yes)* I was a drum major for righteousness. And all of the other shallow things will not matter. *(Yes)* I won't have any money to leave behind. I won't have the fine and luxurious things of life to leave behind. But I just want to leave a com-mitted life behind. *(Amen)* And that's all I want to say.

If I can help somebody as I pass along,
If I can cheer somebody with a word or song,
If I can show somebody he's traveling wrong,
Then my living will not be in vain.
If I can do my duty as a Christian ought,
If I can bring salvation to a world once wrought,

If I can spread the message as the master taught,
Then my living will not be in vain.

Yes, Jesus, I want to be on your right or your left side, *(Yes)* not for any selfish reason. I want to be on your right or your left side, not in terms of some political kingdom or ambition. But I just want to be there in love and in justice and in truth and in commitment to others, so that we can make of this old world a new world.

Delivered at Ebenezer Baptist Church, Atlanta, Georgia, on 4 February 1968.

E. E. CUMMINGS
1894–1962

The two things that everyone seems to know about the poet Edward Estlin Cummings (e.e. cummings) is that he hated capital letters and wasn't all that fond of punctuation. Such facts, however, do little to express the perplexing variety of his poems. Cummings's verses can be bitingly satirical one moment, incurably sentimental the next; they can be brutally sexually explicit or transcendently lyrical. His poems are often syntactically radical yet, just as often, conservative in their form. A painter as well as a writer, Cummings experimented freely with typographical arrangement, scattering words about the page, forcing his readers to read upside down, backwards, and sideways. The same poet, however, was a master of the strict discipline of the sonnet. Some critics deem Cummings's poems immature; some applaud them as poignantly universal. Is it any wonder that critics have a hard time figuring out how to make sense of Cummings's aesthetic?

Cummings grew up in Cambridge, Massachusetts, the son of a reform-minded Harvard sociology professor turned Unitarian minister. A talented student, Cummings became a Harvard undergraduate in 1911 and received a B.A. in English, with a specialization in Greek, in 1915. Intrigued by Romantic and pre-Raphaelite poetry, as well as languages ancient and modern, Cummings stayed an additional year at Harvard and received an M.A. in English in 1916. During his college years, he published poems in the Harvard Advocate *and the* Harvard Monthly, *befriended future novelist John Dos Passos (1896–1970), and future* Dial *magazine entrepreneurs, Scofield Thayer and James Sibley Watson.*

After college, Cummings moved to New York to make a career as a writer, but ended up volunteering for service in World War I as an ambulance driver with an American Red Cross unit stationed in France. In 1917, he was assigned duty in Germaine, a small town in East Picardy that, at the time, was relatively quiet. Cummings and his friend Slater Brown passed long days of inactivity hosing down the amubulances, annoying their superiors, and getting to know the French soldiers who told them horror stories about conditions at the front. Both Brown and Cummings were naive enough to repeat the complaints of the rank and file in their letters home. Soon, both were suspected of being spies for the Germans. They were arrested and shipped to a French concentration camp where Cummings stayed until the end of 1917. His internment resulted in his first book, The Enormous Room, *a fictionalized memoir of his days at the camp, which appeared from Boni and Liveright in 1922.*

At the end of World War I, Cummings once again landed in New York, where he began to publish his poems in little magazines and exhibit his paintings. He also became seriously involved with his good friend Scofield Thayer's wife, Elaine. Thayer urbanely accepted the relationship and, in 1919, Elaine gave birth to Cummings's only child, Nancy (Cummings and Elaine would both marry and divorce in 1923. Nancy was raised to believe that Thayer, not Cummings, was her father). By the end of 1921, Cummings had moved to Paris and written a great many verses, but could not find a publisher willing to take a chance on his rich manuscript of 152 poems, Tulips and Chimneys. *The sexually explicit and blatantly satirical material terrified printers, but a shortened, sanitized selection finally appeared from Thomas Seltzer in 1923. Cummings scattered many of the omitted poems (84 in all) throughout his next three volumes:* & *(1925),* XLI Poems *(1925), and* is 5 *(1926). At the end of 1925, Cummings was granted the* Dial *award "for distinguished service to American letters," an prize also won by Marianne Moore, William Carlos Williams, and T. S. Eliot.*

Drawn to the socialist cause and intrigued by the Soviet experiment that began with the Russian revolution of 1917, Cummings traveled to Russia in 1930 in order to see the results of proletarian rule. Witnessing Communism firsthand, however, convinced Cummings that leftist governments could be as monstrous as those on the right and reconfirmed his sense that the best governments were those that governed least. The individual remained the basis of his politics. As he wrote shortly before his book ViVa *appeared in 1931: "there are two types of human beings, children & prisoners. Prisoners are inhabited by formulae. Children inhabit forms. A formula is something to get out of oneself, to rid oneself of—an arbitrary emphasis deliberately neglecting the invisible and significant entirely. A form is something to wander in . . . a new largeness, dimensionally differing from the socalled real world." Cummings recorded his disparaging observations of the Soviet state in his 1933 narrative* Eimi *(Greek for "I am"). The book was roundly attacked by left-leaning American critics and gave ammunition to those who deemed Cummings's poems less than politically serious. Cummings dedicated his next book of poems,* No Thanks *(1935), to the fourteen publishers who rejected the volume before the tiny Golden Eagle Press agreed to print it.*

Cummings did not secure a commercial publisher until Harcourt Brace printed his Collected Poems *in 1938. The book proved a breakthrough for Cummings in that it finally allowed readers access to poems scattered about in a number of hard-to-find volumes.* Collected Poems *was more widely and charitably reviewed than any of Cummings's previous books and the mature Cummings, now happily ensconced in New York with his long-time partner,*

Marion Morehouse, finally began to enjoy the fruits of his labors. His sense of personal security, however, was tempered by his disgust and horror at the coming of World War II. In 1944, he published 1 X1, a book that contains some of his most sober and haunting poems about the human condition. Xaipe (Greek for "rejoice"), followed in 1950. Throughout the 1950s, Cummings marketed himself as a literary icon. He hit the lecture circuit and filled the Charles Eliot Norton Chair at Harvard for the year 1952–53, delivering a series of six "nonlectures" on topics poetic and personal. Poems 1923–1954 was published in 1954 and in 1958, the same year his final book of new poems, 95 poems, appeared, Cummings was awarded the prestigious Yale Bolligen Prize for poetry.

While the typographical surface of many of Cummings's poems can seem off-putting to beginning readers, his verses do tend to return to a few central themes. Throughout his career, Cummings championed the natural over the artificial, the instinctual over the rational. He maintained a youthful distrust of governments, rules, systems, and collective actions. Like the British Romantic poets who he adored (Keats in particular), Cummings believed that human feeling could put the poet in touch with a natural order or things beyond the reach of human thinking. His verses applaud the spontaneous earth, the clatter of April showers, the flush of first feeling, the incalculable mysteries of the eternal night. His poems despise thoughtless conventions, self-important proprieties, and stale rhetorics. Cummings's poems never fail to remind his readers that they need to be on guard against the words that make up culture, the pronouncements that they somehow take for granted as being "true" even when their guts tell them otherwise.

All of the versions of Cummings's poems quoted here come from George James Firmage's two-volume corrected and expanded edition of Cummings's Complete Poems (1981). Firmage's edition is an eclectic one; the poems here have been "corrected" according to Firmage's scholarly sense of Cummings's literary intentions, and the texts may differ from other published sources.

For Further Reading

Primary Works

The Enormous Room (New York: Boni & Liveright, 1922; London: Cape, 1928); Tulips and Chimneys (New York: Seltzer, 1923; enlarged edition, Mount Vernon, N.Y.: Golden Eagle Press, 1937); & (New York: Privately printed, 1925); XLI Poems (New York: Dial Press, 1925); Is 5 (New York: Boni & Liveright, 1926); Him (New York: Boni & Liveright, 1927), [No Title] (New York: Covici-Friede, 1930); CIOPW (New York: Covici-Friede, 1931); ViVa (New York: Liveright, 1931); Eimi (New York: Covici-Friede, 1933); No Thanks (Mount Vernon, N.Y.: Golden Eagle Press, 1935); Tom (New York: Arrow Editions, 1935); Collected

Poems (New York: Harcourt, Brace, 1938); *50 Poems* (New York: Duell, Sloan & Pearce, 1940); *1 X 1* (New York: Holt, 1944; London: Horizon Press, 1947); *Santa Claus—A Morality* (New York: Holt, 1946); *XAIPE: Seventy-One Poems* (New York: Oxford University Press, 1950); *i: six nonlectures* (Cambridge: Harvard University Press, 1953); *Poems 1923–1954* (New York: Harcourt, Brace, 1954); *E. E. Cummings: A Miscellany,* edited by George Firmage (New York: Argophile Press, 1958; enlarged edition, New York: October House, 1965; London: Owen, 1966); *95 Poems* (New York: Harcourt, Brace, 1958); *100 Selected Poems* (New York: Grove Press, 1959); *Selected Poems, 1923–1958* (London: Faber & Faber, 1960); *Adventures in Value* (New York: Harcourt, Brace & World, 1962); *73 Poems* (New York: Harcourt, Brace & World, 1963; London: Faber & Faber, 1964); *Fairy Tales* (New York: Harcourt, Brace & World, 1965); *Complete Poems 1923–1962,* edited by George Firmage (two volumes, London: MacGibbon & Kee, 1968; 1 volume, New York: Harcourt Brace Jovanovich, 1972); *Poems 1905–1962,* edited by Firmage (London: Marchim Press, 1973); *Tulips & Chimneys: The Original 1922 Manuscript with the 35 Additional Poems from &,* edited by Firmage (New York: Liveright, 1976).

Secondary Works

George J. Firmage, *E. E. Cummings: A Biblioraphy* (Middletown, Conn.: Wesleyan University Press, 1960); Guy L. Rotella, *E. E. Cummings: A Reference Guide* (Boston: G. K. Hall, 1979); Milton A. Cohen, *Poet and Painter: The Aesthetics of E. E. Cummings's Early Work* (Detroit: Wayne State University Press, 1987); Norman Friedman, *E. E. Cummings The Art of His Poetry* (Baltimore: Johns Hopkins University Press, 1960); Norman Friedman, *(Re)valuing Cummings: Further Essays on the Poet, 1962–1993* (Gainesville: University Press of Florida, 1996); Richard S. Kennedy, *Dreams in the Mirror: A Biography of E. E. Cummings* (New York: Liveright, 1980); Richard S. Kennedy, *E. E. Cummings Revisited* (New York: Twayne, 1994); Rushworth M. Kidder, *E. E. Cummings: An Introduction to the Poetry* (New York: Columbia University Press, 1979); Robert E. Wegner, *The Poetry and Prose of E. E. Cummings* (New York: Harcourt, Brace, 1965).

[the Cambridge ladies who live in furnished souls]*

E. E. CUMMINGS

the Cambridge ladies who live in furnished souls
are unbeautiful and have comfortable minds
(also,with the church's protestant blessings
daughters,unscented shapeless spirited)
they believe in Christ and Longfellow,both dead,   5
are invariably interested in so many things—
at the present writing one still finds
delighted fingers knitting for the is it Poles?
perhaps. While permanent faces coyly bandy
scandal of Mrs. N and Professor D   10
.... the Cambridge ladies do not care,above
Cambridge if sometimes in its box of
sky lavender and cornerless,the
moon rattles like a fragment of angry candy

[1922]

EUDORA WELTY
[1909–2001]

"I am a writer who came of a sheltered life," she once wrote. "A sheltered life can be a daring life as well. For all serious daring starts from within." Born in Jackson, Mississippi, Eudora Welty moved only once, from North Congress Street to Pinehurst Street in that sheltered Southern city, but the body of work she created is indeed daring—political, psychological, sprawling but always, like her life, circling back to home. By her death just after the turn of the new century, the gracious, white-haired Welty was a familiar figure in a nation's cultural life, one of America's most beloved writers. But the enduring and original work she left behind—powerful novels and a dazzling wealth of novellas and short stories, set mostly in her native South but not confined by it, and an array of nonfiction that includes an incisive exploration of the writer's craft—can be sharp-edged, even brutal, and always true to life.

Her father, Christian, was the son of Ohio farmers who brought his West Virginia-born wife, Chestina, to Mississippi before Eudora's birth. He loved mechanical objects and knowing how things worked; Eudora's mother loved books. From her father's love came the myriad instruments designed to instruct and fascinate that filled their house during Eudora's youth—clocks, chronometers, cameras, a magnifying glass, a kaleidoscope, and a gyroscope. By their dining room table, to provide support for endless mealtime discussions, sat a dictionary, a set of encyclopedias, and that treasure of all early twentieth century childhoods, the Book of Knowledge. *From her mother's love came a complete set of the works of Charles Dickens (which, in a familiar family story, Chestina Welty had returned to a burning house to rescue), and a sense of storytelling that would always be central to Eudora's writing. But her father's love of knowledge—fact rather than fiction—and his need to explore the workings of everything he encountered, were as much a part of Eudora's narrative voice as the language of her mother's friends, and Chessie's ability to lose herself entirely in novels.*

Throughout Eudora's childhood, the Weltys traveled almost every summer, sometimes by car and sometimes by train, to visit family on both sides. They stayed with the dour Swiss-Yankee Weltys in Ohio and with the rambunctious

Andrews clan of West Virginia, whose household was always filled with music and the laughter of Eudora's five uncles, Chessie's younger brothers. These long, long journeys opened Eudora's eyes to her own place in the world. "On the train," Eudora tells us in her memoir, One Writer's Beginnings (1984), "I saw that world passing my window. . . . Through travel I first became aware of the outside world; it was through travel that I found my own introspective way into becoming a part of it."

Eudora left home in the fall of 1925 for the first and only time. She spent two years at the Mississippi State College for Women in Columbus, two hundred miles north of Jackson, finished her college education at the University of Wisconsin (selected by her father for its reputation as a fine liberal arts institution) and then spent a year at Columbia University's Graduate School of Business. She studied advertising, acquiring the skills that her father, dubious about her desire to write for a living, was convinced she would need. Back in Jackson in 1931, Eudora settled into the new house on Pinehurst Street that her father had designed and built in her absence. That same year her father died. Although she traveled widely and enthusiastically for many years thereafter, it was in that faux Tudor house of bricks and stucco, once out a ways from town and surrounded by pine forest, now absorbed into Jackson proper, that Welty lived and wrote and graciously welcomed visitors for all the rest of her life.

Without a father to provide an income, and with the Great Depression in full swing, Eudora took a part-time job with the local radio station, then soon moved into a full-time position as a junior publicity agent for the Mississippi office of the Works Progress Administration, one of the federal agencies created under Franklin Roosevelt to put people back to work. The WPA sent Welty all over Mississippi with a camera and a pen and pad; her task was to capture in words and pictures the plight of the people of Mississippi. Cameras had always been an important component of the Welty household, but now Eudora understood the real message of photography: "Life doesn't hold still." Photography, she writes, taught her the need to "capture transcience, by being ready to click the shutter at the crucial moment . . . to be prepared to recognize this moment when I saw it."

But finally it was in words, not pictures, that Welty captured those transient moments. What she calls her "first good story" sprang from a sentence repeated to her by a neighbor— "He's gone to borry some fire"—and the "snapshot" of a cabin set into the clay hills glimpsed once from the train. The resulting story, "Death of a Traveling Salesman," was published in 1936 in a small literary magazine, and her first collection of stories, A Curtain of Green, in 1941. Almost immediately, Welty began gathering praise from the literary establishment, and her stories began to appear in magazines such as The Atlantic Monthly. "A Worn Path" won an O. Henry Short Story Prize in 1942, as did the title story of her next collection, "The Wide Net," in 1943.

Welty's first novel, The Robber Bridegroom *(1942), is a fairy tale set on the Natchez Trace in a time (if not a place) very distant from her own. In it, Welty abandons the remarkable psychological insight that characterizes her first collection of stories and instead creates all of the magic and mystery readers might expect from the Brothers Grimm—whose works Eudora had devoured, along with much of the rest of the world of literature, as a child under her mother's eye. The books that followed almost always take place in the South, often on or near the Natchez Trace, and they share a remarkable accuracy of voice, place, and character. They celebrate life in very particular ways. But their narrative range is breathtaking—from a sprawling family saga to a high comic monologue to a volume of interlaced stories—and they brought Welty an ever-growing list of prizes including, a Pulitzer for* The Optimist's Daughter *in 1973.*

Welty is most often described as a Southern regional writer, but her voice is in fact universal—and bust-your-britches funny. One of her best known stories, "Why I Live at the P.O." (1941), is one long comic rant in which the narrator, Sister, explains why she has moved into the local post office, where she holds the job of postmistress, to protest the return of her sister, Stella Rondo, who has earlier run off with Sister's boyfriend. Similarly, in The Ponder Heart *(1954), Edna Earle Ponder pours out the story of her life and her family (before the word "dysfunctional" came into vogue) to a traveling salesman visiting the hotel she runs. When she was asked to speak at colleges or conferences, as she often was in her later years, Welty often read from her works, and often (being wise to the ways of audiences) selected something funny. There is no happier picture in the tale of twentieth century American literature than Eudora Welty, soft white hair in beauty-parlor waves, long-sleeved red velvet gown rising to the primmest of white collars, reading aloud from "Why I Live at the P.O." while audiences roar.*

Welty's accuracy of voice inspired a generation of Southern writers. In a collection of tributes to Welty on her ninetieth birthday, a consistent theme prevailed: I became a writer because I recognized my voice in Eudora Welty's stories. Because she told my stories. Because I heard my parents and my neighbors and my life and my history in the tales of Sister and Edna Earle, of the MacLains and the Raineys in The Golden Apples *(1949) and the Fiarchilds in* Delta Wedding *(1947), of weary old Phoenix Jackson in "A Worn Path," and Granny Vaughan's extended family in* Losing Battles *(1970). And the voices are authentic and complex and varied—a black jazz musician in "Powerhouse" or women whose boundaries are too small in "Petrified Man," both written at the beginning of Welty's career—and perhaps most daringly of all, the voice of the murderer of Medgar Evers in "Where This Voice Is Coming From," written the night after Evers's death in 1963.*

Eudora Welty continued to open the door of her home on Pinehurst Street to strangers and fans until shortly before her death in 2001, and she was generous in talking about her work, but she was notoriously cranky about biography. She believed—and supported her belief aggressively—that the work stands alone. She actively blocked at least one intended biography and consistently refused to interpret the specifics of her work. When an eager young graduate student questioned her about "your choice of marble cake as a symbol of the fusion between dream and reality, between the temporal and the eternal," she famously replied, "Well, it's a lovely cake, and it's a recipe that has been in my family for years."

If all this suggests that Welty was in fact the sweet and gentle lady she often appeared to be—well, indeed she was. She disliked very few people (Carson McCullers, another Southern writer, was one of them). Welty may have suffered initially by reaching the peak of her fame at about the same time yet another Southern woman, Flannery O'Connor, was reaching hers. O'Connor wrote huge, raging stories, filled with questions of grace. Welty's stories follow a more familiar path—characters readers can easily recognize from their own lives, families just as absurd as their own. It is easy to categorize Welty as a remarkable satirist of regional manners and mores, a good observer of human character and foibles—and maybe not much more. But that would be foolish. Reading the life of weary Phoenix Jackson, walking the Natchez Trace in dead winter to get medicine for a sick grandson; or listening to the shocking and repugnant imagined monologue of Medgar Evers's killer suggests a range of human insight that transcends region or satire. Welty's masterworks, particularly her novel Losing Battles, *easily stand with the best of American writing in the twentieth century.*

Once, when Eudora was very old indeed, the writer Willie Morris and his wife took her out driving, with some concern about the heat and her age. Far from the shelter of town, at the crest of a hill, Morris decided to try an even "narrower and darker byway that intersected with the one on which we were traveling. 'Eudora, I'm going to make a left and drive down Paradise Road,' I said.

"'We'd be fools if we didn't,' she replied."

For Further Reading

Primary Works

A Curtain of Green and Other Stories (1941); *The Robber Bridegroom* (1942); *The Wide Net, and Other Stories* (1943); *Delta Wedding* (1946); *The Golden Apples* (1949); *Short Stories* (1950); *The Ponder Heart* (1954); *Selected Stories of Eudora Welty* (1954); *The Bride of Innisfallen, and Other Stories* (1955); *Place in Fiction* (1957); *Three Papers on Fiction* (1962); *The Shoe Bird* (1964); *A Sweet Devouring* (1969); *Losing Battles* (1970); *One Time, One Place: Mississippi in the Depression: A Snapshot Album* (1971); *The Optimist's Daughter* (1972); *A 3*

Pageant of Birds (1974); *Fairy Tales of the Natchez Trace* (1975); *The Eye of the Story: Selected Essays and Reviews* (1978); *Ida M'Toy* (1979); *Women!! Make Turban in Own Home!* (1979); *Acrobats in the Park* (1980); *Bye-bye Brevoort* (1980); *Moon Lake and Other Stories* (1980); *White Fruitcake* (1980); *The Collected Stories of Eudora Welty* (1980); *Miracles of Perception: The Art of Willa Cather* (1980); *Twenty Photographs* (1980); *Retreat* (1981); *Four Photographs by Eudora Welty* (1984); *One Writer's Beginnings* (1984); *The Little Store* (1985); *In Black and White: Photographs of the 30s and 40s* (1985); *A Writer's Eye: Collected Book Reviews* (1994); *Eudora Welty: Complete Novels* (1998); *Eudora Welty: Stories, Essays and Memoir* (1998).

Secondary Works

John F. Desmond, ed., *A Still Moment: Essays on the Art of Eudora Welty* (1979); Peggy Whitman Prenshaw, *Conversations with Eudora Welty* (1984); Harold Bloom, ed., *Modern Critical Views: Eudora Welty* (1986); Laurie Champion, ed., *The Critical Response to Eudora Welty's Fiction* (1994); Pearl Amelia McHaney, *Eudora Welty: Writers' Reflections Upon First Reading Welty* (1999).

Why I Live at the P.O.

EUDORA WELTY

I was getting along fine with Mama, Papa-Daddy and Uncle Rondo until my Sister Stella-Rondo just separated from her husband and came back home again. Mr. Whitaker! Of course I went with Mr. Whitaker first, when he first appeared here in China Grove, taking "Pose Yourself" photos, and Stella-Rondo broke us up. Told him I was one-sided. Bigger on one side than the other, which is a deliberate, calculated falsehood: I'm the same. Stella-Rondo is exactly twelve months to the day younger than I am and for that reason she's spoiled.

She's always had anything in the world she wanted and then she'd throw it away. Papa-Daddy gave her this gorgeous Add-a-Pearl necklace when she was eight years old and she threw it away playing baseball when she was nine, with only two pearls.

So as soon as she got married and moved away from home the first thing she did was separate! From Mr. Whitaker! This photographer with the popeyes she said she trusted. Came home from one of those towns up in Illinois and to our complete surprise brought this child of two.

Mama said she like to made her drop dead for a second. "Here you had this marvelous blonde child and never so much as wrote your mother a word about it," says Mama. "I'm thoroughly ashamed of you." But of course she wasn't.

Stella-Rondo just calmly takes off this *hat*, I wish you could see it. She says, "Why, Mama, Shirky-T.'s adopted. I can prove it."

"How?" says Mama, but all I says was, "H'm!" There I was over the hot stove, trying to stretch two chickens over five people and a completely unexpected child into the bargain, without one moment's notice.

"What do you mean—'H'm!'?" says Stella-Rondo, and Mama says, "I heard that, Sister."

I said that oh, I didn't mean a dung, only that whoever Shirley-T. was, she was the spit-image of Papa-Daddy if he'd cut off his beard, which of course he'd never do in the world. Papa-Daddy's Mama's papa and sulks.

Reprinted from A *Curtain of Green and Other Stories* (1979), Harcourt, Inc.

Stella-Rondo got furious! She said, "Sister, I don't need to tell you you got a lot of time and always did have and I'll thank you to make no future reference to my adopted child whatsoever."

"Very well," I said. "Very well, very well. Of course I noticed at once she looks like Mr. Whitaker's side too. That frown. She looks like a cross between Mr. Whitaker and Papa-Daddy."

"Well, all I can say is she isn't,"

"She looks exactly like Shirley Temple to me," says Mama, but Shirley-T. just ran away from her.

So the first thing Stella-Rondo did at the table was turn Papa-Daddy against me.

"Papa-Daddy," she says. He was trying to cut up his meat. "Papa-Daddy!" I was taken completely by surprise. Papa-Daddy is about a million years old and's got this long-long beard, "Papa-Daddy, Sister says she fails to understand why you don't cut off your beard."

So Papa-Daddy l-a-y-s down his knife and fork! He's real rich. Mama says he is, he says he isn't. So he says, "Have I heard correctly? You don't understand why I don't cut off my beard?"

"Why," I says, "Papa-Daddy, of course I understand, I did not say any such of a thing, the idea!"

He says, "Hussy!"

I says, "Papa-Daddy, you know I wouldn't any more want you to cut off your beard than the man in the moon, it was the farthest thing from my mind! Stella-Rondo sat there and made that up while she was eating breast of chicken."

But he says, "So the postmistress fails to understand why I don't cut off my beard. Which job I got you through my influence with the government. 'Bird's nest'—is that what you call it?"

Not that it isn't the next to smallest P.O. in the entire state of Mississippi.

I says, "Oh, Papa-Daddy," I says, "I didn't say any such of a thing, I never dreamed it was a bird's nest, I have always been grateful though this is the next to smallest P.O. in the state of Mississippi, and I do not enjoy being referred to as a hussy by my own grandfather."

But Stella-Rondo says, "Yes, you did say it too. Anybody in the world could of heard you, that had ears."

"Stop right there." says Mama, looking at me.

So I pulled my napkin straight back through the napkin ring and left the table.

As soon as I was out of the room Mama says, "Call her back, or she'll starve to death," but Papa-Daddy says, "This is the beard I started growing on the Coast when I was fifteen years old." He would of gone on till nightfall if Shirley-T. hadn't lost the Milky Way she ate in Cairo.

So Papa-Daddy says, "I am going out and lie in the hammock, and you can all sit here and remember my words: I'll never cut off my beard as long as I live, even one inch, and I don't appreciate it in you at all." Passed right by me in the hall and went straight out and got in the hammock.

It would be a holiday. It wasn't five minutes before Uncle Rondo suddenly appeared in the hall in one of Stelia-Rondo's flesh-colored kimonos, all cut on the bias, like something Mr. Whitaker probably thought was gorgeous.

"Uncle Rondo!" I says. "I didn't know who that was! Where are you going?"

"Sister," he says, "get out of my way, I'm poisoned."

"If you're poisoned stay away from Papa-Daddy," I says. "Keep out of the hammock. Papa-Daddy will certainly beat you on the head if you come within forty miles of him. He thinks I deliberately said he ought to cut off his beard after he got me the P.O., and I've told him and told him and told him, and he acts like he just don't hear me. Papa-Daddy must of gone stone deaf."

"He picked a fine day to do it then," says Uncle Rondo, and before you could say "Jack Robinson" flew out in the yard.

What he'd really done, he'd drunk another bottle of that prescription. He does it every single Fourth of July as sure as shooting, and it's horribly expensive. Then he falls over in the hammock and snores. So he insisted on zigzagging right on out to the hammock, looking like a half-wit.

Papa-Daddy woke up with this horrible yell and right there without moving an inch he tried to turn Uncle Rondo against me. I heard every word he said. Oh, he told Uncle Rondo I didn't learn to read till I was eight years old and he didn't see how in the world I ever got the mail put up at the P.O., much less read it all, and he said if Uncle Rondo could only fathom the lengths he had gone to get me that job! And he said on the other hand he thought Stella-Rondo had a brilliant mind and deserved credit for getting out of town. All the time he was just lying there swinging as pretty as you please and looping out his beard, and poor Uncle Rondo was *pleading* with him to slow down the hammock, it was making him as dizzy as a witch to watch it. But that's what Papa-Daddy likes about a hammock. So Uncle Rondo was too dizzy to get turned against me for the time being. He's Mama's only brother and is a good case of a one-track mind. Ask anybody. A certified pharmacist.

Just then I heard Stella-Rondo raising the upstairs window. While she was married she got this peculiar idea that it's cooler with the windows shut and locked. So she has to raise the window before she can make a soul hear her outdoors.

So she raises the window and says, "*Oh!*" You would have thought she was mortally wounded.

Uncle Rondo and Papa-Daddy didn't even look up, but kept right on with what they were doing. I had to laugh.

I flew up the stairs and threw the door open! I says, "What in the wide world's the matter, Stella-Rondo? You mortally wounded?"

"No," she says, "I am not mortally wounded but I wish you would do me the favor of looking out that window there and telling me what you see."

So I shade my eyes and look out the window.

"I see the front yard," I says.

"Don't you see any human beings?" she says.

"I see Uncle Rondo trying to run Papa-Daddy out of the hammock," I says. "Nothing more. Naturally, it's so suffocating-hot in the house, with all the windows shut and locked, everybody who cares to stay in their right mind will have to go out and get in the hammock before the Fourth of July is over."

"Don't you notice anything different about Uncle Rondo?" asks Stella-Rondo.

"Why, no, except he's got on some terrible-looking flesh-colored contraption I wouldn't be found dead in, is all I can see," I says.

"Never mind, you won't be found dead in it, because it happens to be part of my trousseau, and Mr. Whitaker took several dozen photographs of me in it," says Stella-Rondo. "What on earth could Uncle Rondo *mean* by wearing part of my trousseau out in the broad open daylight without saying so much as 'Kiss my foot,' *knowing* I only got home this morning after my separation and hung my negligee up on the bathroom door, just as nervous as I could be?"

"I'm sure I don't know, and what do you expect me to do about it?" I says. "Jump out the window?"

"No, I expect nothing of the kind. I simply declare that Uncle Rondo looks like a fool in it, that's all," she says. "It makes me sick to my stomach."

"Well, he looks as good as he can," I says. "As good as anybody in reason could." I stood up for Uncle Rondo, please remember. And I said to Stella-Rondo, "I think I would do well not to criticize so freely if I were you and came home with a two-year-old child I had never said a word about, and no explanation whatever about my separation."

"I asked you the instant I entered this house not to refer one more time to my adopted child, and you gave me your word of honor you would not," was all Stella-Rondo would say, and started pulling out every one of her eyebrows with some cheap Kress tweezers:

So I merely slammed the door behind me and went down and made some green-tomato pickle. Somebody had to do it. Of course Mama had turned both the Negroes loose; she always said no earthly power could hold one anyway on the Fourth of July, so she wouldn't even try. It turned out that Jaypan fell in the lake and came within a very narrow limit of drowning.

So Mama trots in. Lifts up the lid and says, "H'm! Not very good for your Uncle Rondo in his precarious condition, I must say. Or poor little adopted Shirley-T. Shame on you!"

That made me tired. I says, "Well, Stella-Rondo had better thank her lucky stars it was her instead of me came trotting in with that very peculiar-looking child. Now if it had been me that trotted in from Illinois and brought a peculiar-looking child of two, I shudder to think of the reception I'd of got, much less controlled the diet of an entire family."

"But you must remember, Sister that you were never married to Mr. Whitaker in the first place and didn't go up to Illinois to live," says Mama, shaking a spoon in my face. "If you had I would of been just as overjoyed to see you and your little adopted girl as I was to see Stella-Rondo, when you wound up with your separation and came on back home."

"You would not," I says.

"Don't contradict me. I would," says Mama.

But I said she couldn't convince me though she talked till she was blue in the face. Then I said, "Besides, you know as well as I do that that child is not adopted."

"She most certainly is adopted," says Mama, stiff as a poker.

I says, "Why, Mama, Stella-Rondo had her just as sure as anything in this world, and just too stuck up to admit it."

"Why, Sister," said Mama. "Here I thought we were going to have a pleasant Fourth of July, and you start right out not believing a word your own baby sister tells you!"

"Just like Cousin Annie Flo. Went to her grave denying the facts of life," I remind Mama.

"I told you if you ever mentioned Annie Flo's name I'd slap your face," says Mama, and slaps my face.

"All right, you wait and see," I says.

"I," says Mama, "*I* prefer to take my children's word for anything when it's humanly possible." You ought to see Mama, she weighs two hundred pounds and has real tiny feet.

Just then something perfectly horrible occurred to me.

"Mama," I says, "can that child talk?" I simply had to whisper! "Mama, I wonder if that child can be—you know—in any way? Do you realize," I says, "that she hasn't spoken one single, solitary word to a human being up to this minute? This is the way she looks," I says, and I looked like this.

Well, Mama and I just stood there and stared at each other. It was horrible!

"I remember well that Joe Whitaker frequently drank like a fish," says Mama. "I believed to my soul he drank *chemicals*." And without another word she marches to the foot of the stairs and calls Stella-Rondo.

"Stella-Rondo? O-o-o-o-o! Stella-Rondo!"

"What?" says Stella-Rondo from upstairs. Not even the grace to get up off the bed.

"Can that child of yours talk?" asks Mama.

Stella-Rondo says, "Can she what?"

"Talk! Talk!" says Mama. "Burdyburdyburdyburdy!"

So Stella-Rondo yells back, "Who says she can't talk?"

"Sister says so," says Mama.

"You didn't have to tell me, I know whose word of honor don't mean a thing in this house," says Stella-Rondo.

And in a minute the loudest Yankee voice I ever heard in my life yells out, "OE'm Pop-OE the Sailor-r-r-r Ma-a-an!" and then somebody jumps up and down in the upstairs hall. In another second the house would of fallen down.

"Not only talks, she can tap-dance!" calls Stella-Rondo. "Which is more than some people I won't name can do."

"Why, the little precious darling thing!" Mama says, so surprised. "Just as smart as she can be!" Starts talking baby talk right there. Then she turns on me. "Sister, you ought to be thoroughly ashamed! Run upstairs this instant and apologize to Stella-Rondo and Shirley-T."

"Apologize for what?" I says. "I merely wondered if the child was normal, that's all. Now that she's proved she is, why, I have nothing further to say."

But Mama just turned on her heel and flew out, furious. She ran right upstairs and hugged the baby. She believed it was adopted. Stella-Rondo hadn't done a thing but turn her against me from upstairs while I stood there helpless over the hot stove. So that made Mama, Papa-Daddy and the baby all on Stella-Rondo's side.

Next, Uncle Rondo.

I must say that Uncle Rondo has been marvelous to me at various times in the past and I was completely unprepared to be made to jump out of my skin the way it turned out. Once Stella-Rondo did something perfectly horrible to him—broke a chain letter from Flanders Field—and he took the radio back he had given her and gave it to me. Stella-Rondo was furious! For six months we all had to call her Stella instead of Stella-Rondo, or she wouldn't answer. I always thought Uncle Rondo had all the brains of the entire family. Another time he sent me to Mammoth Cave, with all expenses paid.

But this would be the day he was drinking that prescription, the Fourth of July.

So at supper Stella-Rondo speaks up and says she thinks Uncle Rondo ought to try to eat a little something. So finally Uncle Rondo said he would try a little cold biscuits and ketchup, but that was all. So *she* brought it to him.

"Do you think it wise to disport with ketchup in Stella-Rondo's flesh-colored kimono?" I says. Trying to be considerate! If Stella-Rondo couldn't watch out for her trousseau, somebody had to.

"Any objections?" asks Uncle Rondo, just about to pour out all the ketchup.

"Don't mind what she says, Uncle Rondo," says Stella-Rondo. "Sister has been devoting this solid afternoon to sneering out my bedroom window at the way you look."

"What's that?" says Uncle Rondo. Uncle Rondo has got the most terrible temper in the world. Anything is liable to make him tear the house down if it comes at the wrong time.

So Stella-Rondo says, "Sister says, 'Uncle Rondo certainly does look like a fool in that pink kimono!'"

Do you remember who it was really said that?

Uncle Rondo spills out all the ketchup and jumps out of his chair and tears off the kimono and throws it down on the dirty floor and puts his foot on it. It had to be sent all the way to Jackson to the cleaners and re-pleated.

"So that's your opinion of your Uncle Rondo, is it?" he says. "I look like a fool, do I? Well, that's the last straw. A whole day in this house with nothing to do, and then to hear you come out with a remark like that behind my back!"

"I didn't say any such of a thing, Uncle Rondo," I says, "and I'm not saying who did, either. Why, I think you look all right. Just try to take care of yourself and not talk and eat at the same time," I says. "I think you better go lie down."

"Lie down my foot," says Uncle Rondo. I ought to of known by that he was fixing to do something perfectly horrible.

So he didn't do anything that night in the precarious state he was in—just played Casino with Mama and Stella-Rondo and Shirley-T. and gave Shirley-T. a nickel with a head on both sides. It tickled her nearly to death, and she called him "Papa." But at 6:30 A.M. the next morning, he threw a whole five-cent package of some unsold one-inch firecrackers from the store as hard as he could into my bedroom and they every one went off. Not one bad one in the string. Anybody else, there'd be one that wouldn't go off.

Well, I'm just terribly susceptible to noise of any kind, the doctor has always told me I was the most sensitive person he had ever seen in his whole life, and I was simply prostrated. I couldn't eat! People tell me they heard it as far as the cemetery, and old Aunt Jep Patterson, that had been holding her own so good, thought it was Judgment Day and she was going to meet her whole family. It's usually so quiet here.

And I'll tell you it didn't take me any longer than a minute to make up my mind what to do. There I was with the whole entire house on Stella-Rondo's side and turned against me. If I have anything at all I have pride.

So I just decided I'd go straight down to the P.O. There's plenty of room there in the back, I says to myself.

Well! I made no bones about letting the family catch on to what I was up to. I didn't try to conceal it.

The first thing they knew, I marched in where they were all playing Old Maid and pulled the electric oscillating fan out by the plug, and everything got real hot. Next I snatched the pillow I'd done the needlepoint on right off the davenport from behind Papa-Daddy. He went "Ugh!" I beat Stella-Rondo up the stairs and finally found my charm bracelet in her bureau drawer under a picture of Nelson Eddy.

"So that's the way the land lies," says Uncle Rondo. There he was, piecing on the ham. "Well, Sister, I'll be glad to donate my army cot if you got any place to set it up, providing you'll leave right this minute and let me get some peace." Uncle Rondo was in France.

"Thank you kindly for the cot and 'peace' is hardly the word I would select if I had to resort to firecrackers at 6:30 A.M. in a young girl's bedroom," I says back to him. "And as to where I intend to go, you seem to forget my position as postmistress of China Grove, Mississippi," I says. "I've always got the P.O."

Well, that made them all sit up and take notice.

I went out front and started digging up some four-o'clocks to plant around the P.O.

"Ah-ah-ah!" says Mama, raising the window. "Those happen to be my four-o'clocks. Everything planted in that star is mine. I've never known you to make anything grow in your life."

"Very well," I says. "But I take the fern. Even you, Mama, can't stand there and deny that I'm the one watered that fern. And I happen to know where I can send in a box top and get a packet of one thousand mixed seeds, no two the same kind, free."

"Oh, where?" Mama wants to know.

But I says, "Too late. You 'tend to your house, and I'll 'tend to mine. You hear things like that all the time if you know how to listen to the radio. Perfectly marvelous offers. Get anything you want free."

So I hope to tell you I marched in and got that radio, and they could of all bit a nail in two, especially Stella-Rondo, that it used to belong to, and she well knew she couldn't get it back, I'd sue for it like a shot. And I very politely took the sewing-machine motor I helped pay the most on to give Mama for Christmas back in 1920, and a good big calendar, with the first-aid remedies on it. The thermometer and the Hawaiian ukulele certainly were rightfully mine, and I stood on the stepladder and got all my watermelon-rind preserves and every fruit and vegetable I'd put up, every jar. Then I began to pull the tacks out of the bluebird wall vases on the archway to the dining room.

"Who told you you could have those, Miss Priss?" says Mama, fanning as hard as she could.

"I bought 'em and I'll keep track of 'em," I says. "I'll tack 'em up one on each side the post-office window, and you can see 'em when you come to ask me for your mail, if you're so dead to see 'em."

"Not I! I'll never darken the door to that post office again if live to be a hundred," Mama says. "Ungrateful child! After all the money we spent on you at the Normal."[1]

"Me either," says Stella-Rondo. "You can just let my mail lie there and *rot* for all I care. I'll never come and relieve you of a single, solitary piece."

"I should worry," I says. "And who you think's going to sit down and write you all those big fat letters and postcards, by the way? Mr. Whitaker? Just because he was the only man ever dropped down in China Grove and you got him—unfairly—is he going to sit down and write you a lengthy correspondence after you come home giving no rhyme nor reason whatsoever for your separation and no explanation for the presence of that child? I may not have your brilliant mind, but I fail to see it."

So Mama says, "Sister, I've told you a thousand times that Stella-Rondo simply got homesick, and this child is far too big to be hers," and she says, "Now, why don't you all just sit down and play Casino?"

Then Shirley-T. sticks out her tongue at me in this perfectly horrible way. She has no more manners than the man in the moon. I told her she was going to cross her eyes like that some day and they'd stick.

"It's too late to stop me now," I says. "You should have tried that yesterday. I'm going to the P.O. and the only way you can possibly see me is to visit me there."

So Papa-Daddy says, "You'll never catch me setting foot in that post office, even if I should take a notion into my head to write a letter some place." He says, "I won't have you reachin' out of that little old window with a pair of shears and cuttin' off any beard of mine. I'm too smart for you!"

"We all are." says Stella-Rondo.

But I said, "If you're so smart, where's Mr. Whitaker?"

So then Uncle Rondo says, 'I'll thank you from now on to stop reading all the orders I get on postcards and telling everybody in China Grove what you think is the matter with them," but I says, "I draw my own conclusions and will continue in the future to draw them." I says, "If people want to write their inmost secrets on penny postcards, there's nothing in the wide world you can do about it, Uncle Rondo."

"And if you think we'll ever *write* another postcard you're sadly mistaken," says Mama.

---

[1] I.e., normal school, which trained teachers, chiefly for the elementary grades.

"Cutting off your nose to spite your face then," I says. "But if you're all determined to have no more to do with the U.S. mail, think of this: What will Stella-Rondo do now, if she wants to tell Mr. Whitaker to come after her?"

"Wah!" says Stella-Rondo. I knew she'd cry. She had a conniption fit right there in the kitchen.

"It will be interesting to see how long she holds out," I says. "And now— I am leaving."

"Good-bye," says Uncle Rondo.

"Oh, I declare," says Mama, "to think that a family of mine should quarrel on the Fourth of July, or the day after, over Stella-Rondo leaving old Mr. Whitaker and having the sweetest little adopted child! It looks like we'd all be glad!"

"Wah!" says Stella-Rondo, and has a fresh conniption fit.

"He left her—you mark my words," I says. "That's Mr. Whitaker. I know Mr. Whitaker. After all, I knew him first. I said from the beginning he'd up and leave her. I foretold every single thing that's happened."

"Where did he go?" asks Mama.

"Probably to the North Pole, if he knows what's good for him," I says.

But Stella-Rondo just bawled and wouldn't say another word. She flew to her room and slammed the door.

"Now look what you've gone and done, Sister," says Mama. "You go apologize."

"I haven't got time, I'm leaving," I says.

"Well, what are you waiting around for?" asks Uncle Rondo.

So I just picked up the kitchen clock and marched off, without saying "Kiss my foot" or anything, and never did tell Stella-Rondo good-bye.

There was a girl going along on a little wagon right in front.

"Girl," I says, "come help me haul these things down the hill, I'm going to live in the post office."

Took her nine trips in her express wagon. Uncle Rondo came out on the porch and threw her a nickel.

And that's the last I've laid eyes on any of my family or my family laid eyes on me for five solid days and nights. Stella-Rondo may be telling the most horrible tales in the world about Mr. Whitaker, but I haven't heard them. As I tell everybody, I draw my own conclusions.

But oh, I like it here. It's ideal, as I've been saying. You see, I've got everything cater-cornered, the way I like it. Hear the radio? All the war news. Radio, sewing machine, book ends, ironing board and that great big piano lamp—peace, that's what I like. Butter-bean vines planted all along the front where the strings are.

Of course, there's not much mail. My family are naturally the main people in China Grove, and if they prefer to vanish from the face of the earth, for all the mail they get or the mail they write, why, I'm not going to open my mouth. Some of the folks here in town are taking up for me and some turned against me. I know which is which. There are always people who will quit buying stamps just to get on the right side of Papa-Daddy.

But here I am, and here I'll stay. I want the world to know I'm happy.

And if Stella-Rondo should come to me this minute, on bended knees, and attempt to explain the incidents of her life with Mr. Whitaker, I'd simply put my fingers in both my ears and refuse to listen.

SOJOURNER TRUTH
[c. 1797–1883]

When asked to name African-American women of the nineteenth century, most people can identify only two: Harriet Tubman and Sojourner Truth. Both women are rightly remembered for their unique leadership, their success in overcoming almost inconceivable obstacles in life, and their devotion to liberation and human rights. Neither Tubman nor Truth, however, could write, and the popular understanding of both women is based on texts written by white women. The significance of this filtered historical memory is particularly striking in the case of Sojourner Truth, who is remembered primarily for her 1851 speech at a Women's Rights convention in Akron, Ohio, a speech featuring the famous refrain "ar'n't I a woman?" The famous version of this speech was recorded some twelve years after the event by white feminist Frances Dana Gage, and she noted that her record of the speech was only an approximation. But her version of the speech, and the extent to which that version has been identified with Sojourner Truth, emphasizes the importance of recognizing Truth's most famous speech as a particular kind of "fluid text"—for, as several scholars have demonstrated, it is unlikely that the words for which Truth is most remembered are the words she spoke in 1851.

Sojourner Truth was enslaved at birth in Ulster County, New York; her name was Isabella Baumfree. Sold three times before she reached the age of twelve, and raped by one of her owners, Isabella's life is a reminder that the American habit of identifying slavery and its multifarious violations solely with the South is a serious misrepresentation of U.S. national history. Isabella had five children with an enslaved man, Thomas, one of whom, five-year-old Peter, was sold by her owner in 1827, just one year before the end of legal slavery in New York. Isabella escaped, contracted herself to work for another master for one year, and sued successfully to regain custody of her son. She adopted the name of Van Wagener from her last employer and in 1829 moved to New York City. Influenced by evangelical religion—including participation in a then-notorious mystical cult—Isabella experienced visions that led her to change her name to Sojourner Truth and to begin her career as an itinerant preacher in 1843. Truth's political and social education continued in the

1840s during her residence at a communal farm in Massachusetts called the Northampton Association of Education and Industry, one of many communal projects devoted to utopian reform in the nineteenth century. In this community Truth met Olive Gilbert, to whom she dictated the manuscript that she published in 1850, The Narrative of Sojourner Truth: A Bondswoman of Olden Time, *sales of which provided Truth with her primary source of income through the 1850s and 1860s.*

Although the Narrative of Sojourner Truth *was the public record of her life and voice, another voice later came to represent Truth's eloquent advocacy of the related causes of antislavery and women's rights. When Frances Gage recorded her memory of Truth's speech at the 1851 Women's Rights convention in Akron, Ohio, she created an influential representation of Truth's power as a speaker, but it was a distorted representation that reveals much about the racial assumptions and stereotypes that infected the women's movement and influenced even those who considered themselves allies of the cause of African-American rights. Gage's version (included in* History of Woman Suffrage *by Elizabeth Cady Stantion et al. in 1881, and reproduced as well in the 1875 edition of Truth's* Narrative) *is held together by the refrain "ar'n't I a woman?"—a phrase that does not appear in any of the four accounts of Truth's speech published shortly after the convention. It is unlikely, in other words, that this refrain was woven through Truth's speech, if she said it at all. Moreover, Gage's version has Truth talking in stereotypical black Southern dialect or "plantation speech," a highly unlikely representation of the speech patterns of a woman who grew up in upstate New York and spoke Dutch until she was ten. Even in a distorted form, it shows the general direction of Truth's line of thought, the courage with which she faced her adversaries at the convention, and the wisdom with which she broke through the prejudices and pretensions of those around her.*

We can get a sense of Truth's power as a speaker also by reading other speeches she gave on the subject of women's rights. In 1853, for example, Truth spoke at the fourth national Women's Rights Convention in New York City. The event was disrupted continually by various young men who attended the convention simply to ridicule the participants, and Truth, more ridiculed than most other participants, addressed the hecklers with characteristic courage and directness, telling her most vocal critics that, concerning women's rights, "you may hiss as much as you please, like any other lot of geese, but you can't stop it; it's bound to come." Truth understood that the reasons she was so scorned—that is, for being an uneducated black woman— were also the reasons why she had so much to bring to the cause of women's rights, social justice, and moral understanding. In an address at the First Annual Meeting of the American Equal Rights Association in 1867, Truth joined African-American rights with women's rights, noting both the need to attend to women's rights within the black comunity and the need to attend to

African-American rights within the national community. "If colored men get their rights, and not colored women theirs," Truth asserted, "you see the colored men will be masters over the women, and it will be just as bad as it was before. . . . Slavery," Truth observed, had been only "partly destroyed; not entirely. I want it root and branch destroyed."

Throughout her life, Truth continued to advocate for the destruction of slavery's "root and branch," and as the story of her life developed Truth continued to represent both the possibility of and the obstacles to that liberationist vision. Seven editions of The Narrative of Sojourner Truth *were published, and the additions to that life story reveal the problematic cultural frame of the portrait of Sojourner Truth that has become so prominent in American culture. Included in an edition published in 1878 are Truth's "Book of Life," a scrapbook featuring letters and clippings from Truth's expansive public career. In that same edition, however, is Gage's version of Truth's Akron speech, along with a narrative sketch by Harriet Beecher Stowe, author of* Uncle Tom's Cabin, *titled "Sojourner Truth, the Libyan Sibyl," a piece first published in* The Atlantic Monthly *in 1863. Stowe's sketch added considerably to Truth's fame but, as the title of her piece suggests, Stowe offered a portrait that was both particular and generalized, speaking of both the power of Truth's presence and the racialized lens through which many white Americans, then and since, viewed this preacher of truths.*

The woman, both seen through and obscured by that lens, saw the end of slavery and the emergence of a daunting range of problems faced by African-American men and women after the Civil War, when legal slavery was replaced increasingly by a system of racial control, and when those who had been emancipated from slavery faced the prospect of starting anew in a hostile world. Traveling from her home in Battle Creek, Michigan, where she had purchased a house in the 1850s, Truth put her prominence to work for the African-American community. She helped to gather supplies for African-American soldiers during the Civil War and met with President Lincoln in 1864. After the war, she served briefly in the National Freedmen's Relief Association, advising those who had been enslaved, and her experiences led her to campaign for the establishment of a "Negro State" in the West, in the hopes that a separate community might offer African Americans the opportunity to establish economic and social security. Sojourner Truth was, in short, a greater presence across the American cultural landscape than even her legend suggests—and those who set out in search of Truth will have to look far beyond the familiar transcripts of her most famous talks. Scholars today cannot know exactly what Truth said in 1851, though there is considerable reason to distrust the version of her speech for which Truth is remembered, just as there is reason to distrust the generalized myth of Sojourner Truth that has remained prominent through the years. But the records of Truth's most famous speech remain invaluable, for it is possible to compare the different versions of her speeches, and by the fluidity of this and other famous texts, the stream of religious and social vision that leads back to their elusive but formidable source can definitely be traced. Truth is still there to tell those who seek her out, "what time o'night it is."

John Ernest
University of New Hampshire

For Further Reading

Primary Works

Olive Gilbert, *Narrative of Sojourner Truth; A Northern Slave, Emancipated from Bodily Servitude by the State of New York, in 1828* (1850, 1853); Olive Gilbert, *Narrative of Sojourner Truth; A Bondwoman of Olden Time, Emancipated by the New York Legislature in the Early Part of the Present Century; With a History of Her . . . Last Sickness and Death* (1875, 1878, 1884); Speech at Akron, Ohio, May 29, 1851, in *History of Woman Suffrage*, Elizabeth Cady Stanton et al., eds. (1881), 1: 115–17; Speech at New York City, May 9, 1867, in *History of Woman Suffrage*, Elizabeth Cady Stanton et al., eds. (1881), 2: 193–194; Speech at New York City, May 10, 1867, in *History of Woman Suffrage*, Elizabeth Cady Stanton et al., eds. (1881), 2: 222; *Narrative of Sojourner Truth; A Bondswoman of Olden Time, With a History of Her Labors and Correspondence Drawn from Her "Book of Life"* (1991); Suzanne Pullon Fitch and Roseann M. Mandsiuk. *Sojourner Truth as Orator: Wit, Story, and Song* (1997).

Secondary Works

Dorothy Sterling. *We Are Your Sisters: Black Women in the Nineteenth Century* (1984); Jean Fagan Yellin. *Women and Sisters: The Antislavery Feminists in American Culture* (1989); Carleton Mabee. *Sojourner Truth: Slave, Prophet, Legend* (1991); Erlene Stetson and Linda David. *Glorying in Tribulation: The Lifework of Sojourner Truth* (1994); Carla L. Peterson. *"Doers of the Word": African-American Women Speakers and Writers in the North (1830–1880)*, (1995); Nell Irvin Painter. *Sojourner Truth, a Life, a Symbol* (1996).

Women's Rights Convention, Akron, Ohio, May 28, 1851*

SOJOURNER TRUTH

As reported in the *Anti-Slavery Bugle*, June 21, 1851

One of the most unique and interesting speeches of the Convention was made by Sojourner Truth, an emancipated slave. It is impossible to transfer it to paper, or convey any adequate idea of the effect it produced upon the audience. Those only can appreciate it who saw her powerful form, her whole-souled, earnest gestures, and listened to her strong and truthful tones. She came forward to the platform and addressing the President said with a great simplicity:

May I say a few words? Receiving an affirmative answer, she proceeded; I want to say a few words about this matter. I am a woman's rights. I have as much muscle as any man, and can do as much work as any man. I have plowed and reaped and husked and chopped and mowed, and can any man do more than that? I have heard much about the sexes being equal; I can carry as much as any man, and can eat as much too, if I can get it. I am as strong as any man that is now. As for intellect, all I can say is, if woman have a pint and man a quart—why cant she have her little pint full? You need not be afraid to give us our rights for fear we will take too much,—for we cant take more than our pint'll hold. The poor men seem to be all in confusion, and dont know what to do. Why children, if you have woman's rights give it to her and you will feel better. You will have your own rights, and they wont

---

*Sojourner Truth's most famous speech was presented at the Woman's Rights convention in Akron, Ohio, on May 29, 1851. Frances Dana Gage presided over the convention and invited Truth to speak—and it is Gage's version of the speech, reconstructed many years after the event, that has survived. But the accuracy of Gage's version of the speech has been soundly challenged by scholars. Sojourner Truth could not write, so all of her surviving speeches have been preserved only as recorded by others, and this can lead to many unintentional misrepresentations. Scholars believe, for example, that it is unlikely that Truth's speech featured the refrain "Ar'n't I a woman?"; and scholars have noted that Truth was unlikely to speak in the stereotypical Southern black dialect that Gage represents, for Truth grew up in New York state speaking Dutch. The text here reprints three versions of the 1851 speech—two by Frances Gage (showing changes in Gage's representation of Truth's dialect), and the one from the *Anti-Slavery Bugle* account of the event that scholars believe to be the most accurate record of Truth's speech.

be so much trouble. I cant read, but I can hear. I have heard the bible and have learned that Eve caused man to sin. Well if woman upset the world, do give her a chance to set it right side up again. The Lady has spoken about Jesus, how he never spurned woman from him, and she was right. When Lazarus died, Mary and Martha came to him with faith and love and besought him to raise their brother. And Jesus wept—and Lazarus came forth.[1] And how came Jesus into the world? Through God who created him and woman who bore him. Man, where is your part? But the women are coming up blessed be God and a few of the men are coming up with them. But man is in a tight place, the poor slave is on him, woman is coming on him, and he is surely between a hawk and a buzzard.

[1851]

"Sojourner Truth"
By Mrs. F. D. Gage
in the *National Anti-Slavery Standard*, May 2, 1863

"Well, chillen, what dar's so much racket dar must be som'ting out o'kilter. I tink dat 'twixt de niggers of de South and de women at de Norf, all a-talking 'bout rights, de white men will be in a fix pretty soon. But what's all this here talking 'bout? Dat man ober dar say dat woman needs to be helped into carriages, and lifted ober ditches, and to have de best place eberywhar. Nobody eber helps me into carriages, or ober mud-puddles, or gives me any best place,"; and, raising herself to her full height, and her voice to a pitch like rolling thunder, she asked, "And ar'n't I a woman? Look at me. Look at my arm," and she bared her right arm to the shoulder, showing its tremendous muscular power. "I have plowed and planted and gathered into barns, and no man could head me—and ar'n't I a woman? I could work as much and eat as much as a man (when I could get it) and bear de lash as well—and ar'n't I a woman? I have borne thirteen children, and seen 'em mos' all sold off to slavery, and when I cried out with a mother's grief, none but Jesus heard—and ar'n't I a woman? Den dey talks 'bout dis ting in de head. What dis dey call it" "Intellect," whispered some one near. "Dat's it, honey. What's dat got to do with woman's rights or niggers' rights? If my cup won't hold but a pint, and yourn holds a quart, wouldn't ye be mean not to let me have my little half-measure full?" and she pointed her significant finger and sent a keen glance at the minister who had made the argument. The cheering was long and loud. "Den dat little man in black dar, he say woman can't have as much rights as man, 'cause Christ wa'n't a woman. *Whar did your Christ come from?*"

---

[1]*John* 11: 1–44

Rolling thunder could not have stilled that crowd as did those deep, wonderful tones, as she stood there with outstretched arms and eye of fire. Raising her voice still louder, she repeated,—
"Whar did your Christ come from? From God and a woman. Man had not'ing to do with him." Oh, what a rebuke she gave the little man. Turning again to another objector, she took up the defence of Mother Eve. I cannot follow her through it all. It was pointed and witty and solemn, eliciting at almost every sentence defeaning applause, and she ended by asserting: "that if de fust woman God ever made was strong enought to turn de world upside down all her one lone, all dese togeder," and she glanced her eye over us, "ought to be able to turn it back, and git it right side up again, and now dey as asking to, de men better let 'em." (long and continued cheering). "Bleeged to ye for hearin' on me, and now ole Sojourner ha'n't got nothing more to say."

[1863]

Reminescences by Frances D. Gage of Sojourner Truth, for May 28–29, 1851

The leaders of the movement trembled on seeing a tall, gaunt black woman in a gray dress and white turban, surmounted with an uncouth sun-bonnet, march deliberately into the church, walk with the air of a queen up the aisle, and take her seat upon the pulpit steps. A buzz of disapprobation was heard all over the house, and there fell on the listening ear, "An abolition affair!" "Woman's rights and niggers!" "I told you so!" "Go it, darkey!"

I chanced on that occasion to wear my first laurels in public life as president of the meeting. At my request order was restored, and the business of the Convention went on. Morning, afternoon, and evening exercises came and went. Through all these sessions old Sojourner, quiet and reticent as the "Lybian Statue,"[2] sat crouched against the wall on the corner of the pulpit stairs, her sun-bonnet shading her eyes, her elbows on her knees, her chin resting upon her broad, hard palms. At intermission she was busy selling the "Life of Sojourner Truth," a narrative of her own strange and adventurous life. Again and again, timorous and trembling ones came to me and said, with earnestness, "Don't let her speak, Mrs. Gage, it will ruin us. Every newspaper in the land will have our cause mixed up with abolition and niggers, and we shall be utterly denounced." My only answer was, "We shall see when the time comes."

---

[2]This is a reference to William Wetmore Story's sculpture *The Libyan Sibyl*. In her essay "The Libyan Sibyl," Harriet Beecher Stowe claims that her encounter with Sojourner Truth was the inspiration for Story's sculpture.

The second day the work waxed warm. Methodist, Baptist, Episcopal, Presbyterian, and Universalist ministers came in to hear and discuss the resolutions presented. One claimed superior rights and privileges for man, on the ground of "superior intellect"; another, because of the "manhood of Christ; if God had desired the equality of woman, He would have given some token of His will through the birth, life, and death of the Saviour." Another gave us a theological view of the "sin of our first mother."

There were very few women in those days who dared to "speak in meeting"; and the august teachers of the people were seemingly getting the better of us, while the boys in the galleries, and the sneerers among the pews, were hugely enjoying the discomfiture, as they supposed, of the "strong-minded." Some of the tender-skinned friends were on the point of losing dignity, and the atmosphere betokened a storm. When, slowly from her seat in the corner rose Sojourner Truth, who, till now, had scarcely lifted her head. "Don't let her speak!" gasped half a dozen in my ear. She moved slowly and solemnly to the front, laid her old bonnet at her feet, and turned her great speaking eyes to me. There was a hissing sound of disapprobation above and below. I rose and announced "Sojourner Truth," and begged the audience to keep silence for a few moments.

The tumult subsided at once, and every eye was fixed on this almost Amazon form, which stood nearly six feet high, head erect, and eyes piercing the upper air like one in a dream. At her first word there was a profound hush. She spoke in deep tones, which, though not loud, reached every ear in the house, and away through the throng at the doors and windows.

"Wall, chilern, whar dar is so much racket dar must be somethin' out o' kilter. I tink dat 'twixt de niggers of de Souf and de womin at de Norf, all talkin' 'bout rights, de white men will be in a fix pretty soon. But what's all dis here talkin' 'bout?

"Dat man over dar say dat womin needs to be helped into carriages, and lifted ober ditches, and to hab de best place everywhar. Nobody eber helps me into carriages, or ober mud-puddles, or gibs me any best place!" And raising herself to her full height, and her voice to a pitch like rolling thunder, she asked. "And a'n't I a woman? Look at me! Look at my arm! (and she bared her right arm to the shoulder, showing her tremendous muscular power). I have ploughed, and planted, and gathered into barns, and no man could head me! And a'n't I a woman? I could work as much and eat as much as a man—when I could get it—and bear de lash as well! And a'n't I a woman? I have borne thirteen childern, and seen 'em most' all sold off to slavery, and when I cried out with my mother's grief, none but Jesus heard me! And a'n't I a woman?

"Den dey talks 'bout dis ting in de head; what dis dey call it?" ("Intellect," whispered some one near.) "Dat's it, honey. What's dat got to do wid womin's rights or nigger's rights? If my cup won't hold but a pint, and yourn

161

holds a quart, wouldn't ye be mean not to let me have my little half-measure full?" And she pointed her significant finger, and sent a keen glance at the minister who had made the argument. The cheering was long and loud.

"Den dat little man in black dar, he say women can't have as much rights as men, 'cause Christ wan't a woman! Whar did your Christ come from?" Rolling thunder couldn't have stilled that crowd, as did those deep, wonderful tones, as she stood there with outstretched arms and eyes of fire. Raising her voice still louder, she repeated, "Whar did your Christ come from? From God and a woman! Man had nothin' to do wid Him." Oh, what a rebuke that was to that little man.

Turning again to another objector, she took up the defense of Mother Eve. I can not follow her throught it all. It was pointed, and witty, and solemn; eliciting at almost every sentence deafening applause; and she ended by asserting: "If de fust woman God ever made was strong enough to turn de world upside down all alone, dese women togedder (and she glanced her eye over the platform) ought to be able to turn it back, and get it right side up again! And now dey is asking to do it, de men better let 'em." Long-continued cheering greeted this. "Bleeged to ye for hearin' on me, and now ole Sojourner han't got nothin' more to say."

Amid roars of applause, she returned to her corner, leaving more than one of us with streaming eyes, and hearts beating with gratitude. She had taken us up in her strong arms and carried us safely over the slough of difficulty turning the whole tide in our favor. I have never in my life seen anything like the magical influence that subdued the mobbish spirit of the day, and turned the sneers and jeers of an excited crowd into notes of respect and admiration. Hundreds rushed up to shake hands with her, and congratulate the glorious old mother, and bid her God-speed on her mission of "testifyin' agin concerning the wickedness of this 'ere people."

[1881]

LORRAINE VIVIAN HANSBERRY
[1930–1965]

Lorraine Vivian Hansberry's first staged play, A Raisin in the Sun, *brought her immediate international recognition. Directed by Lloyd Richards and produced on Broadway in 1959,* A Raisin in the Sun *is a nonviolent play about an African-American family's conflicts with each other and their struggles against racism in America after World War II. Some critics have argued that the play's appeal lies in its universal themes of aspiration, tragedy, and family relationships. This same attribute—universality—drew criticism from some of the proponents of the 1960s Black Arts movement, who felt the play was too assimilationist and politically benign. Despite these differences of interpretation, the play clearly was and continues to be a success. It was the first play by a black woman to be produced on Broadway. Hansberry was the youngest playwright, the first black, and the fifth woman to win the New York Drama Critics Circle Award for Best Play of the Year. Columbia Pictures made* A Raisin in the Sun *into a film starring Sidney Poitier in 1961, and it received a special award at the Cannes film festival that year. According to critic Margaret Wilkerson, the 1989 "made-for-television version of the play . . . broke television viewing records across the country." Hansberry, who died of cancer at the age of thirty-four, made a significant contribution to American theater that, as Wilkerson puts it, "was more than a simple 'first' to be commemorated in history books and then forgotten.* A Raisin in the Sun *was the turning point for black artists in the professional theater."*

Hansberry was born on May 19, 1930, in Chicago, Illinois, into a prominent, politically active family. Her father, Carl Augustus Hansberry, was a successful realtor and banker. Her mother, Nannie Perry Hansberry, was a schoolteacher trained at Tennessee Agricultural and Industrial University, who later served as a ward commissioner for the Republican Party. Lorraine Hansberry attended Chicago public schools, after which she attended the University of Wisconsin, the Art Institute of Chicago, and Roosevelt College. She also studied in Guadalajara, Mexico (1948–50), then, moving to New York in 1950, attended the New School for Social Research. Hansberry married songwriter and publisher Robert Nemiroff in 1953, but the couple divorced the year before she died.

Growing up in a politically active family undoubtedly influenced Hansberry's own activism. She had been president of the Young Progressive League at the University of Wisconsin. She also worked as a reporter and an editor for a progressive black newspaper, Freedom, in the early 1950s. In fact, Hansberry met her husband while covering a protest of discriminatory practices against black athletes at New York University. As Hansberry's political interests grew, she turned her attention to the theater, believing that she could reach a greater audience. She wrote a number of plays that challenged people all over the world to examine the mistreatment of nonwhite people in postcolonial systems. Indeed, themes such as those explored in A Raisin in the Sun pushed her to the forefront of the Civil Rights movement.

The title of her best-known play was taken from Langston Hughes's famous poem "Harlem," part of a sequence titled Montage of a Dream Deferred (1951). It was a title extremely relevant for the times because so many African-American families were struggling to actualize their economic dreams only to have them "dry up/ like a raisin in the sun," as in Hughes's poem. Lena (Mama) Younger, the matriarch of the family, wants to use the insurance settlement from her husband's suspicious death to purchase a house for her family and to send her college-aged daughter to medical school. Mama is convinced that a home in the suburbs and her daughter's education will help her family claim a piece of the American Dream. The audience quickly learns that each member of the family has his or her own personal interpretation of the American Dream, as well as different desires for using the insurance money. Mama uses some of the money for a down payment on a house, but in a white neighborhood that doesn't want blacks. She entrusts the rest to her son, Walter Lee, who selfishly invests and loses most of the money, including his sister's college tuition, in a risky scheme to buy a liquor store. Devastated by the loss of his family's money and thereby his own dreams of success, Walter Lee decides to accept an offer made by a representative of the white neighborhood to buy out the Youngers to avoid racial integration. At the last moment, however, he rejects the offer, saving the family's dignity. The play thus ends on a somewhat tragic note as each family member realizes that the American Dream is not readily accessible to African Americans. Yet, although their initial hopes and dreams are shattered, they refuse to be defeated. This realistic drama challenges audiences to question the possibilities of human survival after dreams have been deferred.

Hansberry was consistent in advocating social change in both her plays and her extra-literary work. Her speech "The Negro Writer and His Roots" was delivered in 1959, at a black writers' conference in which she spoke of what she believed to be the black writer's mission. During the Civil Rights movement, she helped to raise money for the Student Nonviolent Coordinating Committee. In March of 1964, though seriously ill, she completed a project titled The Movement: Documentary of a Struggle for Equality, and in May she left the *hospital to deliver a speech to the winners of a writing contest sponsored by the United Negro College Fund. It was with this speech that she coined the phrase "Young, gifted and black." A month after this speech, she participated in a debate titled "The Black Revolution and the White Backlash."*

Hansberry's The Sign in Sidney Brustein's Window *is a play about a 1950s Jewish intellectual living in Greenwich Village, and it is based on the American labor demonstrations of the 1930s. It opened on Broadway in October 1964, with a predominantly white cast, but did not enjoy the success of* A Raisin in the Sun. *Ironically, it closed on January 12, 1965, the day Hansberry died. Her other works have been staged and published posthumously. In his capacity as a literary executor, her former husband, Robert Nemiroff, compiled Hansberry's notes, letters, and early writings into a performative text aptly titled "To Be Young, Gifted, and Black: A Portrait of Lorraine Hansberry in Her Own Words," which was produced off-Broadway in 1969 (later published in 1971). It ran for 538 performances, the longest running drama of the 1968–69 off-Broadway season. He also edited three of her unpublished plays under the title* Les Blancs: The Collected Last Plays of Lorraine Hansberry *(1972). The collection includes* Les Blancs, *unfinished at the time of her death;* The Drinking Gourd; *and* What Use Are Flowers? *Of the last three plays published,* Les Blancs *was the only one produced on Broadway. Nemiroff collaborated with Charlotte Zaltzberg on a musical version of* A Raisin in the Sun, *titled* Raisin *(1978), which won a Tony Award. The current literary executor, Dr. Jewell Gresham Nemiroff, continues to release more of Hansberry's unpublished work and papers, making them available for further study and ensuring that this important American playwright is remembered.*

Jasmin L. Lambert, Assistant Professor of Theater
The College of William and Mary

For Further Reading

Primary Works

A Raisin in the Sun: A Drama in Three Acts (New York: Random House, 1959); *The Sign in Sidney Brustein's Window: A Drama in Three Acts* (New York: Samuel French, 1965); *To Be Young, Gifted, and Black* (New York: Samuel French, 1971); *To Be Young, Gifted and Black: Lorraine Hansberry in Her Own Words* (New York: Vintage Books, 1995); *Les Blancs: The Collected Last Plays of Lorraine Hansberry*, Robert Nemiroff, ed., includes *Les Blancs*, *The Drinking Gourd*, and *What Use Are Flowers?* (New York: Random House, 1972); *The Collected Last Plays* (New York: Vintage Books, 1994); *Raisin* (New York: Samuel French, 1978); *A Raisin in the Sun: The Unfilmed Original Screenplay*, Robert Nemiroff, ed. (New York: Penguin Books, 1992).

Nonfiction: *The Movement: Documentary of a Struggle for Equality* (New York: Simon & Schuster, 1964); *To Be Young, Gifted, and Black: Lorraine Hansberry in Her Own Words*, Robert Nemiroff, ed., with an introduction by James Baldwin (Englewood Cliffs, N.J.: Prentice-Hall, 1969). **Fiction:** "All the Dark and Beautiful Warriors," in *Village Voice* (August 16, 1983); 1, 11–16, 18–19; "The Buck Williams Tennessee Memorial Association," in *Southern Exposure* (September-October 1984); 28–30. **Selected Essays:** "Willy Loman, Walter Lee Younger, and He Who Must Live," in *Village Voice* (August 12, 1959), 7–8; "The Black Revolution and the White Backlash," in *National Guardian* (July 4, 1964), 5–9; "The Negro Writer and His Roots: Toward a New Romanticism," in *Black Scholar* 12 (March-April 1981): 2–12.

Secondary Works

Baraka, Amiri (LeRoi Jones). "Raisin in the Sun's Enduring Passion," in *Washington Post* (November 16, 1986); Bigsby, C. W. E. *Modern American Drama, 1945–1990* (New York: Cambridge University Press, 1992); Bond, Jean Carey, ed. *Lorraine Hansberry: At of Thunder, Vision of Light. Freedomways* 19 (1979); Carter, Steven R. *Hansberry's Drama: Commitment and Complexity* (Urbana: University of Illinois Press, 1991); Domina, Lynn. *Understanding "A Raisin in the Sun": A Student Casebook to Issues, Sources, and Historical Documents* (Westport, Conn.: Greenwood Press, 1998); Keppel, Ben. *The Work of Democracy: Ralph Bunche, Kenneth B. Clark, Lorraine Hansberry, and the Cultural Politics of Race* (Cambridge, Mass.: Harvard University Press, 1995); Scheader, Catherine. *Lorraine Hansberry: Playwright and Voice of Justice* (Berkeley Heights, N.J.: Enslow Publishers, 1998); Tripp, Janet. *Lorraine Hansberry* (San Diego: Lucent Books, 1998); Wilkerson, Margaret B. "From Harlem to Broadway: African American Women Playwrights at Mid-Century," in *The Cambridge Companion to American Women Playwrights*, Brenda Murphy, ed. (Cambridge: Cambridge University Press, 1999); Wilkerson, Margaret B. "Lorraine Hansberry." In *African American Writers*, second edition, vol. 1, Valerie Smith, ed. (New York: Charles Scribner's Sons, 2001).

Bibliographies

Kaiser, Ernest and Robert Nemiroff. "A Lorraine Hansberry Bibliography," in *Lorraine Hansberry: Art of Thunder, Vision of Light. Freedomways* 19 (1979); Leeson, Richard M. *Lorraine Hansberry: A Research and Production Sourcebook* (Westport, Conn.: Greenwood Press, 1997).

A Raisin in the Sun

LORRAINE HANSBERRY

What happens to a dream deferred?
Does it dry up
Like a raisin in the sun?
Or fester like a sore—
And then run?
Does it stink like rotten meat?
Or crust and sugar over—
Like a syrupy sweet?

Maybe it just sags
Like a heavy load.

Or does it explode?

    —LANGSTON HUGHES

Characters

Ruth Younger
Travis Younger
Walter Lee Younger (Brother)
Beneatha Younger
Lena Younger (Mama)
Joseph Asagai
George Murchison
Karl Lindner
Bobo
Moving Men

The action of the play is set in Chicago's Southside, sometime between World War II and the present.

Act One

SCENE 1 *Friday morning.*
SCENE 2 *The following morning.*

Act Two

SCENE 1 *Later, the same day.*
SCENE 2 *Friday night, a few weeks later.*
SCENE 3 *Moving day, one week later.*

Act Three

An hour later.

Act I
Scene 1

The Younger living room would be a comfortable and well-ordered room if it were not for a number of indestructible contradictions to this state of being. Its furnishings are typical and undistinguished and their primary feature now is that they have clearly had to accommodate the living of too many people for too many years—and they are tired. Still, we can see that at some time, a time probably no longer remembered by the family (except perhaps for Mama), the furnishings of this room were actually selected with care and love and even hope—and brought to this apartment and arranged with taste and pride.

That was a long time ago. Now the once loved pattern of the couch upholstery has to fight to show itself from under acres of crocheted doilies and couch covers which have themselves finally come to be more important than the upholstery. And here a table or a chair has been moved to disguise the worn places in the carpet; but the carpet has fought back by showing its weariness, with depressing uniformity, elsewhere on its surface.

Weariness has, in fact, won in this room. Everything has been polished, washed, sat on, used, scrubbed too often. All pretenses but living itself have long since vanished from the very atmosphere of this room.

Moreover, a section of this room, for it is not really a room unto itself, though the landlord's lease would make it seem so, slopes backward to provide a small kitchen area, where the family prepares the meals that are eaten in the living room proper, which must also serve as dining room. The single window that has been provided for these "two" rooms is located in this kitchen area. The sole natural light the family may enjoy in the course of a day is only that which fights its way through this little window.

At left, a door leads to a bedroom which is shared by Mama and her daughter, Beneatha. At right, opposite, is a second room (which in the beginning of the life of this apartment was probably a breakfast room) which serves as a bedroom for Walter and his wife, Ruth.

TIME: *Sometime between World War II and the present.*

PLACE: *Chicago's Southside.*

At rise: It is morning dark in the living room. Travis is asleep on the make-down bed at center. An alarm clock sounds from within the bedroom at right, and presently Ruth enters from that room and closes the door behind her. She crosses sleepily toward the window. As she passes her sleeping son she reaches down and shakes him a little. At the window she raises the shade and a dusky Southside morning light comes in feebly. She fills a pot with water and puts it on to boil. She calls to the boy, between yawns, in a slightly muffled voice.

Ruth is about thirty. We can see that she was a pretty girl, even exceptionally so, but now it is apparent that life has been little that she expected, and disappointment has already begun to hang in her face. In a few years, before thirty-five even, she will be known among her people as a "settled woman."

She crosses to her son and gives him a good, final, rousing shake.

Ruth. Come on now, boy, it's seven thirty! *(Her son sits up at last, in a stupor of sleepiness)* I say hurry up, Travis! You ain't the only person in the world got to use a bathroom! *(The child, a sturdy, handsome little boy of ten or eleven, drags himself out of the bed and almost blindly takes his towels and "today's clothes" from drawers and a closet and goes out to the bathroom, which is in an outside hall and which is shared by another family or families on the same floor. Ruth crosses to the bedroom door at right and opens it and calls in to her husband)* Walter Lee! ... It's after seven thirty! Lemme see you do some waking up in there now! *(She waits)* You better get up from there, man! It's after seven thirty I tell you. *(She waits again)* All right, you just go ahead and lay there and next thing you know Travis be finished and Mr. Johnson'll be in there and you'll be fussing and cussing round here like a mad man! And be late too! *(She waits, at the end of patience)* Walter Lee—it's time for you to get up!

(She waits another second and then starts to go into the bedroom, but is apparently satisfied that her husband has begun to get up. She stops, pulls the door to, and returns to the kitchen area. She wipes her face with a moist cloth and runs her fingers through her sleep-disheveled hair in a vain effort and ties an apron around her housecoat. The bedroom door at right opens and her husband stands in the doorway in his pajamas, which are rumpled and mismated. He is a lean, intense young man in his middle thirties, inclined to quick nervous movements and erratic speech habits—and always in his voice there is a quality of indictment)

Walter. Is he out yet?

Ruth. What you mean *out?* He ain't hardly got in there good yet.

Walter (Wandering in, still more oriented to sleep than to a new day). Well, what was you doing all that yelling for if I can't even get in there yet? *(Stopping and thinking)* Check coming today?

Ruth. They *said* Saturday and this is just Friday and I hopes to God you ain't going to get up here first thing this morning and start talking to me 'bout no money—'cause I 'bout don't want to hear it.

Walter. Something the matter with you this morning?

Ruth. No—I'm just sleepy as the devil. What kind of eggs you want?

Walter. Not scrambled. *(Ruth starts to scramble eggs)* Paper come? *(Ruth points impatiently to the rolled up* Tribune *on the table, and he gets it and spreads it out and vaguely reads the front page)* Set off another bomb yesterday.

Ruth (Maximum indifference). Did they?

Walter (Looking up). What's the matter with you?

Ruth. Ain't nothing the matter with me. And don't keep asking me that this morning.

Walter. Ain't nobody bothering you. *(Reading the news of the day absently again)* Say Colonel McCormick is sick.

Ruth (Affecting tea-party interest). Is he now? Poor thing.

Walter (Sighing and looking at his watch). Oh, me. *(He waits)* Now what is that boy doing in that bathroom all this time? He just going to have to start getting up earlier. I can't be being late to work on account of him fooling around in there.

Ruth (Turning on him). Oh, no he ain't going to be getting up no earlier no such thing! It ain't his fault that he can't get to bed no earlier nights 'cause he got a bunch of crazy good-for-nothing clowns sitting up running their mouths in what is supposed to be his bedroom after ten o'clock at night . . .

Walter. That's what you mad about, ain't it? The things I want to talk about with my friends just couldn't be important in your mind, could they?

(He rises and finds a cigarette in her handbag on the table and crosses to the little window and looks out, smoking and deeply enjoying this first one)

Ruth (Almost matter of factly, a complaint too automatic to deserve emphasis). Why you always got to smoke before you eat in the morning?

Walter *(At the window).* Just look at 'em down there . . . Running and racing to work . . . *(He turns and faces his wife and watches her a moment at the stove, and then, suddenly)* You look young this morning, baby.

Ruth (Indifferently). Yeah?

Walter. Just for a second—stirring them eggs. It's gone now—just for a second it was—you looked real young again. *(Then, drily)* It's gone now—you look like yourself again.

Ruth. Man, if you don't shut up and leave me alone.

Walter (Looking out to the street again). First thing a man ought to learn in life is not to make love to no colored woman first thing in the morning. You all some evil people at eight o'clock in the morning.

(Travis appears in the hall doorway, almost fully dressed and quite wide awake now, his towels and pajamas across his shoulders. He opens the door and signals for his father to make the bathroom in a hurry)

Travis (Watching the bathroom). Daddy, come on! *(Walter gets his bathroom utensils and flies out to the bathroom)*
Ruth.   Sit down and have your breakfast, Travis.
Travis.   Mama, this is Friday. *(Gleefully)* Check coming tomorrow, huh?
Ruth.   You get your mind off money and eat your breakfast.
Travis (Eating). This is the morning we supposed to bring the fifty cents to school.
Ruth.   Well, I ain't got no fifty cents this morning.
Travis.   Teacher say we have to.
Ruth.   I don't care what teacher say. I ain't got it. Eat your breakfast, Travis.
Travis.   I *am* eating.
Ruth.   Hush up now and just eat!

(The boy gives her an exasperated look for her lack of understanding, and eats grudgingly)

Travis.   You think grandmama would have it?
Ruth.   No! And I want you to stop asking your grandmother for money, you hear me?
Travis (Outraged). Gaaaleee! I don't ask her, she just gimme it sometimes!
Ruth.   Travis Willard Younger—I got too much on me this morning to be—
Travis.   Maybe Daddy—
Ruth.   Travis!

(The boy hushes abruptly. They are both quiet and tense for several seconds)

Travis (Presently). Could I maybe go carry some groceries in front of the supermarket for a little while after school then?
Ruth.   Just hush, I said. *(Travis jabs his spoon into his cereal bowl viciously, and rests his head in anger upon his fists)* If you through eating, you can get over there and make up your bed.

(The boy obeys stiffly and crosses the room, almost mechanically, to the bed and more or less carefully folds the covering. He carries the bedding into his mother's room and returns with his books and cap)

Travis (Sulking and standing apart from her unnaturally). I'm gone.

171

Ruth (Looking up from the stove to inspect him automatically). Come here. *(He crosses to her and she studies his head)* If you don't take this comb and fix this here head, you better! *(Travis puts down his books with a great sigh of oppression, and crosses to the mirror. His mother mutters under her breath about his "slubbornness")* 'Bout to march out of here with that head looking just like chickens slept in it! I just don't know where you get your slubborn ways . . . And get your jacket, too. Looks chilly out this morning.
Travis (With conspicuously brushed hair and jacket). I'm gone.
Ruth. Get carfare and milk money—*(Waving one finger)*—and not a single penny for no caps, you hear me?
Travis (With sullen politeness). Yes'm.

(He turns in outrage to leave. His mother watches after him as in his frustration he approaches the door almost comically. When she speaks to him, her voice has become a very gentle tease)

Ruth (Mocking; as she thinks he would say it). Oh, Mama makes me so mad sometimes, I don't know what to do! *(She waits and continues to his back as he stands stock-still in front of the door)* I wouldn't kiss that woman good-bye for nothing in this world this morning! *(The boy finally turns around and rolls his eyes at her, knowing the mood has changed and he is vindicated; he does not, however, move toward her yet)* Not for nothing in this world! *(She finally laughs aloud at him and holds out her arms to him and we see that it is a way between them, very old and practiced. He crosses to her and allows her to embrace him warmly but keeps his face fixed with masculine rigidity. She holds him back from her presently and looks at him and runs her fingers over the features of his face. With utter gentleness—)* Now—whose little old angry man are you?
Travis (The masculinity and gruffness start to fade at last). Aw gaalee—Mama . . .
Ruth (Mimicking). Aw—gaaaaalleeeee, Mama! *(She pushes him, with rough playfulness and finality, toward the door)* Get on out of here or you going to be late.
Travis (In the face of love, new aggressiveness). Mama, could I *please* go carry groceries?
Ruth. Honey, it's starting to get so cold evenings.
Walter (Coming in from the bathroom and drawing a make-believe gun from a make-believe holster and shooting at his son). What is it he wants to do?
Ruth. Go carry groceries after school at the supermarket.
Walter. Well, let him go . . .
Travis (Quickly, to the ally). I have to—she won't gimme the fifty cents . . .
Walter (To his wife only). Why not?
Ruth (Simply, and with flavor). 'Cause we don't have it.

172

Walter (To Ruth only). What you tell the boy things like that for? *(Reaching down into his pants with a rather important gesture)* Here, son—

(He hands the boy the coin, but his eyes are directed to his wife's. Travis takes the money happily)

Travis. Thanks, Daddy.

(He starts out. Ruth watches both of them with murder in her eyes. Walter stands and stares back at her with defiance, and suddenly reaches into his pocket again on an afterthought)

Walter (Without even looking at his son, still staring hard at his wife). In fact, here's another fifty cents . . . Buy yourself some fruit today—or take a taxicab to school or something!
Travis. Whoopee—

(He leaps up and clasps his father around the middle with his legs, and they face each other in mutual appreciation; slowly Walter Lee peeks around the boy to catch the violent rays from his wife's eyes and draws his head back as if shot)

Walter. You better get down now—and get to school, man.
Travis (At the door). O.K. Good-bye.

(He exits)

Walter (After him, pointing with pride). That's my boy. *(She looks at him in disgust and turns back to her work)* You know what I was thinking 'bout in the bathroom this morning?
Ruth. No.
Walter. How come you always try to be so pleasant!
Ruth. What is there to be pleasant 'bout!
Walter. You want to know what I was thinking 'bout in the bathroom or not!
Ruth. I know what you thinking 'bout.
Walter (Ignoring her). 'Bout what me and Willy Harris was talking about last night.
Ruth (Immediately—a refrain). Willy Harris is a good-for-nothing loud mouth.
Walter. Anybody who talks to me has got to be a good-for-nothing loud mouth, ain't he? And what you know about who is just a good-for-nothing loud mouth? Charlie Atkins was just a "good-for-nothing loud mouth" too, wasn't he! When he wanted me to go in the dry-cleaning business with him. And now—he's grossing a hundred thousand a year. A hundred thousand dollars a year! You still call *him* a loud mouth!
Ruth (Bitterly). Oh, Walter Lee . . .

173

(She folds her head on her arms over the table)

Walter *(Rising and coming to her and standing over her)*. You tired, ain't you? Tired of everything. Me, the boy, the way we live—this beat-up hole—everything. Ain't you? *(She doesn't look up, doesn't answer)* So tired—moaning and groaning all the time, but you wouldn't do nothing to help, would you? You couldn't be on my side that long for nothing, could you?

Ruth. Walter, please leave me alone.

Walter. A man needs for a woman to back him up . . .

Ruth. Walter—

Walter. Mama would listen to you. You know she listen to you more than she do me and Bennie. She think more of you. All you have to do is just sit down with her when you drinking your coffee one morning and talking 'bout things like you do and—*(He sits down beside her and demonstrates graphically what he thinks her methods and tone should be)*—you just sip your coffee, see, and say easy like that you been thinking 'bout that deal Walter Lee is so interested in, 'bout the store and all, and sip some more coffee, like what you saying ain't really that important to you—And the next thing you know, she be listening good and asking you questions and when I come home—I can tell her the details. This ain't no fly-by-night proposition, baby. I mean we figured it out, me and Willy and Bobo.

Ruth (With a frown). Bobo?

Walter. Yeah. You see, this little liquor store we got in mind cost seventy-five thousand and we figured the initial investment on the place be 'bout thirty thousand, see. That be ten thousand each. Course, there's a couple of hundred you got to pay so's you don't spend your life just waiting for them clowns to let your license get approved—

Ruth. You mean graft?

Walter (Frowning impatiently). Don't call it that. See there, that just goes to show you what women understand about the world. Baby, don't *nothing* happen for you in this world 'less you pay *somebody* off!

Ruth. Walter, leave me alone! *(She raises her head and stares at him vigorously—then says, more quietly)* Eat your eggs, they gonna be cold.

Walter (Straightening up from her and looking off). That's it. There you are. Man say to his woman: I got me a dream. His woman say: Eat your eggs. *(Sadly, but gaining in power)* Man say: I got to take hold of this here world, baby! And a woman will say: Eat your eggs and go to work. *(Passionately now)* Man say: I got to change my life, I'm choking to death, baby! And his woman say—*(In utter anguish as he brings his fists down on his thighs)*—Your eggs is getting cold!

Ruth (Softly). Walter, that ain't none of our money.

Walter (Not listening at all or even looking at her). This morning, I was lookin' in the mirror and thinking about it . . . I'm thirty-five years old; I

been married eleven years and I got a boy who sleeps in the living room—
(Very, very quietly)—and all I got to give him is stories about how rich
white people live . . .

Ruth. Eat your eggs, Walter.

Walter. Damn my eggs . . . *damn all the eggs that ever was!*

Ruth. Then go to work.

Walter (Looking up at her). See—I'm trying to talk to you 'bout myself—
(Shaking his head with the repetition)—and all you can say is eat them
eggs and go to work.

Ruth (Wearily). Honey, you never say nothing new. I listen to you every
day, every night and every morning, and you never say nothing new.
(Shrugging) So you would rather *be* Mr. Arnold than be his chauffeur.
So—I would *rather* be living in Buckingham Palace.

Walter. That is just what is wrong with the colored woman in this
world . . . Don't understand about building their men up and making 'em
feel like they somebody. Like they can do something.

Ruth (Drily, but to hurt). There *are* colored men who do things.

Walter. No thanks to the colored woman.

Ruth. Well, being a colored woman, I guess I can't help myself none.

*(She rises and gets the ironing board and sets it up and attacks a huge pile of
rough-dried clothes, sprinkling them in preparation for the ironing and then
rolling them into tight fat balls)*

Walter (Mumbling). We one group of men tied to a race of women with small
minds.

*(His sister Beneatha enters. She is about twenty, as slim and intense as her
brother. She is not as pretty as her sister-in-law, but her lean, almost intellectual face has a handsomeness of its own. She wears a bright-red flannel
nightie, and her thick hair stands wildly about her head. Her speech is a mixture of many things; it is different from the rest of the family's insofar as education has permeated her sense of English—and perhaps the Midwest rather
than the South has finally—at last—won out in her inflection; but not altogether, because over all of it is a soft slurring and transformed use of vowels
which is the decided influence of the Southside. She passes through the room
without looking at either Ruth or Walter and goes to the outside door and
looks, a little blindly, out to the bathroom. She sees that it has been lost to the
Johnsons. She closes the door with a sleepy vengeance and crosses to the table
and sits down a little defeated)*

Beneatha. I am going to start timing those people.

Walter. You should get up earlier.

Beneatha (Her face in her hands. She is still fighting the urge to go back to bed). Really—would you suggest dawn? Where's the paper?

Walter (Pushing the paper across the table to her as he studies her almost clinically, as though he has never seen her before). You a horrible-looking chick at this hour.

Beneatha (Drily). Good morning, everybody.

Walter (Senselessly). How is school coming?

Beneatha (In the same spirit). Lovely. Lovely. And you know, biology is the greatest. *(Looking up at him)* I dissected something that looked just like you yesterday.

Walter. I just wondered if you've made up your mind and everything.

Beneatha (Gaining in sharpness and impatience). And what did I answer yesterday morning—and the day before that?

Ruth (From the ironing board, like someone disinterested and old). Don't be so nasty, Bennie.

Beneatha (Still to her brother). And the day before that and the day before that!

Walter (Defensively). I'm interested in you. Something wrong with that? Ain't many girls who decide—

Walter and Beneatha (In unison). —"to be a doctor."

(Silence)

Walter. Have we figured out yet just exactly how much medical school is going to cost?

Ruth. Walter Lee, why don't you leave that girl alone and get out of here to work?

Beneatha (Exits to the bathroom and bangs on the door). Come on out of there, please!

(She comes back into the room)

Walter (Looking at his sister intently). You know the check is coming tomorrow.

Beneatha (Turning on him with a sharpness all her own). That money belongs to Mama, Walter, and it's for her to decide how she wants to use it. I don't care if she wants to buy a house or a rocket ship or just nail it up somewhere and look at it. It's hers. Not ours—*hers.*

Walter (Bitterly). Now ain't that fine! You just got your mother's interest at heart, ain't you, girl? You such a nice girl—but if Mama got that money she can always take a few thousand and help you through school too—can't she?

Beneatha. I have never asked anyone around here to do anything for me!

Walter. No! And the line between asking and just accepting when the time comes is big and wide—ain't it it!

Beneatha (With fury). What do you want from me, Brother—that I quit school or just drop dead, which!

Walter. I don't want nothing but for you to stop acting holy 'round here. Me and Ruth done made some sacrifices for you—why can't you do something for the family?

Ruth. Walter, don't be dragging me in it.

Walter. You are in it—Don't you get up and go work in somebody's kitchen for the last three years to help put clothes on her back?

Ruth. Oh, Walter—that's not fair . . .

Walter. It ain't that nobody expects you to get on your knees and say thank you, Brother; thank you, Ruth; thank you, Mama—and thank you, Travis, for wearing the same pair of shoes for two semesters—

Beneatha (Dropping to her knees). Well—I *do*—all right?—thank everybody . . . and forgive me for ever wanting to be anything at all . . . forgive me, forgive me!

Ruth. Please stop it! Your mama'll hear you.

Walter. Who the hell told you you had to be a doctor? If you so crazy 'bout messing 'round with sick people—then go be a nurse like other women—or just get married and be quiet . . .

Beneatha. Well—you finally got it said . . . It took you three years but you finally got it said. Walter, give up; leave me alone—it's Mama's money.

Walter. *He was my father, too!*

Beneatha. So what? He was mine, too—and Travis' grandfather—but the insurance money belongs to Mama. Picking on me is not going to make her give it to you to invest in any liquor stores—*(Underbreath, dropping into a chair)*—and I for one say, God bless Mama for that!

Walter (To Ruth). See—did you hear? Did you hear!

Ruth. Honey, please go to work.

Walter. Nobody in this house is ever going to understand me.

Beneatha. Because you're a nut.

Walter. Who's a nut?

Beneatha. You—you are a nut. Thee is mad, boy.

Walter (Looking at his wife and his sister from the door, very sadly). The world's most backward race of people, and that's a fact.

Beneatha (Turning slowly in her chair). And then there are all those prophets who would lead us out of the wilderness—*(Walter slams out of the house)*—into the swamps!

Ruth. Bennie, why you always gotta be pickin' on your brother? Can't you be a little sweeter sometimes? *(Door opens. Walter walks in)*

Walter (To Ruth). I need some money for carfare.

Ruth (Looks at him, then warms; teasing, but tenderly). Fifty cents? *(She goes to her bag and gets money)* Here, take a taxi.

(Walter exits. Mama enters. She is a woman in her early sixties, full-bodied and strong. She is one of those women of a certain grace and beauty who wear it so unobtrusively that it takes a while to notice. Her dark-brown face is surrounded by the total whiteness of her hair, and, being a woman who has adjusted to many things in life and overcome many more, her face is full of strength. She has, we can see, wit and faith of a kind that keep her eyes lit and full of interest and expectancy. She is, in a word, a beautiful woman. Her bearing is perhaps most like the noble bearing of the women of the Hereros of Southwest Africa—rather as if she imagines that as she walks she still bears a basket or a vessel upon her head. Her speech, on the other hand, is as careless as her carriage is precise—she is inclined to slur everything—but her voice is perhaps not so much quiet as simply soft)

Mama. Who that 'round here slamming doors at this hour?

(She crosses through the room, goes to the window, opens it, and brings in a feeble little plant growing doggedly in a small pot on the window sill. She feels the dirt and puts it back out)

Ruth. That was Walter Lee. He and Bennie was at it again.
Mama. My children and they tempers. Lord, if this little old plant don't get more sun than it's been getting it ain't never going to see spring again. *(She turns from the window)* What's the matter with you this morning, Ruth? You looks right peaked. You aiming to iron all them things? Leave some for me. I'll get to 'em this afternoon. Bennie honey, it's too drafty for you to be sitting 'round half dressed. Where's your robe?
Beneatha. In the cleaners.
Mama. Well, go get mine and put it on.
Beneatha. I'm not cold, Mama, honest.
Mama. I know—but you so thin . . .
Beneatha (Irritably). Mama, I'm not cold.
Mama (Seeing the make-down bed as Travis has left it). Lord have mercy, look at that poor bed. Bless his heart—he tries, don't he?

(She moves to the bed Travis has sloppily made up)

Ruth. No—he don't half try at all 'cause he knows you going to come along behind him and fix everything. That's just how come he don't know how to do nothing right now—you done spoiled that boy so.
Mama. Well—he's a little boy. Ain't supposed to know 'bout housekeeping. My baby, that's what he is. What you fix for his breakfast this morning?
Ruth (Angrily). I feed my son, Lena!

Mama. I ain't meddling—*(Underbreath; busy-bodyish)* I just noticed all last week he had cold cereal, and when it starts getting this chilly in the fall a child ought to have some hot grits or something when he goes out in the cold—
Ruth (Furious). I gave him hot oats—is that all right!
Mama. I ain't meddling. *(Pause)* Put a lot of nice butter on it? *(Ruth shoots her an angry look and does not reply)* He likes lots of butter.
Ruth (Exasperated). Lena—
Mama (To Beneatha. Mama is inclined to wander conversationally sometimes). What was you and your brother fussing 'bout this morning?
Beneatha. It's not important, Mama.

(She gets up and goes to look out at the bathroom, which is apparently free, and she picks up her towels and rushes out)

Mama. What was they fighting about?
Ruth. Now you know as well as I do.
Mama (Shaking her head). Brother still worrying hisself sick about that money?
Ruth. You know he is.
Mama. You had breakfast?
Ruth. Some coffee.
Mama. Girl you better start eating and looking after yourself better. You almost thin as Travis.
Ruth. Lena—
Mama. Un-hunh?
Ruth. What are you going to do with it?
Mama. Now don't you start, child. It's too early in the morning to be talking about money. It ain't Christian.
Ruth. It's just that he got his heart set on that store—
Mama. You mean that liquor store that Willy Harris want him to invest in?
Ruth. Yes—
Mama. We ain't no business people, Ruth. We just plain working folks.
Ruth. Ain't nobody business people till they go into business. Walter Lee say colored people ain't never going to start getting ahead till they start gambling on some different kinds of things in the world—investments and things.
Mama. What done got into you, girl? Walter Lee done finally sold you on investing.
Ruth. No. Mama, something is happening between Walter and me. I don't know what it is—but he needs something—something I can't give him any more. He needs this chance, Lena.
Mama (Frowning deeply). But liquor, honey—

Ruth. Well—like Walter say—I spec people going to always be drinking themselves some liquor.

Mama. Well—whether they drinks it or not ain't none of my business. But whether I go into business selling it to 'em *is,* and I don't want that on my ledger this late in life. *(Stopping suddenly and studying her daughter-in-law)* Ruth Younger, what's the matter with you today? You look like you could fall over right there.

Ruth. I'm tired.

Mama. Then you better stay home from work today.

Ruth. I can't stay home. She'd be calling up the agency and screaming at them, "My girl didn't come in today—send me somebody! My girl didn't come in!" Oh, she just have a fit . . .

Mama. Well, let her have it. I'll just call her up and say you got the flu—

Ruth (Laughing). Why the flu?

Mama. 'Cause it sounds respectable to 'em. Something white people get, too. They know 'bout the flu. Otherwise they think you been cut up or something when you tell 'em you sick.

Ruth. I got to go in. We need the money.

Mama. Somebody would of thought my children done all but starved to death the way they talk about money here late. Child, we got a great big old check coming tomorrow.

Ruth (Sincerely, but also self-righteously). Now that's your money. It ain't got nothing to do with me. We all feel like that—Walter and Bennie and me—even Travis.

Mama (Thoughtfully, and suddenly very far away). Ten thousand dollars—

Ruth. Sure is wonderful.

Mama. Ten thousand dollars.

Ruth. You know what you should do, Miss Lena? You should take yourself a trip somewhere. To Europe or South America or someplace—

Mama (Throwing up her hands at the thought). Oh, child!

Ruth. I'm serious. Just pack up and leave! Go on away and enjoy yourself some. Forget about the family and have yourself a ball for once in your life—

Mama (Drily). You sound like I'm just about ready to die. Who'd go with me? What I look like wandering 'round Europe by myself?

Ruth. Shoot—these here rich white women do it all the time. They don't think nothing of packing up they suitcases and piling on one of them big steamships and—swoosh!—they gone, child.

Mama. Something always told me I wasn't no rich white woman.

Ruth. Well—what are you going to do with it then?

Mama. I ain't rightly decided. *(Thinking. She speaks now with emphasis)* Some of it got to be put away for Beneatha and her schoolin'—and ain't nothing going to touch that part of it. Nothing. *(She waits several seconds, trying to make up her mind about something, and looks at Ruth a little tentatively before going on)* Been thinking that we maybe could meet the notes on a little old two-story somewhere, with a yard where Travis could play in the summertime, if we use part of the insurance for a down payment and everybody kind of pitch in. I could maybe take on a little day work again, few days a week—

Ruth (Studying her mother-in-law furtively and concentrating on her ironing, anxious to encourage without seeming to). Well, Lord knows, we've put enough rent into this here rat trap to pay for four houses by now . . .

Mama (Looking up at the words "rat trap" and then looking around and leaning back and sighing—in a suddenly reflective mood—). "Rat trap"— yes, that's all it is. *(Smiling)* I remember just as well the day me and Big Walter moved in here. Hadn't been married but two weeks and wasn't planning on living here no more than a year. *(She shakes her head at the dissolved dream)* We was going to set away, little by little, don't you know, and buy a little place out in Morgan park. We had even picked out the house. *(Chuckling a little)* Looks right dumpy today. But Lord, child, you should know all the dreams I had 'bout buying that house and fixing it up and making me a little garden in the back—*(She waits and stops smiling)* And didn't none of it happen.

(Dropping her hands in a futile gesture)

Ruth (Keeps her head down, ironing). Yes, life can be a barrel of disappointments, sometimes.

Mama. Honey, Big Walter would come in here some nights back then and slump down on that couch there and just look at the rug, and look at me and look at the rug and then back at me—and I'd know he was down then . . . really down. *(After a second very long and thoughtful pause; she is seeing back to times that only she can see)* And then, Lord, when I lost that baby—little Claude—I almost thought I was going to lose Big Walter too. Oh, that man grieved hisself! He was one man to love his children.

Ruth. Ain't nothin' can tear at you like losin' your baby.

Mama. I guess that's how come that man finally worked hisself to death like he done. Like he was fighting his own war with this here world that took his baby from him.

Ruth. He sure was a fine man, all right. I always liked Mr. Younger.

Mama. Crazy 'bout his children! God knows there was plenty wrong with Walter Younger—hard-headed, mean, kind of wild with women—plenty wrong with him. But he sure loved his children. Always wanted them to have something—be something. That's where Brother gets all these notions, I reckon. Big Walter used to say, he'd get right wet in the eyes sometimes, lean his head back with the water standing in his eyes and say,

"Seem like God didn't see fit to give the black man nothing but dreams—but He did give us children to make them dreams seem worth while." *(She smiles)* He could talk like that, don't you know.
Ruth.   Yes, he sure could. He was a good man, Mr. Younger.
Mama.   Yes, a fine man—just couldn't never catch up with his dreams, that's all.

(Beneatha comes in, brushing her hair and looking up to the ceiling, where the sound of a vacuum cleaner has started up)

Beneatha.   What could be so dirty on that woman's rugs that she has to vacuum them every single day?
Ruth.   I wish certain young women 'round here who I could name would take inspiration about certain rugs in a certain apartment I could also mention.
Beneatha (Shrugging).   How much cleaning can a house need, for Christ's sakes.
Mama (Not liking the Lord's name used thus).   Bennie!
Ruth.   Just listen to her—just listen!
Beneatha.   Oh, God!
Mama.   If you use the Lord's name just one more time—
Beneatha (A bit of a whine).   Oh, Mama—
Ruth.   Fresh—just fresh as salt, this girl!
Beneatha (Drily).   Well—if the salt loses its savor—
Mama.   Now that will do. I just ain't going to have you 'round here reciting the scriptures in vain—you hear me?
Beneatha.   How did I manage to get on everybody's wrong side by just walking into a room?
Ruth.   If you weren't so fresh—
Beneatha.   Ruth, I'm twenty years old.
Mama.   What time you be home from school today?
Beneatha.   Kind of late. *(With enthusiasm)* Madeline is going to start my guitar lessons today.

(Mama and Ruth look up with the same expression)

Mama.   Your *what* kind of lessons?
Beneatha.   Guitar.
Ruth.   Oh, Father!
Mama.   How come you done taken it in your mind to learn to play the guitar?
Beneatha.   I just want to, that's all.
Mama (Smiling).   Lord, child, don't you know what to do with yourself? How long it going to be before you get tired of this now—like you got

tired of that little play-acting group you joined last year? *(Looking at Ruth)* And what was it the year before that?

Ruth. The horseback-riding club for which she bought that fifty-five-dollar riding habit that's been hanging in the closet ever since!

Mama (To Beneatha). Why you got to flit so from one thing to another, baby?

Beneatha (Sharply). I just want to learn to play the guitar. Is there anything wrong with that?

Mama. Ain't nobody trying to stop you. I just wonders sometimes why you has to flit so from one thing to another all the time. You ain't never done nothing with all that camera equipment you brought home—

Beneatha. I don't flit! I—I experiment with different forms of expression—

Ruth. Like riding a horse?

Beneatha. —People have to express themselves one way or another.

Mama. What is it you want to express?

Beneatha (Angrily). Me! *(Mama and Ruth look at each other and burst into raucous laughter)* Don't worry—I don't expect you to understand.

Mama (To change the subject). Who you going out with tomorrow night?

Beneatha (With displeasure). George Murchison again.

Mama (Pleased). Oh—you getting a little sweet on him?

Ruth. You ask me, this child ain't sweet on nobody but herself—*(Underbreath)* Express herself!

(They laugh)

Beneatha. Oh—I like George all right, Mama. I mean I like him enough to go out with him and stuff, but—

Ruth (For devilment). What does *and stuff* mean?

Beneatha. Mind your own business.

Mama. Stop picking at her now, Ruth. *(A thoughtful pause, and then a suspicious sudden look at her daughter as she turns in her chair for emphasis)* What *does* it mean?

Beneatha (Wearily). Oh, I just mean I couldn't ever really be serious about George. He's—he's so shallow.

Ruth. Shallow—what do you mean he's shallow? He's *Rich!*

Mama. Hush, Ruth.

Beneatha. I know he's rich. He knows he's rich, too.

Ruth. Well—what other qualities a man got to have to satisfy you, little girl?

Beneatha. You wouldn't even begin to understand. Anybody who married Walter could not possibly understand.

Mama (Outraged). What kind of way is that to talk about your brother?

Beneatha. Brother is a flip—let's face it.

Mama (To Ruth, helplessly). What's a flip?

Ruth (Glad to add kindling). She's saying he's crazy.

Beneatha. Not crazy. Brother isn't really crazy yet—he—he's an elaborate neurotic.

Mama. Hush your mouth!

Beneatha. As for George. Well. George looks good—he's got a beautiful car and he takes me to nice places and, as my sister-in-law says, he is probably the richest boy I will ever get to know and I even like him sometimes—but if the Youngers are sitting around waiting to see if their little Bennie is going to tie up the family with the Murchisons, they are wasting their time.

Ruth. You mean you wouldn't marry George Murchison if he asked you someday? That pretty, rich thing? Honey, I knew you was odd—

Beneatha. No I would not marry him if all I felt for him was what I feel now. Besides, George's family wouldn't really like it.

Mama. Why not?

Beneatha. Oh, Mama—The Murchisons are honest-to-God-real-*live*-rich colored people, and the only people in the world who are more snobbish than rich white people are rich colored people. I thought everybody knew that. I've met Mrs. Murchison. She's a scene!

Mama. You must not dislike people 'cause they well off, honey.

Beneatha. Why not? It makes just as much sense as disliking people 'cause they are poor, and lots of people do that.

Ruth (A wisdom-of-the-ages manner. To Mama). Well, she'll get over some of this—

Beneatha. Get over it? What are you talking about, Ruth? Listen, I'm going to be a doctor. I'm not worried about who I'm going to marry yet—if I ever get married.

Mama and Ruth. If!

Mama. Now, Bennie—

Beneatha. Oh, I probably will ... but first I'm going to be a doctor, and George, for one, still thinks that's pretty funny. I couldn't be bothered with that. I am going to be a doctor and everybody around here better understand that!

Mama (Kindly). 'Course you going to be a doctor, honey, God willing.

Beneatha (Drily). God hasn't got a thing to do with it.

Mama. Beneatha—that just wasn't necessary.

Beneatha. Well—neither is God. I get sick of hearing about God.

Mama. Beneatha!

Beneatha. I mean it! I'm just tired of hearing about God all the time. What has He got to do with anything? Does he pay tuition?

Mama. You 'bout to get your fresh little jaw slapped!

Ruth. That's just what she needs, all right!

Beneatha.   Why? Why can't I say what I want to around here, like every-body else?

Mama.   It don't sound nice for a young girl to say things like that—you wasn't brought up that way. Me and your father went to trouble to get you and Brother to church every Sunday.

Beneatha.   Mama, you don't understand. It's all a matter of ideas, and God is just one idea I don't accept. It's not important. I am not going out and be immoral or commit crimes because I don't believe in God. I don't even think about it. It's just that I get tired of Him getting credit for all the things the human race achieves through its own stubborn effort. There simply is no blasted God—there is only man and it is he who makes miracles!

(Mama absorbs this speech, studies her daughter and rises slowly and crosses to Beneatha and slaps her powerfully across the face. After, there is only silence and the daughter drops her eyes from her mother's face, and Mama is very tall before her)

Mama.   Now—you say after me, in my mother's house there is still God. *(There is a long pause and Beneatha stares at the floor wordlessly. Mama repeats the phrase with precision and cool emotion)* In my mother's house there is still God.

Beneatha.   In my mother's house there is still God.

(A long pause)

Mama (Walking away from Beneatha, too disturbed for triumphant posture. Stopping and turning back to her daughter). There are some ideas we ain't going to have in this house. Not long as I am at the head of this family.

Beneatha.   Yes, ma'am.

(Mama walks out of the room)

Ruth (Almost gently, with profound understanding). You think you a woman, Bennie—but you still a little girl. What you did was childish—so you got treated like a child.

Beneatha.   I see. *(Quietly)* I also see that everybody thinks it's all right for Mama to be a tyrant. But all the tyranny in the world will never put a God in the heavens!

(She picks up her books and goes out)

Ruth (Goes to Mama's door). She said she was sorry.

185

Mama (Coming out, going to her plant). They frightens me, Ruth. My children.
Ruth. You got good children, Lena. They just a little off sometimes—but they're good.
Mama. No—there's something come down between me and them that don't let us understand each other and I don't know what it is. One done almost lost his mind thinking 'bout money all the time and the other done commence to talk about things I can't seem to understand in no form or fashion. What is it that's changing, Ruth?
Ruth (Soothingly, older than her years). Now . . . you taking it all too seriously. You just got strong-willed children and it takes a strong woman like you to keep 'em in hand.
Mama (Looking at her plant and sprinkling a little water on it). They spirited all right, my children. Got to admit they got spirit—Bennie and Walter. Like this little old plant that ain't never had enough sunshine or nothing—and look at it . . .

(She has her back to Ruth, who has had to stop ironing and lean against something and put the back of her hand to her forehead)

Ruth (Trying to keep Mama from noticing). You . . . sure . . . loves that little old thing, don't you?
Mama. Well, I always wanted me a garden like I used to see sometimes at the back of the houses down home. This plant is close as I ever got to having one. *(She looks out of the window as she replaces the plant)* Lord, ain't nothing as dreary as the view from this window on a dreary day, is there? Why ain't you singing this morning, Ruth? Sing that "No Ways Tired." That song always lifts me up so—*(She turns at last to see that Ruth has slipped quietly into a chair, in a state of semiconsciousness)* Ruth! Ruth honey—what's the matter with you . . . Ruth!

CURTAIN

Scene II

It is the following morning; a Saturday morning, and house cleaning is in progress at the Youngers. Furniture has been shoved hither and yon and Mama is giving the kitchen-area walls a washing down. Beneatha, in dungarees, with a handkerchief tied around her face, is spraying insecticide into the cracks in the walls. As they work, the radio is on and a Southside disk-jockey program is inappropriately filling the house with a rather exotic saxophone blues. Travis, the sole idle one, is leaning on his arms, looking out of the window.

Travis. Grandmama, that stuff Bennie is using smells awful. Can I go downstairs, please?

Mama. Did you get all them chores done already? I ain't seen you doing much.

Travis Yes'm—finished early. Where did Mama go this morning?

Mama (Looking at Beneatha). She had to go on a little errand.

Travis. Where?

Mama. To tend to her business.

Travis. Can I go outside then?

Mama. Oh, I guess so. You better stay right in front of the house, though . . . and keep a good lookout for the postman.

Travis. Yes'm. *(He starts out and decides to give his Aunt Beneatha a good swat on the legs as he passes her)* Leave them poor little old cockroaches alone, they ain't bothering you none.

(He runs as she swings the spray gun at him both viciously and playfully. Walter enters from the bedroom and goes to the phone)

Mama. Look out there, girl, before you be spilling some of that stuff on that child!

Travis (Teasing). That's right—look out now!

(He exits)

Beneatha (Drily). I can't imagaine that it would hurt him—it has never hurt the roaches.

Mama. Well, little boys' hides ain't as tough as Southside roaches.

Walter (Into phone). Hello—Let me talk to Willy Harris.

Mama. You better get over there behind the bureau. I seen one marching out of there like Napoleon yesterday.

Walter. Hello, Willy? It ain't come yet. It'll be here in a few minutes. Did the lawyer give you the papers?

Beneatha. There's really only one way to get rid of them, Mama—

Mama. How?

Beneatha. Set fire to this building.

Walter. Good. Good. I'll be right over.

Beneatha. Where did Ruth go, Walter?

Walter. I don't know.

(He exits abruptly)

Beneatha. Mama, where did Ruth go?

Mama (Looking at her with meaning). To the doctor, I think.

187

Beneatha. The doctor? What's the matter? *(They exchange glances)* You don't think—

Mama (With her sense of drama). Now I ain't saying what I think. But I ain't never been wrong 'bout a woman neither.

(The phone rings)

Beneatha (At the phone). Hay-lo . . . *(Pause, and a moment of recognition)* Well—when did you get back! . . . And how was it? . . . Of course I've missed you—in my way . . . This morning? No . . . house cleaning and all that and Mama hates it if I let people come over when the house is like this . . . You *have*? Well, that's different . . . What is it—Oh, what the hell, come on over . . . Right, see you then.

(She hangs up)

Mama (Who has listened vigorously, as is her habit). Who is that you inviting over here with this house looking like this? You ain't got the pride you was born with!

Beneatha. Asagai doesn't care how houses look, Mama—he's an intellectual.

Mama. Who?

Beneatha. Asagai—Joseph Asagai. He's an African boy I met on campus. He's been studying in Canada all summer.

Mama. What's his name?

Beneatha. Asagai, Joseph. Ah-sah-guy . . . He's from Nigeria.

Mama. Oh, that's the little country that was founded by slaves way back . . .

Beneatha. No, Mama—that's Liberia.

Mama. I don't think I never met no African before.

Beneatha. Well, do me a favor and don't ask him a whole lot of ignorant questions about Africans. I mean, do they wear clothes and all that—

Mama. Well, now, I guess if you think we so ignorant 'round here maybe you shouldn't bring your friends here—

Beneatha. It's just that people ask such crazy things. All anyone seems to know about when it comes to Africa is Tarzan—

Mama (Indignantly). Why should I know anything about Africa?

Beneatha. Why do you give money at church for the missionary work?

Mama. Well, that's to help save people.

Beneatha. You mean save them from *heathenism*—

Mama (Innocently). Yes.

Beneatha. I'm afraid they need more salvation from the British and the French.

(Ruth comes in forlornly and pulls off her coat with dejection. They both turn to look at her)

Ruth (Dispiritedly). Well, I guess from all the happy faces—everybody knows.
Beneatha. You pregnant?
Mama. Lord have mercy, I sure hope it's a little old girl. Travis ought to have a sister.

(Beneatha and Ruth give her a hopeless look for this grandmotherly enthusiasm)

Beneatha. How far along are you?
Ruth. Two months.
Beneatha. Did you mean to? I mean did you plan it or was it an accident?
Mama. What do you know about planning or not planning?
Beneatha. Oh, Mama.
Ruth (Wearily). She's twenty years old, Lena.
Beneatha. Did you plan it, Ruth?
Ruth. Mind your own business.
Beneatha. It is my business—where is he going to live, on the *roof? (There is silence following the remark as the three women react to the sense of it)* Gee—I didn't mean that, Ruth, honest. Gee, I don't feel like that at all. I—I think it is wonderful.
Ruth (Dully). Wonderful.
Beneatha. Yes—really.
Mama (Looking at Ruth, worried). Doctor say everything going to be all right?
Ruth (Far away). Yes—she says everything is going to be fine . . .
Mama (Immediately suspicious). "She" —What doctor you went to?

(Ruth folds over, near hysteria)

Mama (Worriedly hovering over Ruth). Ruth honey—what's the matter with you—you sick?

(Ruth has her fists clenched on her thighs and is fighting hard to suppress a scream that seems to be rising in her)

Beneatha. What's the matter with her, Mama?
Mama (Working her fingers in Ruth's shoulder to relax her) She be all right. Women gets right depressed sometimes when they get her way. *(Speaking softly, expertly, rapidly)* Now you just relax. That's right . . . just lean back, don't think 'bout nothing at all . . . nothing at all—
Ruth. I'm all right . . .

(The glassy-eyed look melts and then she collapses into a fit of heavy sobbing. The bell rings)

Beneatha. Oh, my God—that must be Asagai.
Mama (To Ruth) Come on now, honey. You need to lie down and rest awhile . . . then have some nice hot food.

(They exit, Ruth's weight on her mother-in-law. Beneatha, herself profoundly disturbed, opens the door to admit a rather dramatic-looking young man with a large package)

Asagai. Hello, Alaiyo—
Beneatha (Holding the door open and regarding him with pleasure). Hello . . . *(Long pause)* Well—come in. And please excuse everything. My mother was very upset about my letting anyone come here with the place like this.
Asagai (Coming into the room). You look disturbed too . . . Is something wrong?
Beneatha (Still at the door, absently). Yes . . . we've all got acute ghetto-itus. *(She smiles and comes toward him, finding a cigarette and sitting)* So—sit down! How was Canada?
Asagai (A sophisticate). Canadian.
Beneatha (Looking at him). I'm very glad you are back.
Asagai (Looking back at her in turn). Are you really?
Beneatha. Yes—very.
Asagai. Why—you were quite glad when I went away. What happened?
Beneatha. You went away.
Asagai. Ahhhhhhhh.
Beneatha. Before—you wanted to be so serious before there was time.
Asagai. How much time must there be before one knows what one feels?
Beneatha (Stalling this particular conversation. Her hands pressed together, in a deliberately childish gesture). What did you bring me?
Asagai (Handing her the package). Open it and see.
Beneatha (Eagerly opening the package and drawing out some records and the colorful robes of a Nigerian woman). Oh, Asagai! . . . You got them for me! . . . How beautiful . . . and the records too! *(She lifts out the robes and runs to the mirror with them and holds the drapery up in front of herself)*
Asagai (Coming to her at the mirror). I shall have to teach you how to drape it properly. *(He flings the material about her for the moment and stands back to look at her)* Ah—Oh-pay-gay-day, oh-gbah-mu-shay. *(A Yoruba exclamation for admiration)* You wear it well . . . very well . . . mutilated hair and all.
Beneatha (Turning suddenly). My hair—what's wrong with my hair?
Asagai (Shrugging). Were you born with it like that?
Beneatha (Reaching up to touch it). No . . . of course not.

(She looks back to the mirror, disturbed)

Asagai (Smiling). How then?

Beneatha. You know perfectly well how . . . as crinkly as yours . . . that's how.

Asagai. And it is ugly to you that way?

Beneatha (Quickly). Oh, no — not ugly . . . *(More slowly, apologetically)* But it's so hard to manage when it's, well — raw.

Asagai. And so to accommodate that — you mutilate it every week?

Beneatha. It's not mutilation!

Asagai (Laughing aloud at her seriousness). Oh . . . please! I am only teasing you because you are so very serious about these things. *(He stands back from her and folds his arms across his chest as he watches her pulling at her hair and frowning in the mirror)* Do you remember the first time you met me at school? . . . *(He laughs)* You came up to me and you said — and I thought you were the most serious little thing I had ever seen — you said: *(He imitates her)* "Mr. Asagai — I want very much to talk with you. About Africa. You see, Mr. Asagai, I am looking for my *identity*!"

(He laughs)

Beneatha (Turning to him, not laughing). Yes —

(Her face is quizzical, profoundly disturbed)

Asagai (Still teasing and reaching out and taking her face in his hands and turning her profile to him). Well . . . it is true that this is not so much a profile of a Hollywood queen as perhaps a queen of the Nile — *(A mock dismissal of the importance of the question)* But what does it matter? Assimilationism is so popular in your country.

Beneatha (Wheeling, passionately, sharply). I am not an assimilationist!

Asagai (The protest hangs in the room for a moment and Asagai studies her, his laughter fading). Such a serious one. *(There is a pause)* So — you like the robes? You must take excellent care of them — they are from my sister's personal wardrobe.

Beneatha (With incredulity). You — you sent all the way home — for me?

Asagai (With charm). For you — I would do much more . . . Well, that is what I came for. I must go.

Beneatha. Will you call me Monday?

Asagai. Yes . . . We have a great deal to talk about. I mean about identity and time and all that.

Beneatha. Time?

Asagai. Yes. About how much time one needs to know what one feels.

Beneatha. You never understood that there is more than one kind of feeling which can exist between a man and a woman — or, at least, there should be.

Asagai (Shaking his head negatively but gently). No. Between a man and a woman there need be only one kind of feeling. I have that for you . . . Now even . . . right this moment . . .

Beneatha. I know—and by itself—it won't do. I can find that anywhere.

Asagai. For a woman it should be enough.

Beneatha. I know—because that's what it says in all the novels that men write. But it isn't. Go ahead and laugh—but I'm not interested in being someone's little episode in America or—*(With feminine vengeance)*—one of them! *(Asagai has burst into laughter again)* That's funny as hell, huh!

Asagai. It's just that every American girl I have known has said that to me. White—black—in this you are all the same. And the same speech, too!

Beneatha (Angrily). Yuk, yuk, yuk!

Asagai. It's how you can be sure that the world's most liberated women are not liberated at all. You all talk about it too much!

(Mama enters and is immediately all social charm because of the presence of a guest)

Beneatha. Oh—Mama—this is Mr. Asagai.

Mama. How do you do?

Asagai (Total politeness to an elder). How do you do, Mrs. Younger. Please forgive me for coming at such an outrageous hour on a Saturday.

Mama. Well, you are quite welcome. I just hope you understand that our house don't always look like this. *(Chatterish)* You must come again. I would love to hear all about—*(Not sure of the name)*—your country. I think it's so sad the way our American Negroes don't know nothing about Africa 'cept Tarzan and all that. And all that money they pour into these churches when they ought to be helping you people over there drive out them French and Englishmen done taken away your land.

(The mother flashes a slightly superior look at her daughter upon completion of the recitation)

Asagai (Taken aback by this sudden and acutely unrelated expression of sympathy). Yes . . . yes . . .

Mama (Smiling at him suddenly and relaxing and looking him over). How many miles is it from here to where you come from?

Asagai. Many thousands.

Mama (Looking at him as she would Walter). I bet you don't half look after yourself, being away from your mama either. I spec you better come 'round here from time to time and get yourself some decent homecooked meals . . .

Asagai (Moved). Thank you. Thank you very much. *(They are all quiet, then—)* Well . . . I must go, I will call you Monday, Alaiyo.

192

Mama. What's that he call you?

Asagai. Oh—"Alaiyo." I hope you don't mind. It is what you would call a nickname, I think. It is a Yoruba word. I am a Yoruba.

Mama (Looking at Beneatha). I—I thought he was from—

Asagai (Understanding). Nigeria is my country. Yoruba is my tribal origin—

Beneatha. You didn't tell us what Alaiyo means . . . for all I know, you might be calling me Little Idiot or something . . .

Asagai. Well . . . let me see . . . I do not know how just to explain it . . . The sense of a thing can be so different when it changes languages.

Beneatha. You're evading.

Asagai. No—really it is difficult . . . *(Thinking)* It means . . . it means One for Whom Bread—Food—Is Not Enough. *(He looks at her)* Is that all right?

Beneatha (Understanding, softly). Thank you.

Mama (Looking from one to the other and not understanding any of it). Well . . . that's nice . . . You must come see us again—Mr.—

Asagai. Ah-sah-guy . . .

Mama. Yes . . . Do come again.

Asagai. Good-bye.

(He exits)

Mama (After him). Lord, that's a pretty thing just went out here! *(Insinuatingly, to her daughter)* Yes, I guess I see why we done commence to get so interested in Africa 'round here. Missionaries my aunt Jenny!

(She exits)

Beneatha. Oh, Mama! . . .

(She picks up the Nigerian dress and holds it up to her in front of the mirror again. She sets the headdress on haphazardly and then notices her hair again and clutches at it and then replaces the headdress and frowns at herself Then she starts to wriggle in front of the mirror as she thinks a Nigerian woman might. Travis enters and regards her)

Travis. You cracking up?

Beneatha. Shut up.

(She pulls the headdress off and looks at herself in the mirror and clutches at her hair again and squinches her eyes as if trying to imagine something. Then, suddenly, she gets her raincoat and kerchief and hurriedly prepares for going out)

Mama (Coming back into the room). She's resting now. Travis, baby, run next door and ask Miss Johnson to please let me have a little kitchen cleanser. This here can is empty as Jacob's kettle.

Travis. I just came in.

Mama. Do as you told. *(He exits and she looks at her daughter)* Where you going?

Beneatha (Halting at the door). To become a queen of the Nile!

(She exits in a breathless blaze of glory. Ruth appears in the bedroom doorway)

Mama. Who told you to get up?

Ruth. Ain't nothing wrong with me to be lying in no bed for. Where did Bennie go?

Mama (Drumming her fingers). Far as I could make out—to Egypt. *(Ruth just looks at her)* What time is it getting to?

Ruth. Ten twenty. And the mailman going to ring that bell this morning just like he done every morning for the last umpteen years.

(Travis comes in with the cleanser can)

Travis. She say to tell you that she don't have much.

Mama (Angrily). Lord, some people I could name sure is tight-fisted! *(Directing her grandson)* Mark two cans of cleanser down on the list there. If she that hard up for kitchen cleanser, I sure don't want to forget to get her none!

Ruth. Lena—maybe the woman is just short on cleanser—

Mama (Not listening). —Much baking powder as she done borrowed from me all these years, she could of done gone into the baking business!

(The bell sounds suddenly and sharply and all three are stunned—serious and silent—mid-speech. In spite of all the other conversations and distractions of the morning, this is what they have been waiting for, even Travis, who looks helplessly from his mother to his grandmother. Ruth is the first to come to life again)

Ruth (To Travis). Get down them steps, boy!

(Travis snaps to life and flies out to get the mail)

Mama (Her eyes wide, her hand to her breast). You mean it done really come?

Ruth (Excited). Oh, Miss Lena!

Mama (Collecting herself). Well . . . I don't know what we all so excited about 'round here for. We known it was coming for months.

Ruth. That's a whole lot different from having it come and being able to hold it in your hands . . . a piece of paper worth ten thousand dollars . . . *(Travis bursts back into the room. He holds the envelope high above his head, like a little dancer, his face is radiant and he is breathless. He moves to his grand-mother with sudden slow ceremony and puts the envelope into her hands. She accepts it, and then merely holds it and looks at it)* Come on! Open it . . . Lord have mercy, I wish Walter Lee was here!

Travis. Open it, Grandmama!

Mama (Staring at it). Now you all be quiet. It's just a check.

Ruth. Open it . . .

Mama (Still staring at it). Now don't act silly . . . We ain't never been no people to act silly 'bout no money—

Ruth (Swiftly). We ain't never had none before—open it!

(Mama finally makes a good strong tear and pulls out the thin blue slice of paper and inspects it closely. The boy and his mother study it raptly over Mama's shoulders)

Mama. Travis! *(She is counting off with doubt).* Is that the right number of zeros.

Travis. Yes'm . . . ten thousand dollars. Gaalee, Grandmama, you rich.

Mama (She holds the check away from her, still looking at it. Slowly her face sobers into a mask of unhappiness). Ten thousand dollars. *(She hands it to Ruth)* Put it away somewhere, Ruth. *(She does not look at Ruth; her eyes seem to be seeing something somewhere very far off)* Ten thousand dollars they give you. Ten thousand dollars.

Travis (To his mother, sincerely). What's the matter with Grandmama—don't she want to be rich?

Ruth (Distractedly). You go on out and play now, baby. *(Travis exits. Mama starts wiping dishes absently, humming intently to herself. Ruth turns to her, with kind exasperation)* You've gone and got yourself upset.

Mama (Not looking at her). I spec if it wasn't for you all . . . I would just put that money away or give it to the church or something.

Ruth. Now what kind of talk is that. Mr. Younger would just be plain mad if he could hear you talking foolish like that.

Mama (Stopping and staring off). Yes . . . he sure would. *(Sighing)* We got enough to do with that money, all right. *(She halts then, and turns and looks at her daughter-in-law hard; Ruth avoids her eyes and Mama wipes her hands with finality and starts to speak firmly to Ruth)* Where did you go today, girl?

Ruth. To the doctor.

Mama (Impatiently). Now, Ruth . . . you know better than that. Old Doctor Jones is strange enough in his way but there ain't nothing 'bout him make somebody slip and call him "she"—like you done this morning.

Ruth. Well, that's what happened—my tongue slipped.

Mama. You went to see that woman, didn't you?
Ruth (Defensively, giving herself away). What woman you talking about?
Mama (Angrily). That woman who—

(Walter enters in great excitement)

Walter. Did it come?
Mama (Quietly). Can't you give people a Christian greeting before you start asking about money?
Walter (To Ruth). Did it come? *(Ruth unfolds the check and lays it quietly before him, watching him intently with thoughts of her own. Walter sits down and grasps it close and counts off the zeros)* Ten thousand dollars— *(He turns suddenly, frantically to his mother and draws some papers out of his breast pocket)* Mama—look. Old Willy Harris put everything on paper—
Mama. Son—I think you ought to talk to your wife . . . I'll go on out and leave you alone if you want—
Walter. I can talk to her later—Mama, look—
Mama. Son—
Walter. WILL SOMEBODY PLEASE LISTEN TO ME TODAY!
Mama (Quietly). I don't 'low no yellin' in this house, Walter Lee, and you know it—*(Walter stares at them in frustration and starts to speak several times)* And there ain't going to be no investing in no liquor stores. I don't aim to have to speak on that again.

(A long pause)

Walter. Oh—so you don't aim to have to speak on that again? So *you* have decided . . . *(Crumpling his papers)* Well, *you* tell that to my boy tonight when you put him to sleep on the living-room couch . . . *(Turning to Mama and speaking directly to her)* Yeah—and tell it to my wife, Mama, tomorrow when she has to go out of here to look after somebody else's kids. And tell it to *me*, Mama, every time we need a new pair of curtains and I have to watch *you* go out and work in somebody's kitchen. Yeah, you tell me then!

(Walter starts out)

Ruth. Where you going?
Walter. I'm going out!
Ruth. Where?
Walter. Just out of this house somewhere—
Ruth (Getting her coat). I'll come too.

Walter. I don't want you to come!

Ruth. I got something to talk to you about, Walter.

Walter. That's too bad.

Mama (Still quietly). Walter Lee—*(She waits and he finally turns and looks at her)* Sit down.

Walter. I'm a grown man, Mama.

Mama. Ain't nobody said you wasn't grown. But you still in my house and my presence. And as long as you are—you'll talk to your wife civil. Now sit down.

Ruth (Suddenly). Oh, let him go on out and drink himself to death! He makes me sick to my stomach! *(She flings her coat against him)*

Walter (Violently). And you turn mine too, baby! *(Ruth goes into their bedroom and slams the door behind her)* That was my greatest mistake—

Mama (Still quietly). Walter, what is the matter with you?

Walter. Matter with me? Ain't nothing the matter with *me*!

Mama. Yes there is. Something eating you up like a crazy man. Something more than me not giving you this money. The past few years I been watching it happen to you. You get all nervous acting and kind of wild in the eyes—*(Walter jumps up impatiently at her words)* I said sit there now, I'm talking to you!

Walter. Mama—I don't need no nagging at me today.

Mama. Seem like you getting to a place where you always tied up in some kind of knot about something. But if anybody ask you 'bout it you just yell at 'em and bust out the house and go out and drink somewheres. Walter Lee, people can't live with that. Ruth's a good, patient girl in her way— but you getting to be too much. Boy, don't make the mistake of driving that girl away from you.

Walter. Why—what she do for me?

Mama. She loves you.

Walter. Mama—I'm going out. I want to go off somewhere and be by myself for a while.

Mama. I'm sorry 'bout your liquor store, son. It just wasn't the thing for us to do. That's what I want to tell you about—

Walter. I got to go out, Mama—

(He rises)

Mama. It's dangerous, son.

Walter. What's dangerous?

Mama. When a man goes outside his home to look for peace.

Walter (Beseechingly). Then why can't there never be no peace in this house then?

Mama. You done found it in some other house?

197

Walter.   No—there ain't no woman! Why do women always think there's a woman somewhere when a man gets restless. *(Coming to her)* Mama— Mama—I want so many things . . .

Mama.   Yes, son—

Walter.   I want so many things that they are driving me kind of crazy . . . Mama—look at me.

Mama.   I'm looking at you. You a good-looking boy. You got a job, a nice wife, a fine boy and—

Walter.   A job. *(Looks at her)* Mama, a job? I open and close car doors all day long. I drive a man around in his limousine and I say, "Yes, sir; no, sir; very good, sir; shall I take the Drive, sir?" Mama, that ain't no kind of job . . . that ain't nothing at all. *(Very quietly)* Mama, I don't know if I can make you understand.

Mama.   Understand what, baby?

Walter (Quietly).   Sometimes it's like I can see the future stretched out in front of me—just plain as day. The future, Mama. Hanging over there at the edge of my days. Just waiting for me—a big, looming blank space— full of *nothing*. Just waiting for me. *(Pause)* Mama—sometimes when I'm downtown and I pass them cool, quiet-looking restaurants where them white boys are sitting back and talking 'bout things . . . sitting there turn- ing deals worth millions of dollars . . . sometimes I see guys don't look much older than me—

Mama.   Son—how come you talk so much 'bout money?

Walter (With immense passion).   Because it is life, Mama!

Mama (Quietly).   Oh—*(Very quietly)* So now it's life. Money is life. Once upon a time freedom used to be life—now it's money. I guess the world really do change . . .

Walter.   No—it was always money, Mama. We just didn't know about it.

Mama.   No . . . something has changed. *(She looks at him)* You something new, boy. In my time we was worried about not being lynched and getting to the North if we could and how to stay alive and still have a pinch of dignity too . . . Now here come you and Beneatha—talking 'bout things we ain't never even thought about hardly, me and your daddy. You ain't satisfied or proud of nothing we done. I mean that you had a home; that we kept you out of trouble till you was grown; that you don't have to ride to work on the back of nobody's streetcar—You my children—but how different we done become.

Walter.   You just don't understand, Mama, you just don't understand.

Mama.   Son—do you know your wife is expecting another baby? *(Walter stands, stunned, and absorbs what his mother has said)* That's what she wanted to talk to you about. *(Walter sinks down into a chair)* This ain't for me to be telling—but you ought to know. *(She waits)* I think Ruth is thinking 'bout getting rid of that child.

Walter (Slowly understanding). No—no—Ruth wouldn't do that.
Mama. When the world gets ugly enough—a woman will do anything for her family. The part that's already living.
Walter. You don't know Ruth, Mama, if you think she would do that.

(Ruth opens the bedroom door and stands there a little limp)

Ruth (Beaten). Yes I would too, Walter. *(Pause)* I gave her a five-dollar down payment.

(There is total silence as the man stares at his wife and the mother stares at her son)

Mama (Presently). Well—*(Tightly)* Well—son, I'm waiting to hear you say something . . . I'm waiting to hear how you be your father's son. Be the man he was . . . *(Pause)* Your wife say she going to destroy your child. And I'm waiting to hear you talk like him and say we a people who give children life, not who destroys them— *(She rises)* I'm waiting to see you stand up and look like your daddy and say we done give up one baby to poverty and that we ain't going to give up nary another one . . . I'm waiting.
Walter. Ruth—
Mama. If you a son of mine, tell her! *(Walter turns, looks at her and can say nothing. She continues, bitterly)* You . . . you are a disgrace to your father's memory. Somebody get me my hat.

CURTAIN

Act II

Scene I

Time: *Later the same day.*
    At rise: Ruth is ironing again. She has the radio going. Presently Beneatha's bedroom door opens and Ruth's mouth falls and she puts down the iron in fascination.

Ruth. What have we got on tonight!
Beneatha (Emerging grandly from the doorway so that we can see her thoroughly robed in the costume Asagai brought). You are looking at what a well-dressed Nigerian woman wears—*(She parades for Ruth, her hair completely hidden by the headdress; she is coquettishly fanning herself with*

an ornate oriental fan, mistakenly more like Butterfly than any Nigerian that ever was) Isn't it beautiful? *(She promenades to the radio and, with an arrogant flourish, turns off the good loud blues that is playing)* Enough of this assimilationist junk! *(Ruth follows her with her eyes as she goes to the phonograph and puts on a record and turns and waits ceremoniously for the music to come up. Then, with a shout—)* OCOMOGOSIAY!

(Ruth jumps. The music comes up, a lovely Nigerian melody. Beneatha listens, enraptured, her eyes far away—"back to the past." She begins to dance. Ruth is dumfounded)

Ruth.   What kind of dance is that?
Beneatha.   A folk dance.
Ruth (Pearl Bailey). What kind of folks do that, honey?
Beneatha.   It's from Nigeria. It's a dance of welcome.
Ruth.   Who you welcoming?
Beneatha.   The men back to the village.
Ruth.   Where they been?
Beneatha.   How should I know—out hunting or something. Anyway, they are coming back now . . .
Ruth.   Well, that's good.
Beneatha (With the record).
   Alundi, alundi
   Alundi alunya
   Jop pu a jeepua
   Ang gu sooooooooooo

   Ai yai yae . . .
   Ayehaye—alundi . . .

(Walter comes in during this performance; he has obviously been drinking. He leans against the door heavily and watches his sister, at first with distaste. Then his eyes look off—"back to the past"—as he lifts both his fists to the roof screaming)

Walter.   YEAH . . . AND ETHIOPIA STRETCH FORTH HER HANDS AGAIN! . . .
Ruth (Drily, looking at him). Yes—and Africa sure is claiming her own tonight. *(She gives them both up and starts ironing again)*
Walter (All in a drunken, dramatic shout). Shut up! . . . I'm digging them drums . . . them drums move me! . . . *(He makes his weaving way to his wife's face and leans in close to her)* In my heart of hearts—*(He thumps his chest)*—I am much warrior!

Ruth (Without even looking up). In your heart of hearts you are much drunkard.

Walter (Coming away from her and starting to wander around the room, shouting) Me and Jomo . . . *(Intently, in his sister's face. She has stopped dancing to watch him in this unknown mood)* That's my man, Kenyatta. *(Shouting and thumping his chest)* FLAMING SPEAR! HOT DAMN! *(He is suddenly in possession of an imaginary spear and actively spearing enemies all over the room)* OCOMOGOSIAY . . . THE LION IS WAK-ING . . . OWIMOWEH! *(He pulls his shirt open and leaps up on a table and gestures with his spear. The bell rings. Ruth goes to answer)*

Beneatha (To encourage Walter, thoroughly caught up with this side of him). OCOMOGOSIAY, FLAMING SPEAR!

Walter (On the table, very far gone, his eyes pure glass sheets. He sees what we cannot, that he is a leader of his people, a great chief a descendant of Chaka, and that the hour to march has come). Listen, my black brothers—

Beneatha. OCOMOGOSIAY!

Walter. —Do you hear the waters rushing against the shores of the coast-lands—

Beneatha. OCOMOGOSIAY!

Walter. —Do you hear the screeching of the cocks in yonder hills beyond where the chiefs meet in council for the coming of the mighty war—

Beneatha. OCOMOGOSIAY!

Walter. —Do you hear the beating of the wings of the birds flying low over the mountains and the low places of our land—

(Ruth opens the door. George Murchison enters)

Beneatha. OCOMOGOSIAY!

Walter. —Do you hear the singing of the women, singing the war songs of our fathers to the babies in the great houses . . . singing the sweet war songs? OH, DO YOU HEAR, MY BLACK BROTHERS!

Beneatha (Completely gone). We hear you, Flaming Spear—

Walter. Telling us to prepare for the greatness of the time—*(To George)* Black Brother!

(He extends his hand for the fraternal clasp)

George. Black Brother, hell!

Ruth (Having had enough, and embarrassed for the family). Beneatha, you got company—what's the matter with you? Walter Lee Younger, get down off that table and stop acting like a fool . . .

(Walter comes down off the table suddenly and makes a quick exit to the bathroom)

Ruth.   He's had a little to drink . . . I don't know what her excuse is.

George (To Beneatha). Look honey, we're going *to* the theatre—we're not going to be *in* it . . . so go change, huh?

Ruth.   You expect this boy to go out with you looking like that?

Beneatha (Looking at George). That's up to George. If he's ashamed of his heritage—

George.   Oh, don't be so proud of yourself, Bennie—just because you look eccentric.

Beneatha.   How can something that's natural be eccentric?

George.   That's what being eccentric means—being natural. Get dressed.

Beneatha.   I don't like that, George.

Ruth.   Why must you and your brother make an argument out of everything people say?

Beneatha.   Because I hate assimilationist Negroes!

Ruth.   Will somebody please tell me what assimila-whoever means!

George.   Oh, it's just a college girl's way of calling people Uncle Toms—but that isn't what it means at all.

Ruth.   Well, what does it mean?

Beneatha (Cutting George off and staring at him as she replies to Ruth). It means someone who is willing to give up his own culture and submerge himself completely in the dominant, and in this case, oppressive culture!

George.   Oh, dear, dear, dear! Here we go! A lecture on the African past! On our Great West African Heritage! In one second we will hear all about the great Ashanti empires; the great Songhay civilizations; and the great sculpture of Bénin—and then some poetry in the Bantu—and the whole monologue will end with the word *heritage!* (*Nastily*) Let's face it, baby, your heritage is nothing but a bunch of raggedy-assed spirituals and some grass huts!

Beneatha.   Grass huts! (*Ruth crosses to her and forcibly pushes her toward the bedroom*) See there . . . you are standing there in your splendid ignorance talking about people who were the first to smelt iron on the face of the earth! (*Ruth is pushing her through the door*) The Ashanti were performing surgical operations when the English—(*Ruth pulls the door to, with Beneatha on the other side, and smiles graciously at George. Beneatha opens the door and shouts the end of the sentence defiantly at George*)— were still tatooing themselves with blue dragons . . . (*She goes back inside*)

Ruth.   Have a seat, George. (*They both sit. Ruth folds her hands rather primly on her lap, determined to demonstrate the civilization of the family*) Warm, ain't it? I mean for September. (*Pause*) Just like they always say about Chicago weather: If it's too hot or cold for you, just wait a minute and it'll change. (*She smiles happily at this cliché of clichés*) Everybody say it's got to do with them bombs and things they keep setting off. (*Pause*) Would you like a nice cold beer?

George.   No, thank you. I don't care for beer. *(He looks at his watch)* I hope she hurries up.

Ruth.   What time is the show?

George.   It's an eight-thirty curtain. That's just Chicago, though. In New York standard curtain time is eight forty.

(He is rather proud of this knowledge)

Ruth (Properly appreciating it). You get to New York a lot?

George (Offhand). Few times a year.

Ruth.   Oh—that's nice. I've never been to New York.

(Walter enters. We feel he has relieved himself but the edge of unreality is still with him)

Walter.   New York ain't got nothing Chicago ain't. Just a bunch of hustling people all squeezed up together—being "Eastern."

(He turns his face into a screw of displeasure)

George.   Oh—you've been?

Walter.   *Plenty* of times.

Ruth (Shocked at the lie). Walter Lee Younger!

Walter (Staring her down). Plenty! *(Pause)* What we got to drink in this house? Why don't you offer this man some refreshment. *(To* George) They don't know how to entertain people in this house, man.

George.   Thank you—I don't really care for anything.

Walter (Feeling his head; sobriety coming). Where's Mama?

Ruth.   She ain't come back yet.

Walter (Looking Murchison over from head to toe, scrutinizing his carefully casual tweed sports jacket over cashmere V-neck sweater over soft eyelet shirt and tie, and soft slacks, finished off with white buckskin shoes). Why all you college boys wear them fairyish-looking white shoes?

Ruth.   Walter Lee!

(George Murchison ignores the remark)

Walter (To Ruth). Well, they look crazy as hell—white shoes, cold as it is.

Ruth (Crushed). You have to excuse him—

Walter.   No he don't! Excuse me for what? What you always excusing me for! I'll excuse myself when I needs to be excused! *(A pause)* They look as funny as them black knee socks Beneatha wears out of here all the time.

Ruth.   It's the college *style*, Walter.

Walter. Style, hell. She looks like she got burnt legs or something!

Ruth. Oh, Walter —

Walter. (An irritable mimic) Oh, Walter! Oh, Walter! *(To Murchison)* How's your old man making out? I understand you all going to buy that big hotel on the Drive? *(He finds a beer in the refrigerator, wanders over to Murchison, sipping and wiping his lips with the back of his hand, and straddling a chair backwards to talk to the other man)* Shrewd move. Your old man is all right, man. *(Tapping his head and half winking for emphasis)* I mean he knows how to operate. I mean he thinks *big,* you know what I mean, I mean for a *home,* you know? But I think he's kind of running out of ideas now. I'd like to talk to him. Listen, man, I got some plans that could turn this city upside down. I mean I think like he does. *Big.* Invest big, gamble big, hell, lose *big* if you have to, you know what I mean. It's hard to find a man on this whole Southside who understands my kind of thinking — you dig? *(He scrutinizes Murchison again, drinks his beer, squints his eyes and leans in close, confidential, man to man)* Me and you ought to sit down and talk sometimes, man. Man, I got me some ideas . . .

Murchison. (With boredom). Yeah — sometimes we'll have to do that, Walter.

Walter (Understanding the indifference, and offended). Yeah — well, when you get the time, man. I know you a busy little boy.

Ruth. Walter, please —

Walter (Bitterly, hurt). I know ain't nothing in this world as busy as you colored college boys with your fraternity pins and white shoes . . .

Ruth (Covering her face with humiliation). Oh, Walter Lee —

Walter. I see you all all the time — with the books tucked under your arms — going to your *(British A — a mimic)* "clahsses." And for what! What the hell you learning over there? Filling up your heads — *(Counting off on his fingers)* — with the sociology and the psychology — but they teaching you how to be a man? How to take over and run the world? They teaching you how to run a rubber plantation or a steel mill? Naw — just to talk proper and read books and wear white shoes . . .

George (Looking at him with distaste, a little above it all). You're all wacked up with bitterness, man.

Walter (Intently, almost quietly, between the teeth, glaring at the boy). And you — ain't you bitter, man? Ain't you just about had it yet? Don't you see no stars gleaming that you can't reach out and grab? You happy? — You contented son-of-a-bitch — you happy? You got it made? Bitter? Man, I'm a volcano. Bitter? Here I am a giant — surrounded by ants! Ants who can't even understand what it is the giant is talking about.

Ruth (Passionately and suddenly). Oh, Walter — ain't you with nobody!

Walter (Violently). No! 'Cause ain't nobody with me! Not even my own mother!

Ruth. Walter, that's a terrible thing to say!

(Beneatha enters, dressed for the evening in a cocktail dress and earrings)

George. Well—hey, you look great.
Beneatha. Let's go, George. See you all later.
Ruth. Have a nice time.
George. Thanks. Good night. *(To Walter, sarcastically,)* Good night, Prometheus.

(Beneatha and George exit)

Walter (To Ruth). Who is Prometheus?
Ruth. I don't know. Don't worry about it.
Walter (In fury, pointing after George). See there—they get to a point where they can't insult you man to man—they got to go talk about something ain't nobody never heard of!
Ruth. How do you know it was an insult? *(To humor him)* Maybe Prometheus is a nice fellow.
Walter. Prometheus! I bet there ain't even no such thing! I bet that simple-minded clown—
Ruth. Walter—

(She stops what she is doing and looks at him)

Walter (Yelling). Don't start!
Ruth. Start what?
Walter. Your nagging! Where was I? Who was I with? How much money did I spend?
Ruth (Plaintively). Walter Lee—why don't we just try to talk about it . . .
Walter (Not listening). I been out talking with people who understand me. People who care about the things I got on my mind.
Ruth (Wearily). I guess that means people like Willy Harris.
Walter. Yes, people like Willy Harris.
Ruth (With a sudden flash of impatience). Why don't you all just hurry up and go into the banking business and stop talking about it!
Walter. Why? You want to know why? 'Cause we all tied up in a race of people that don't know how to do nothing but moan, pray and have babies!

(The line is too bitter even for him and he looks at her and sits down)

Ruth. Oh, Walter . . . *(Softly)* Honey, why can't you stop fighting me?
Walter (Without thinking). Who's fighting you? Who even cares about you?

(This line begins the retardation of his mood)

205

Ruth. Well—*(She waits a long time, and then with resignation starts to put away her things)* I guess I might as well go on to bed . . . *(More or less to herself)* I don't know where we lost it . . . but we have . . . *(Then, to him)* I—I'm sorry about this new baby, Walter. I guess maybe I better go on and do what I started . . . I guess I just didn't realize how bad things was with us . . . I guess I just didn't really realize—*(She starts out to the bedroom and stops)* You want some hot milk?

Walter. Hot milk?

Ruth. Yes—hot milk.

Walter. Why hot milk?

Ruth. 'Cause after all that liquor you come home with you ought to have something hot in your stomach.

Walter. I don't want no milk.

Ruth. You want some coffee then?

Walter. No, I don't want no coffee. I don't want nothing hot to drink. *(Almost plaintively)* Why you always trying to give me something to eat?

Ruth (Standing and looking at him helplessly). What else can I give you, Walter Lee Younger?

(She stands and looks at him and presently turns to go out again. He lifts his head and watches her going away from him in a new mood which began to emerge when he asked her "Who cares about you?")

Walter. It's been rough, ain't it, baby? *(She hears and stops but does not turn around. and he continues to her back)* I guess between two people there ain't never as much understood as folks generally thinks there is. I mean like between me and you—*(She turns to face him)* How we gets to the place where we scared to talk softness to each other. *(He waits, thinking hard himself)* Why you think it got to be like that? *(He is thoughtful, almost as a child would be)* Ruth, what is it gets into people ought to be close?

Ruth. I don't know, honey. I think about it a lot.

Walter. On account of you and me, you mean? The way things are with us. The way something done come down between us.

Ruth. There ain't so much between us, Walter . . . Not when you come to me and try to talk to me. Try to be with me . . . a little even.

Walter (Total honesty). Sometimes . . . sometimes . . . I don't even know how to try.

Ruth. Walter—

Walter. Yes?

Ruth (Coming to him, gently and with misgiving, but coming to him). Honey . . . life don't have to be like this. I mean sometimes people can do things so that things are better . . . You remember how we used to talk when Travis was born . . . about the way we were going to live . . . the kind of house ... *(She is stroking his head)* Well, it's all starting to slip away from us ...

(Mama enters, and Walter jumps up and shouts at her)

Walter. Mama, where have you been?
Mama. My—them steps is longer than they used to be. Whew! *(She sits down and ignores him)* How you feeling this evening, Ruth?

(Ruth shrugs, disturbed some at having been prematurely interrupted and watching her husband knowingly)

Walter. Mama, where have you been all day?
Mama (Still ignoring him and leaning on the table and changing to more comfortable shoes). Where's Travis?
Ruth. I let him go out earlier and he ain't come back yet. Boy, is he going to get it!
Walter. Mama!
Mama (As if she has heard him for the first time). Yes, son?
Walter. Where did you go this afternoon?
Mama. I went downtown to tend to some business that I had to tend to.
Walter. What kind of business?
Mama. You know better than to question me like a child, Brother.
Walter (Rising and bending over the table). Where were you, Mama? *(Bringing his fists down and shouting)* Mama, you didn't go do something with that insurance money, something crazy?

(The front door opens slowly, interrupting him, and Travis peeks his head in, less than hopefully)

Travis (To his mother). Mama, I—
Ruth. "Mama I" nothing! You're going to get it, boy! Get on in that bedroom and get yourself ready!
Travis. But I—
Mama. Why don't you all never let the child explain hisself.
Ruth. Keep out of it now, Lena.

(Mama clamps her lips together, and Ruth advances toward her son menacingly)

Ruth. A thousand times I have told you not to go off like that—
Mama (Holding out her arms to her grandson). Well—at least let me tell him something. I want him to be the first one to hear ... Come here, Travis *(The boy obeys, gladly)* Travis—*(She takes him by the shoulder and looks into his face)*—you know that money we got in the mail this morning?
Travis. Yes'm—

Mama. Well—what you think your grandmama gone and done with that money?

Travis. I don't know, Grandmama.

Mama (Putting her finger on his nose for emphasis). She went out and she bought you a house! *(The explosion comes from Walter at the end of the revelation and he jumps up and turns away from all of them in a fury. Mama continues, to Travis)* You glad about the house? It's going to be yours when you get to be a man.

Travis. Yeah—I always wanted to live in a house.

Mama. All right, gimme some sugar then—*(Travis puts his arms around her neck as she watches her son over the boy's shoulder. Then, to Travis, after the embrace)* Now when you say your prayers tonight, you thank God and your grandfather—'cause it was him who give you the house—in his way.

Ruth (Taking the boy from Mama and pushing him toward the bedroom). Now you get out of here and get ready for your beating.

Travis. Aw, Mama—

Ruth. Get on in there—*(Closing the door behind him and turning radiantly to her mother-in-law)* So you went and did it!

Mama (Quietly, looking at her son with pain). Yes, I did.

Ruth (Raising both arms classically). Praise God! *(Looks at Walter a moment, who says nothing. She crosses rapidly to her husband)* Please, honey—let me be glad . . . you be glad too. *(She has laid her hands on his shoulders, but he shakes himself free of her roughly, without turning to face her)* Oh, Walter . . . a home . . . a home. *(She comes back to Mama)* Well—where is it? How big is it? How much it going to cost?

Mama. Well—

Ruth. When we moving?

Mama (Smiling at her). First of the month.

Ruth (Throwing back her head with jubilance). Praise God!

Mama (Tentatively, still looking at her son's back turned against her and Ruth) It's— it's a nice house too . . . *(She cannot help speaking directly to him. An imploring quality in her voice, her manner, makes her almost like a girl now)* Three bedrooms—nice big one for you and Ruth . . . Me and Beneatha still have to share our room, but Travis have one of his own—and *(With difficulty)* I figure if the—new baby—is a boy, we could get one of them double-decker outfits . . . And there's a yard with a little patch of dirt where I could maybe get to grow me a few flowers . . . And a nice big basement . . .

Ruth. Walter honey, be glad—

Mama (Still to his back, fingering things on the table). 'Course I don't want to make it sound fancier than it is . . . It's just a plain little old house—but it's made good and solid—and it will be *ours.* Walter Lee—it makes a difference in a man when he can walk on floors that belong to *him* . . .

Ruth. Where is it?

Mama (Frightened at this telling). Well—well—it's out there in Clybourne Park—

(Ruth's radiance fades abruptly, and Walter finally turns slowly to face his mother with incredulity and hostility)

Ruth. Where?

Mama (Matter-of-factly). Four o six Clybourne Street, Clybourne Park.

Ruth. Clybourne Park? Mama, there ain't no colored people living in Clybourne Park.

Mama (Almost idiotically). Well, I guess there's going to be some now.

Walter (Bitterly). So that's the peace and comfort you went out and bought for us today!

Mama (Raising her eves to meet his finally). Son—I just tried to find the nicest place for the least amount of money for my family.

Ruth (Trying to recover from the shock). Well—well—'course I ain't one never been 'fraid of no crackers, mind you—but—well, wasn't there no other houses nowhere?

Mama. Them houses they put up for colored in them areas way out all seem to cost twice as much as other houses. I did the best I could.

Ruth (Struck senseless with the news, in its various degrees of goodness and trouble, she sits a moment, her fists propping her chin in thought, and then she starts to rise, bringing her fists down with vigor, the radiance spreading from cheek to cheek again). Well—well!—All I can say is—if this is my time in life—my time—to say good-bye—*(And she builds with momentum as she starts to circle the room with exuberant, almost tearfully happy release)*—to these Goddamned cracking walls!—*(She pounds the walls)*—and these marching roaches!—*(She wipes at an imaginary army of marching roaches)*—and this cramped little closet which ain't now or never was no kitchen! . . . then I say it loud and good, Hallelujah! and goodbye misery . . . I don't never want to see your ugly face again! *(She laughs joyously, having practically destroyed the apartment, and flings her arms up and lets them come down happily, slowly, reflectively, over her abdomen, aware for the first time perhaps that the life therein pulses with happiness and not despair)* Lena?

Mama (Moved, watching her happiness). Yes, honey?

Ruth (Looking off). Is there—is there a whole lot of sunlight?

Mama (Understanding). Yes, child, there's a whole lot of sunlight.

(Long pause)

Ruth (Collecting herself and going to the door of the room Travis is in). Well—I guess I better see 'bout Travis. *(To Mama)* Lord, I sure don't feel like whipping nobody today!

209

(She exits)

Mama *(The mother and son are left alone now and the mother waits a long time, considering deeply, before she speaks)*. Son—you—you understand what I done, don't you? *(Walter is silent and sullen)* I—I just seen my family falling apart today . . . just falling to pieces in front of my eyes . . . We couldn't of gone on like we was today. We was going backwards 'stead of forwards—talking 'bout killing babies and wishing each other was dead . . . When it gets like that in life—you just got to do something different, push on out and do something bigger . . . *(She waits)* I wish you say something, son . . . I wish you'd say how deep inside you you think I done the right thing—

Walter *(Crossing slowly to his bedroom door and finally turning there and speaking measuredly)*. What you need me to say you done right for? *You* the head of this family. You run our lives like you want to. It was your money and you did what you wanted with it. So what you need for me to say it was all right for? *(Bitterly, to hurt her as deeply as he knows is possible)* So you butchered up a dream of mine—you—who always talking 'bout your children's dreams . . .

Mama. Walter Lee—

(He just closes the door behind him. Mama sits alone, thinking heavily)

CURTAIN

Scene II

Time: *Friday night. A few weeks later.*
  At rise: Packing crates mark the intention of the family to move. Beneatha and George come in, presumably from an evening out again.

George. O.K. . . . O.K., whatever you say . . . *(They both sit on the couch. He tries to kiss her. She moves away)* Look, we've had a nice evening; let's not spoil it, huh?

(He again turns her head and tries to nuzzle in and she turns away from him, not with distaste but with momentary lack of interest; in a mood to pursue what they were talking about)

Beneatha. I'm *trying* to talk to you.
George. We always talk.

Beneatha. Yes—and I love to talk.

George (Exasperated; rising). I know it and I don't mind it sometimes ... I want you to cut it out, see—The moody stuff, I mean. I don't like it. You're a nice-looking girl ... all over. That's all you need, honey, forget the atmosphere. Guys aren't going to go for the atmosphere—they're going to go for what they see. Be glad for that. Drop the Garbo routine. It doesn't go with you. As for myself, I want a nice—*(Groping)*—simple *(Thoughtfully)*—sophisticated girl ... not a poet—O.K.?

(She rebuffs him again and he starts to leave)

Beneatha. Why are you angry?

George. Because this is stupid! I don't go out with you to discuss the nature of "quiet desperation" or to hear all about your thoughts—because the world will go on thinking what it thinks regardless—

Beneatha. Then why read books? Why go to school?

George (With artificial patience, counting on his fingers). It's simple. You read books—to learn facts—to get grades—to pass the course—to get a degree. That's all—it has nothing to do with thoughts.

(A long pause)

Beneatha. I see. *(A longer pause as she looks at him)* Good night, George.

(George looks at her a little oddly, and starts to exit. He meets Mama coming in)

George. Oh—hello, Mrs. Younger.

Mama. Hello, George, how you feeling?

George. Fine—fine, how are you?

Mama. Oh, a little tired. You know them steps can get you after a day's work. You all have a nice time tonight?

George. Yes—a fine time. Well, good night.

Mama. Good night. *(He exits. Mama closes the door behind her)* Hello, honey. What you sitting like that for?

Beneatha. I'm just sitting.

Mama. Didn't you have a nice time?

Beneatha. No.

Mama. No? What's the matter?

Beneatha. Mama, George is a fool—honest. *(She rises)*

Mama (Hustling around unloading the packages she has entered with. She stops). Is he, baby?

Beneatha. Yes.

(Beneatha makes up Travis' bed as she talks)

211

Mama. You sure?

Beneatha. Yes.

Mama. Well—I guess you better not waste your time with no fools.

(Beneatha looks up at her mother, watching her put groceries in the refrigerator. Finally she gathers up her things and starts into the bedroom. At the door she stops and looks back at her mother)

Beneatha. Mama—

Mama. Yes, baby—

Beneatha. Thank you.

Mama. For what?

Beneatha. For understanding me this time.

(She exits quickly and the mother stands, smiling a little, looking at the place where Beneatha just stood. Ruth enters)

Ruth. Now don't you fool with any of this stuff, Lena—

Mama. Oh, I just thought I'd sort a few things out.

(The phone rings. Ruth answers)

Ruth *(At the phone).* Hello—Just a minute. *(Goes to door)* Walter, it's Mrs. Arnold. *(Waits. Goes back to the phone. Tense)* Hello. Yes, this is his wife speaking . . . He's lying down now. Yes . . . well, he'll be in tomorrow. He's been very sick. Yes—I know we should have called, but we were so sure he'd be able to come in today. Yes—yes, I'm very sorry. Yes . . . Thank you very much. *(She hangs up. Walter is standing in the doorway of the bedroom behind her)* That was Mrs. Arnold.

Walter (Indifferently). Was it?

Ruth. She said if you don't come in tomorrow that they are getting a new man . . .

Walter. Ain't that sad—ain't that crying sad.

Ruth. She said Mr. Arnold has had to take a cab for three days . . . Walter, you ain't been to work for three days! *(This is a revelation to her)* Where you been, Walter Lee Younger? *(Walter looks at her and starts to laugh)* You're going to lose your job.

Walter. That's right . . .

Ruth. Oh, Walter, and with your mother working like a dog every day—

Walter. That's sad too—Everything is sad.

Mama. What you been doing for these three days, son?

Walter. Mama—you don't know all the things a man what got leisure can find to do in this city . . . What's this—Friday night? Well—Wednesday I

212

borrowed Willy Harris' car and I went for a drive . . . just me and myself and I drove and drove . . . Way out . . . way past South Chicago, and I parked the car and I sat and looked at the steel mills all day long. I just sat in the car and looked at them big black chimneys for hours. Then I drove back and I went to the Green Hat. *(Pause)* And Thursday—Thursday I borrowed the car again and I got in it and I pointed it the other way and I drove the other way—for hours—way, way up to Wisconsin, and I looked at the farms. I just drove and looked at the farms. Then I drove back and I went to the Green Hat. *(Pause)* And today—today I didn't get the car. Today I just walked. All over the Southside. And I looked at the Negroes and they looked at me and finally I just sat down on the curb at Thirty-ninth and South Parkway and I just sat there and watched the Negroes go by. And then I went to the Green Hat. You all sad? You all depressed? And you know where I am going right now—

(Ruth goes out quietly)

Mama.   Oh, Big Walter, is this the harvest of our days?
Walter.   You know what I like about the Green Hat? *(He turns the radio on and a steamy, deep blues pours into the room)* I like this little cat they got there who blows a sax . . . He blows. He talks to me. He ain't but 'bout five feet tall and he's got a conked head and his eyes is always closed and he's all music—
Mama (Rising and getting some papers out of her handbag). Walter—
Walter.   And there's this other guy who plays the piano . . . and they got a sound. I mean they can work on some music . . . They got the best little combo in the world in the Green Hat . . . You can just sit there and drink and listen to them three men play and you realize that don't nothing matter worth a damn, but just being there—
Mama.   I've helped do it to you, haven't I, son? Walter, I been wrong.
Walter.   Naw—you ain't never been wrong about nothing, Mama.
Mama.   Listen to me, now. I say I been wrong, son. That I been doing to you what the rest of the world been doing to you. *(She stops and he looks up slowly at her and she meets his eyes pleadingly)* Walter—what you ain't never understood is that I ain't got nothing, don't own nothing, ain't never really wanted nothing that wasn't for you. There ain't nothing as precious to me . . . There ain't nothing worth holding on to, money, dreams, nothing else—if it means—if it means it's going to destroy my boy. *(She puts her papers in front of him and he watches her without speaking or moving)* I paid the man thirty-five hundred dollars down on the house. That leaves sixty-five hundred dollars. Monday morning I want you to take this money and take three thousand dollars and put it in a savings account for Beneatha's medical schooling. The rest you put in a

checking account—with your name on it. And from now on any penny that come out of it or that go in it is for you to look after. For you to decide. *(She drops her hands a little helplessly)* It ain't much, but it's all I got in the world and I'm putting it in your hands. I'm telling you to be the head of this family from now on like you supposed to be.

Walter (Stares at the money). You trust me like that, Mama?

Mama. I ain't never stop trusting you. Like I ain't never stop loving you.

(She goes out, and Walter sits looking at the money on the table as the music continues in its idiom, pulsing in the room. Finally, in a decisive gesture, he gets up, and, in mingled joy and desperation, picks up the money. At the same moment, Travis enters for bed)

Travis. What's the matter, Daddy? You drunk?

Walter (Sweetly, more sweetly than we have ever known him). No, Daddy ain't drunk. Daddy ain't going to never be drunk again . . .

Travis. Well, good night, Daddy.

(The Father has come from behind the couch and leans over, embracing his son)

Walter. Son, I feel like talking to you tonight.

Travis. About what?

Walter. Oh, about a lot of things. About you and what kind of man you going to be when you grow up. . . . Son—son, what do you want to be when you grow up?

Travis. A bus driver.

Walter (Laughing a little). A what? Man, that ain't nothing to want to be!

Travis. Why not?

Walter. 'Cause, man—it ain't big enough—you know what I mean.

Travis. I don't know then. I can't make up my mind. Sometimes Mama asks me that too. And sometimes when I tell her I just want to be like you— she says she don't want me to be like that and sometimes she says she does. . . .

Walter (Gathering him up in his arms). You know what, Travis? In seven years you going to be seventeen years old. And things is going to be very different with us in seven years, Travis. . . . One day when you are seventeen I'll come home—home from my office downtown somewhere—

Travis. You don't work in no office, Daddy.

Walter. No—but after tonight. After what your daddy gonna do tonight, there's going to be offices—a whole lot of offices. . . .

Travis. What you gonna do tonight, Daddy?

Walter. You wouldn't understand yet, son, but your daddy's gonna make a transaction . . . a business transaction that's going to change our lives. . . .

That's how come one day when you 'bout seventeen years old I'll come home and I'll be pretty tired, you know what I mean, after a day of conferences and secretaries getting things wrong the way they do . . . 'cause an executive's life is hell, man—*(The more he talks the farther away he gets)* And I'll pull the car up on the driveway . . . just a plain black Chrysler, I think, with white walls—no—black tires. More elegant. Rich people don't have to be flashy . . . though I'll have to get something a little sportier for Ruth—maybe a Cadillac convertible to do her shopping in . . . And I'll come up the steps to the house and the gardener will be clipping away at the hedges and he'll say, "Good evening, Mr. Younger." And I'll say, "Hello, Jefferson, how are you this evening?" And I'll go inside and Ruth will come downstairs and meet me at the door and we'll kiss each other and she'll take my arm and we'll go up to your room to see you sitting on the floor with the catalogues of all the great schools in America around you. . . . All the great schools in the world! And—and I'll say, all right son—it's your seventeenth birthday, what is it you've decided? . . . Just tell me where you want to go to school and you'll go. Just tell me, what it is you want to be—and you'll *be* it. . . . Whatever you want to be—Yessir! *(He holds his arms open for* Travis*)* You just name it, son . . . *(Travis leaps into them)* and I hand you the world!

(Walter's voice has risen in pitch and hysterical promise and on the last line he lifts Travis high)

(BLACKOUT)

Scene III

Time: *Saturday, moving day, one week later.*
  Before the curtain rises, Ruth's voice, a strident, dramatic church alto, cuts through the silence.
  It is, in the darkness, a triumphant surge, a penetrating statement of expectation: "Oh, Lord, I don't feel no ways tired! Children, oh, glory hallelujah!"
  As the curtain rises we see that Ruth is alone in the living room, finishing up the family's packing. It is moving day. She is nailing crates and tying cartons. Beneatha enters, carrying a guitar case, and watches her exuberant sister-in-law.

Ruth. Hey!
Beneatha (Putting away the case). Hi.
Ruth (Pointing at a package). Honey—look in that package there and see what I found on sale this morning at the South Center. *(Ruth gets up and moves to the package and draws out some curtains)* Lookahere—hand-turned hems!

215

Beneatha. How do you know the window size out there?

Ruth (Who hadn't thought of that). Oh—Well, they bound to fit something in the whole house. Anyhow, they was too good a bargain to pass up. *(Ruth slaps her head, suddenly remembering something)* Oh, Bennie—I meant to put a special note on that carton over there. That's your mama's good china and she wants 'em to be very careful with it.

Beneatha. I'll do it.

(Beneatha finds a piece of paper and starts to draw large letters on it)

Ruth. You know what I'm going to do soon as I get in that new house?

Beneatha. What?

Ruth. Honey—I'm going to run me a tub of water up to here . . . *(With her fingers practically up to her nostrils)* And I'm going to get in it—and I am going to sit . . . and sit . . . and sit in that hot water and the first person who knocks to tell *me* to hurry up and come out—

Beneatha. Gets shot at sunrise.

Ruth (Laughing happily). You said it, sister! *(Noticing how large Beneatha is absentmindedly making the note)* Honey, they ain't going to read that from no airplane.

Beneatha (Laughing herself). I guess I always think things have more emphasis if they are big, somehow.

Ruth (Looking up at her and smiling). You and your brother seem to have that as a philosophy of life. Lord, that man—done changed so 'round here. You know— you know what we did last night? Me and Walter Lee?

Beneatha. What?

Ruth (Smiling to herself). We went to the movies. *(Looking at Beneatha to see if she understands)* We went to the movies. You know the last time me and Walter went to the movies together?

Beneatha. No.

Ruth. Me neither. That's how long it been. *(Smiling again)* But we went last night. The picture wasn't much good, but that didn't seem to matter. We went—and we held hands.

Beneatha. Oh, Lord!

Ruth. We held hands—and you know what?

Beneatha. What?

Ruth. When we come out of the show it was late and dark and all the stores and things was closed up . . . and it was kind of chilly and there wasn't many people on the streets . . . and we was still holding hands, me and Walter.

Beneatha. You're killing me.

(Walter enters with a large package. His happiness is deep in him; he cannot keep still with his new-found exuberance. He is singing and wiggling and

snapping his fingers. He puts his package in a corner and puts a phonograph record, which he has brought in with him, on the record player. As the music comes up he dances over to Ruth and tries to get her to dance with him. She gives in at last to his raunchiness and in a fit of giggling allows herself to be drawn into his mood and together they deliberately burlesque an old social dance of their youth)

Beneatha *(Regarding them a long time as they dance, then drawing in her breath for a deeply exaggerated comment which she does not particularly mean).* Talk about—olddddddddddd-fashionedddddddd—Negroes!
Walter *(Stopping momentarily).* What kind of Negroes?

(He says this in fun. He is not angry with her today, nor with anyone. He starts to dance with his wife again)

Beneatha.   Old-fashioned.
Walter *(As he dances with Ruth).* You know, when these *New Negroes* have their convention—*(Pointing at his sister)*—that is going to be the chairman of the Committee on Unending Agitation. *(He goes on dancing, then stops)* Race, race, race! . . . Girl, I do believe you are the first person in the history of the entire human race to successfully brainwash yourself. *(Beneatha breaks up and he goes on dancing. He stops again, enjoying his tease)* Damn, even the N double A C P takes a holiday sometimes! *(Beneatha and Ruth laugh. He dances with Ruth some more and starts to laugh and stops and pantomimes someone over an operating table)* I can just see that chick someday looking down at some poor cat on an operating table before she starts to slice him, saying . . . *(Pulling his sleeves back maliciously)* "By the way, what are your views on civil rights down there? . . ."

(He laughs at her again and starts to dance happily. The bell sounds)

Beneatha.   Sticks and stones may break my bones but . . . words will never hurt me!

(Beneatha goes to the door and opens it as Walter and Ruth go on with the clowning. Beneatha is somewhat surprised to see a quiet-looking middle-aged white man in a business suit holding his hat and a briefcase in his hand and consulting a small piece of paper)

Man.   Uh—how do you do, miss. I am looking for a Mrs.—*(He looks at the slip of paper)* Mrs. Lena Younger?
Beneatha *(Smoothing her hair with slight embarrassment).* Oh—yes, that's my mother. Excuse me. *(She closes the door and turns to quiet the other*

217

two) Ruth! Brother! Somebody's here. *(Then she opens the door. The man casts a curious quick glance at all of them)* Uh—come in please.

Man (Coming in). Thank you.

Beneatha. My mother isn't here just now. Is it business?

Man. Yes . . . well, of a sort.

Walter (Freely, the Man of the House). Have a seat. I'm Mrs. Younger's son. I look after most of her business matters.

(Ruth and Beneatha exchange amused glances)

Man (Regarding Walter, and sitting). Well—My name is Karl Lindner . . .

Walter (Stretching out his hand). Walter Younger. This is my wife—*(Ruth nods politely)*—and my sister.

Lindner. How do you do.

Walter (Amiably, as he sits himself easily on a chair, leaning with interest forward on his knees and looking expectantly into the newcomer's face). What can we do for you, Mr. Lindner!

Lindner (Some minor shuffling of the hat and briefcase on his knees). Well—I am a representative of the Clybourne Park Improvement Association—

Walter (Pointing). Why don't you sit your things on the floor?

Lindner. Oh—yes. Thank you. *(He slides the briefcase and hat under the chair)* And as I was saying—I am from the Clybourne Park Improvement Association and we have had it brought to our attention at the last meeting that you people—or at least your mother—has bought a piece of residential property at—*(He digs for the slip of paper again)*—four o six Clybourne Street . . .

Walter. That's right. Care for something to drink? Ruth, get Mr. Lindner a beer.

Lindner (Upset for some reason). Oh—no, really. I mean thank you very much, but no thank you.

Ruth (Innocently). Some coffee?

Lindner. Thank you, nothing at all.

(Beneatha is watching the man carefully)

Lindner. Well, I don't know how much you folks know about our organization. *(He is a gentle man; thoughtful and somewhat labored in his manner)* It is one of these community organizations set up to look after—oh, you know, things like block up-keep and special projects and we also have what we call our New Neighbors Orientation Committee . . .

Beneatha (Drily). Yes—and what do they do?

Lindner (Turning a little to her and then returning the main force to Walter). Well—it's what you might call a sort of welcoming committee, I guess. I mean they, we, I'm the chairman of the committee—go around and see the new people who move into the neighborhood and sort of give them the lowdown on the way we do things out in Clybourne Park.

Beneatha (With appreciation of the two meanings, which escape Ruth and Walter). Un-huh.

Lindner. And we also have the category of what the association calls — *(He looks elsewhere)* — uh — special community problems . . .

Beneatha. Yes — and what are some of those?

Walter. Girl, let the man talk.

Lindner (With understated relief). Thank you. I would sort of like to explain this thing in my own way. I mean I want to explain to you in a certain way.

Walter. Go ahead.

Lindner. Yes. I'm going to try to get right to the point. I'm sure we'll all appreciate that in the long run.

Beneatha. Yes.

Walter. Be still now!

Lindner. Well —

Ruth (Still innocently). Would you like another chair — you don't look comfortable.

Lindner (More frustrated than annoyed). No, thank you very much. Please. Well — to get right to the point I — *(A great breath, and he is off at last)* I am sure you people must be aware of some of the incidents which have happened in various parts of the city when colored people have moved into certain areas — *(Beneatha exhales heavily and starts tossing a piece of fruit up and down in the air)* Well — because we have what I think is going to be a unique type of organization in American community life — not only do we deplore that kind of thing — but we are trying to do something about it. *(Beneatha stops tossing and turns with a new and quizzical interest to the man)* We feel — *(gaining confidence in his mission because of the interest in the faces of the people he is talking to)* — we feel that most of the trouble in this world, when you come right down to it — *(He hits his knee for emphasis)* — most of the trouble exists because people just don't sit down and talk to each other.

Ruth (Nodding as she might in church, pleased with the remark). You can say that again, mister.

Lindner (More encouraged by such affirmation). That we don't try hard enough in this world to understand the other fellow's problem. The other guy's point of view.

Ruth. Now that's right.

(Beneatha and Walter merely watch and listen with genuine interest)

Lindner. Yes — that's the way we feel out in Clybourne Park. And that's why I was elected to come here this afternoon and talk to you people.

Friendly like, you know, the way people should talk to each other and see if we couldn't find some way to work this thing out. As I say, the whole business is a matter of *caring* about the other fellow. Anybody can see that you are a nice family of folks, hard working and honest I'm sure. *(Beneatha frowns slightly, quizzically, her head tilted regarding him)* Today everybody knows what it means to be on the outside of *something.* And of course, there is always somebody who is out to take the advantage of people who don't always understand.

Walter.   What do you mean?

Lindner.   Well—you see our community is made up of people who've worked hard as the dickens for years to build up that little community. They're not rich and fancy people; just hard-working, honest people who don't really have much but those little homes and a dream of the kind of community they want to raise their children in. Now, I don't say we are perfect and there is a lot wrong in some of the things they want. But you've got to admit that a man, right or wrong, has the right to want to have the neighborhood he lives in a certain kind of way. And at the moment the overwhelming majority of our people out there feel that people get along better, take more of a common interest in the life of the community, when they share a common background. I want you to believe me when I tell you that race prejudice simply doesn't enter into it. It is a matter of the people of Clybourne Park believing, rightly or wrongly, as I say, that for the happiness of all concerned that our Negro families are happier when they live in their *own* communities.

Beneatha (With a grand and bitter gesture). This, friends, is the Welcoming Committee!

Walter (Dumfounded, looking at Lindner). Is this what you came marching all the way over here to tell us?

Lindner.   Well, now we've been having a fine conversation. I hope you'll hear me all the way through.

Walter (Tightly). Go ahead, man.

Lindner.   You see—in the face of all things I have said, we are prepared to make your family a very generous offer . . .

Beneatha.   Thirty pieces and not a coin less!

Walter.   Yeah?

Lindner (Putting on his glasses and drawing a form out of the briefcase). Our association is prepared, through the collective effort of our people, to buy the house from you at a financial gain to your family.

Ruth.   Lord have mercy, ain't this the living gall!

Walter.   All right, you through?

Lindner.   Well, I want to give you the exact terms of the financial arrangement—

Walter.   We don't want to hear no exact terms of no arrangements. I want to know if you got any more to tell us 'bout getting together?

Lindner (Taking off his glasses). Well—I don't suppose that you feel . . .
Walter. Never mind how I feel—you got any more to say 'bout how people ought to sit down and talk to each other? . . . Get out of my house, man.

(He turns his back and walks to the door)

Lindner (Looking around at the hostile faces and reaching and assembling his hat and briefcase). Well—I don't understand why you people are reacting this way. What do you think you are going to gain by moving into a neighborhood where you just aren't wanted and where some elements— well—people can get awful worked up when they feel that their whole way of life and everything they've ever worked for is threatened.
Walter. Get out.
Lindner (At the door, holding a small card). Well—I'm sorry it went like this.
Walter. Get out.
Lindner (Almost sadly regarding Walter). You just can't force people to change their hearts, son.

(He turns and puts his card on a table and exits. Walter pushes the door to with stinging hatred, and stands looking at it. Ruth just sits and Beneatha just stands. They say nothing. Mama and Travis enter)

Mama. Well—this all the packing got done since I left out of here this morning. I testify before God that my children got all the energy of the dead. What time the moving men due?
Beneatha. Four o'clock. You had a caller, Mama.

(She is smiling, teasingly)

Mama. Sure enough—who?
Beneatha (Her arms folded saucily). The Welcoming Committee.

(Walter and Ruth giggle)

Mama (Innocently). Who?
Beneatha. The Welcoming Committee. They said they're sure going to be glad to see you when you get there.
Walter (Devilishly). Yeah, they said they can't hardly wait to see your face.

(Laughter)

Mama (Sensing their facetiousness). What's the matter with you all?
Walter. Ain't nothing the matter with us. We just telling you 'bout the gentleman who came to see you this afternoon. From the Clybourne Park Improvement Association.

Mama. What he want?
Ruth (In the same mood as Beneatha and Walter). To welcome you, honey.
Walter. He said they can't hardly wait. He said the one thing they don't have, that they just *dying* to have out there is a fine family of colored people! *(To Ruth and Beneatha)* Ain't that right!
Ruth and Beneatha (Mockingly). Yeah! He left his card in case—

(They indicate the card, and Mama picks it up and throws it on the floor— understanding and looking off as she draws her chair up to the table on which she has put her plant and some sticks and some cord)

Mama. Father, give us strength. *(Knowingly—and without fun)* Did he threaten us?
Beneatha. Oh—Mama—they don't do it like that any more. He talked Brotherhood. He said everybody ought to learn how to sit down and hate each other with good Christian fellowship.

(She and Walter shake hands to ridicule the remark)

Mama (Sadly). Lord, protect us . . .
Ruth. You should hear the money those folks raised to buy the house from us. All we paid and then some.
Beneatha. What they think we going to do—eat 'em?
Ruth. No, honey, marry 'em.
Mama (Shaking her head). Lord, Lord, Lord . . .
Ruth. Well—that's the way the crackers crumble. Joke.
Beneatha (Laughingly noticing what her mother is doing). Mama, what are you doing?
Mama. Fixing my plant so it won't get hurt none on the way . . .
Beneatha. Mama, you going to take *that* to the new house?
Mama. Un-huh—
Beneatha. That raggedy-looking old thing?
Mama (Stopping and looking at her). It expresses me.
Ruth (With delight, to Beneatha). So there, Miss Thing!

(Walter comes to Mama suddenly and bends down behind her and squeezes her in his arms with all his strength. She is overwhelmed by the suddenness of it and, though delighted, her manner is like that of Ruth with Travis)

Mama. Look out now, boy! You make me mess up my thing here!
Walter (His face lit, he slips down on his knees beside her, his arms still about her). Mama . . . you know what it means to climb up in the chariot?
Mama (Gruffly, very happy). Get on away from me now . . .
Ruth (Near the gift-wrapped package, trying to catch Walter's eye). Psst—

222

Walter. What the old song say, Mama . . .
Ruth. Walter—Now?

(She is pointing at the package)

Walter (Speaking the lines, sweetly, playfully, in his mother's face).

I got wings . . . you got wings . . .
All God's children got wings . . .

Mama. Boy—get out of my face and do some work . . .
Walter.

When I get to heaven gonna put on my wings,
Gonna fly all over God's heaven . . .

Beneatha (Teasingly, from across the room). Everybody talking 'bout heaven ain't going there!
Walter (To Ruth, who is carrying the box across to them). I don't know, you think we ought to give her that . . . Seems to me she ain't been very appreciative around here.
Mama (Eying the box, which is obviously a gift). What is that?
Walter (Taking it from Ruth and putting it on the table in front of Mama). Well—what you all think? Should we give it to her?
Ruth. Oh—she was pretty good today.
Mama. I'll good you —

(She turns her eyes to the box again)

Beneatha. Open it, Mama.

(She stands up, looks at it, turns and looks at all of them, and then presses her hands together and does not open the package)

Walter (Sweetly). Open it, Mama. It's for you. *(Mama looks in his eyes. It is the first present in her life without its being Christmas. Slowly she opens her package and lifts out, one by one, a brand-new sparkling set of gardening tools. Walter continues, prodding)* Ruth made up the note—read it . . .
Mama (Picking up the card and adjusting her glasses). "To our own Mrs. Miniver—Love from Brother, Ruth and Beneatha." Ain't that lovely . . .
Travis (Tugging at his father's sleeve). Daddy, can I give her mine now?
Walter. All right, son. *(Travis flies to get his gift)* Travis didn't want to go in with the rest of us, Mama. He got his own. *(Somewhat amused)* We don't know what it is . . .
Travis (Racing back in the room with a large hatbox and putting it in front of his grandmother). Here!

223

Mama.   Lord have mercy, baby. You done gone and bought your grand-mother a hat?
Travis (Very proud). Open it!

(She does and lifts out an elaborate, but very elaborate, wide gardening hat, and all the adults break up at the sight of it)

Ruth.   Travis, honey, what is that?
Travis (Who thinks it is beautiful and appropriate). It's a gardening hat! Like the ladies always have on in the magazines when they work in their gardens.
Beneatha (Giggling fiercely). Travis—we were trying to make Mama Mrs. Miniver—not Scarlett O'Hara!
Mama (Indignantly). What's the matter with you all! This here is a beautiful hat! *(Absurdly)* I always wanted me one just like it!

(She pops it on her head to prove it to her grandson, and the hat is ludicrous and considerably oversized)

Ruth.   Hot dog! Go, Mama!
Walter (Doubled over with laughter). I'm sorry, Mama—but you look like you ready to go out and chop you some cotton sure enough!

(They all laugh except Mama, out of deference to Travis' feelings)

Mama (Gathering the boy up to her) Bless your heart—this is the prettiest hat I ever owned—*(Walter, Ruth and Beneatha chime in—noisily, festively and insincerely congratulating Travis on his gift)* What are we all standing around here for? We ain't finished packin' yet. Bennie, you ain't packed one book.

(The bell rings)

Beneatha.   That couldn't be the movers . . . it's not hardly two good yet—

(Beneatha goes into her room. Mama starts for door)

Walter (Turning, stiffening). Wait—wait—I'll get it.

(He stands and looks at the door)

Mama.   You expecting company, son?
Walter (Just looking at the door). Yeah—yeah . . .

(Mama looks at Ruth, and they exchange innocent and unfrightened glances)

Mama (Not understanding). Well, let them in, son.

Beneatha (From her room). We need some more string.
Mama. Travis—you run to the hardware and get me some string cord.

(Mama goes out and Walter turns and looks at Ruth. Travis goes to a dish for money)

Ruth. Why don't you answer the door, man?
Walter (Suddenly bounding across the floor to her). 'Cause sometimes it hard to let the future begin! *(Stooping down in her face)*

I got wings! You got wings!
All God's children got wings!

(He crosses to the door and throws it open. Standing there is a very slight little man in a not too prosperous business suit and with haunted frightened eyes and a hat pulled down tightly, brim up, around his forehead. Travis passes between the men and exits. Walter leans deep in the man's face, still in his jubilance)

When I get to heaven gonna put on my wings,
Gonna fly all over God's heaven . . .

(The little man just stares at him)

Heaven—

(Suddenly he stops and looks past the little man into the empty hallway)

Where's Willy, man?
Bobo. He ain't with me.
Walter (Not disturbed). Oh—come on in. You know my wife.
Bobo (Dumbly, taking off his hat). Yes—h'you, Miss Ruth.
Ruth (Quietly, a mood apart from her husband already, seeing Bobo). Hello, Bobo.
Walter. You right on time today . . . Right on time. That's the way! *(He slaps Bobo on his back)* Sit down . . . lemme hear.

(Ruth stands stiffly and quietly in back of them, as though somehow she senses death, her eyes fixed on her husband)

Bobo (His frightened eyes on the floor, his hat in his hands). Could I please get a drink of water, before I tell you about it, Walter Lee?

(Walter does not take his eyes off the man. Ruth goes blindly to the tap and gets a glass of water and brings it to Bobo)

Walter. There ain't nothing wrong, is there?

Bobo. Lemme tell you—

Walter. Man—didn't nothing go wrong?

Bobo. Lemme tell you—Walter Lee. *(Looking at Ruth and talking to her more than to Walter)* You know how it was. I got to tell you how it was. I mean first I got to tell you how it was all the way . . . I mean about the money I put in, Walter Lee . . .

Walter (With taut agitation now). What about the money you put in?

Bobo. Well—it wasn't much as we told you—me and Willy—*(He stops)* I'm sorry, Walter. I got a bad feeling about it. I got a real bad feeling about it . . .

Walter. Man, what you telling me about all this for? . . . Tell me what happened in Springfield . . .

Bobo. Springfield.

Ruth (Like a dead woman). What was supposed to happen in Springfield?

Bobo (To her). This deal that me and Walter went into with Willy—Me and Willy was going to go down to Springfield and spread some money 'round so's we wouldn't have to wait so long for the liquor license . . . That's what we were going to do. Everybody said that was the way you had to do, you understand, Miss Ruth?

Walter. Man—what happened down there?

Bobo (A pitiful man, near tears). I'm trying to tell you, Walter.

Walter (Screaming at him suddenly). THEN TELL ME, GODDAMMIT . . . WHAT'S THE MATTER WITH YOU?

Bobo. Man . . . I didn't go to no Springfield, yesterday.

Walter (Halted, life hanging in the moment). Why not?

Bobo (The long way, the hard way to tell). 'Cause I didn't have no reasons to . . .

Walter. Man, what are you talking about!

Bobo. I'm talking about the fact that when I got to the train station yesterday morning—eight o'clock like we planned . . . Man—*Willy didn't never show up.*

Walter. Why . . . where was he . . . where is he?

Bobo. That's what I'm trying to tell you . . . I don't know . . . I waited six hours . . . I called his house . . . and I waited . . . six hours . . . I waited in that train station six hours . . . *(Breaking, into tears)* That was all the extra money I had in the world . . . *(Looking up at Walter with the tears running down his face)* Man, *Willy is gone.*

Walter. Gone, what you mean Willy is gone? Gone where? You mean he went by himself. You mean he went off to Springfield by himself—to take care of getting the license—*(Turns and looks anxiously at Ruth)* You mean maybe he didn't want too many people in on the business down there? *(Looks to Ruth again, as before)* You know Willy got his own ways.

226

(Looks back to Bobo) Maybe you was late yesterday and he just went on down there without you. Maybe—maybe—he's been callin' you at home tryin' to tell you what happened or something. Maybe—maybe—he just got sick. He's somewhere—he's got to be somewhere. We just got to find him—me and you got to find him. *(Grabs Bobo senselessly by the collar and starts to shake him)* We got to!

Bobo *(In sudden angry, frightened agony)*. What's the matter with you, Walter! *When a cat take off with your money he don't leave you no maps!*

Walter *(Turning madly, as though he is looking for Willy in the very room)*. Willy! . . . Willy . . . don't do it . . . Please don't do it . . . Man, not with that money . . . Man, please, not with that money . . . Oh, God . . . Don't let it be true . . . *(He is wandering around, crying out for Willy and looking for him or perhaps for help from God)* Man . . . I trusted you . . . Man, I put my life in your hands . . . *(He starts to crumple down on the floor as Ruth just covers her face in horror. Mama opens the door and comes into the room, with Beneatha behind her)* Man . . . *(He starts to pound the floor with his fists, sobbing wildly)* That money is made out of my father's flesh . . .

Bobo *(Standing over him helplessly)*. I'm sorry, Walter . . . *(Only Walter's sobs reply. Bobo puts on his hat)* I had my life staked on this deal, too . . .

(He exits)

Mama *(To Walter)*. Son—*(She goes to him, bends down to him, talks to his bent head)* Son . . . Is it gone? Son, I gave you sixty-five hundred dollars. Is it gone? All of it? Beneatha's money too?

Walter *(Lifting his head slowly)*. Mama . . . I never . . . went to the bank at all . . .

Mama *(Not wanting to believe him)*. You mean . . . your sister's school money . . . you used that too . . . Walter?

Walter. Yessss! . . . All of it . . . It's all gone

(There is total silence. Ruth stands with her face covered with her hands; Beneatha leans forlornly against a wall, fingering a piece of red ribbon from the mother's gift. Mama stops and looks at her son without recognition and then, quite without thinking about it, starts to beat him senselessly in the face. Beneatha goes to them and stops it)

Beneatha. Mama!

(Mama stops and looks at both of her children and rises slowly and wanders vaguely, aimlessly away from them)

Mama. I seen . . . him . . . night after night . . . come in . . . and look at that rug . . . and then look at me . . . the red showing in his eyes . . . the veins

moving in his head . . . I seen him grow thin and old before he was
forty . . . working and working and working like somebody's old
horse . . . killing himself . . . and you—you give it all away in a day . . .
Beneatha. Mama—
Mama. Oh, God . . . *(She looks up to Him)* Look down here—and show
me the strength.
Beneatha. Mama—
Mama (Folding over). Strength . . .
Beneatha (Plaintively). Mama . . .
Mama. Strength!

CURTAIN

Act III

An hour later
   *At curtain, there is a sullen light of gloom in the living room, gray light not unlike
that which began the first scene of Act One. At left we can see Walter within his room,
alone with himself. He is stretched out on the bed, his shirt out and open, his arms
under his head. He does not smoke, he does not cry out, he merely lies there, looking
up at the ceiling, much as if he were alone in the world.*
   *In the living room Beneatha sits at the table, still surrounded by the now almost
ominous packing crates. She sits looking off. We feel that this is a mood struck perhaps
an hour before, and it lingers now, full of the empty sound of profound disappointment. We see on a line from her brother's bedroom the sameness of their attitudes.
Presently the bell rings and Beneatha rises without ambition or interest in answering.
It is Asagai, smiling broadly, striding into the room with energy and happy expectation
and conversation.*

Asagai. I came over . . . I had some free time. I thought I might help with
the packing. Ah, I like the look of packing crates! A household in prepar-
ation for a journey! It depresses some people . . . but for me . . . it is
another feeling. Something full of the flow of life, do you understand?
Movement, progress . . . It makes me think of Africa.
Beneatha. Africa!
Asagai. What kind of a mood is this? Have I told you how deeply you
move me?
Beneatha. He gave away the money, Asagai . . .
Asagai. Who gave away what money?
Beneatha. The insurance money. My brother gave it away.
Asagai. Gave it away?
Beneatha. He made an investment! With a man even Travis wouldn't have
trusted.

Asagai.   And it's gone?

Beneatha.   Gone!

Asagai.   I'm very sorry . . . And you, now?

Beneatha.   Me? . . . Me?   . . . Me I'm nothing . . . Me. When I was very small . . . we used to take our sleds out in the wintertime and the only hills we had were the ice-covered stone steps of some houses down the street. And we used to fill them in with snow and make them smooth and slide down them all day . . . and it was very dangerous you know . . . far too steep . . . and sure enough one day a kid named Rufus came down too fast and hit the sidewalk . . . and we saw his face just split open right there in front of us . . . And I remember standing there looking at his bloody open face thinking that was the end of Rufus. But the ambulance came and they took him to the hospital and they fixed the broken bones and they sewed it all up . . . and the next time I saw Rufus he just had a little line down the middle of his face . . . I never got over that . . .

(Walter sits up, listening on the bed. Throughout this scene it is important that we feel his reaction at all times, that he visibly respond to the words of his sister and Asagai)

Asagai.   What?

Beneatha.   That that was what one person could do for another, fix him up—sew up the problem, make him all right again. That was the most marvelous thing in the world . . . I wanted to do that. I always thought it was the one concrete thing in the world that a human being could do. Fix up the sick, you know—and make them whole again. This was truly being God . . .

Asagai.   You wanted to be God?

Beneatha.   No—I wanted to cure. It used to be so important to me. I wanted to cure. It used to matter. I used to care. I mean about people and how their bodies hurt . . .

Asagai.   And you've stopped caring?

Beneatha.   Yes—I think so.

Asagai.   Why?

(Walter rises, goes to the door of his room and is about to open it, then stops and stands listening, leaning on the door jamb)

Beneatha.   Because it doesn't seem deep enough, close enough to what ails mankind—I mean this thing of sewing up bodies or administering drugs. Don't you understand? It was a child's reaction to the world. I thought that doctors had the secret to all the hurts. . . . That's the way a child sees things—or an idealist.

Asagai.   Children see things very well sometimes—and idealists even better.

Beneatha.   I know that's what you think. Because you are still where I left off—you still care. This is what you see for the world, for Africa. You with the dreams of the future will patch up all Africa—you are going to cure the Great Sore of colonialism with Independence—

Asagai.   Yes!

Beneatha.   Yes—and you think that one word is the penicillin of the human spirit: "Independence!" But then what?

Asagai.   That will be the problem for another time. First we must get there.

Beneatha.   And where does it end?

Asagai.   End? Who even spoke of an end? To life? To living?

Beneatha.   An end to misery!

Asagai (Smiling).   You sound like a French intellectual.

Beneatha.   No! I sound like a human being who just had her future taken right out of her hands! While I was sleeping in my bed in there, things were happening in this world that directly concerned me—and nobody asked me, consulted me—they just went out and did things—and changed my life. Don't you see there isn't any real progress, Asagai, there is only one large circle that we march in, around and around, each of us with our own little picture—in front of us—our own little mirage that we think is the future.

Asagai.   That is the mistake.

Beneatha.   What?

Asagai.   What you just said—about the circle. It isn't a circle—it's simply a long line—as in geometry, you know, one that reaches into infinity. And because we cannot see the end—we also cannot see how it changes. And it is very odd but those who see the changes are called "idealists"—and those who cannot, or refuse to think, they are the "realists." It is very strange, and amusing too, I think.

Beneatha.   You—you are almost religious.

Asagai.   Yes . . . I think I have the religion of doing what is necessary in the world— and of worshipping man—because he is so marvelous, you see.

Beneatha.   Man is foul! And the human race deserves its misery!

Asagai.   You see: *you* have become the religious one in the old sense. Already, and after such a small defeat, you are worshipping despair.

Beneatha.   From now on, I worship the truth—and the truth is that people are puny, small and selfish. . . .

Asagai.   Truth? Why is it that you despairing ones always think that only you have the truth? I never thought to see *you* like that. You! Your brother made a stupid, childish mistake—and you are grateful to him. So that now you can give up the ailing human race on account of it. You talk about what good is struggle; what good is anything? Where are we all going? And why are we bothering?

Beneatha. And you cannot answer it! All your talk and dreams about Africa and Independence. Independence and then what? What about all the crooks and petty thieves and just plain idiots who will come into power to steal and plunder the same as before—only now they will be black and do it in the name of the new Independence—You cannot answer that.

Asagai (Shouting over her). I live the answer! (Pause) In my village at home it is the exceptional man who can even read a newspaper . . . or who ever *sees* a book at all. I will go home and much of what I will have to say will seem strange to the people of my village . . . But I will teach and work and things will happen, slowly and swiftly. At times it will seem that nothing changes at all . . . and then again . . . the sudden dramatic events which make history leap into the future. And then quiet again. Retrogression even. Guns, murder, revolution. And I even will have moments when I wonder if the quiet was not better than all that death and hatred. But I will look about my village at the illiteracy and disease and ignorance and I will not wonder long. And perhaps . . . perhaps I will be a great man . . . I mean perhaps I will hold on to the substance of truth and find my way always with the right course . . . and perhaps for it I will be butchered in my bed some night by the servants of empire . . .

Beneatha. The martyr!

Asagai. . . . or perhaps I shall live to be a very old man, respected and esteemed in my new nation . . . And perhaps I shall hold office and this is what I'm trying to tell you, Alaiyo; perhaps the things I believe now for my country will be wrong and outmoded, and I will not understand and do terrible things to have things my way or merely to keep my power. Don't you see that there will be young men and women, not British soldiers then, but my own black countrymen . . . to step out of the shadows some evening and slit my then useless throat? Don't you see they have always been there . . . that they always will be. And that such a thing as my own death will be an advance? They who might kill me even . . . actually replenish me!

Beneatha. Oh, Asagai, I know all that.

Asagai. Good! Then stop moaning and groaning and tell me what you plan to do.

Beneatha. Do?

Asagai. I have a bit of a suggestion.

Beneatha. What?

Asagai (Rather quietly for him). That when it is all over—that you come home with me—

Beneatha (Slapping herself on the forehead with exasperation born of misunderstanding). Oh—Asagai—at this moment you decide to be romantic!

Asagai (Quickly understanding the misunderstanding). My dear, young creature of the New World—I do not mean across the city—I mean across the ocean; home—to Africa.

Beneatha (Slowly understanding and turning to him with murmured amazement). To—to Nigeria?

Asagai. Yes!...*(Smiling and lifting his arms playfully)* Three hundred years later the African Prince rose up out of the seas and swept the maiden back across the middle passage over which her ancestors had come—

Beneatha (Unable to play). Nigeria?

Asagai. Nigeria. Home. *(Coming to her with genuine romantic flippancy)* I will show you our mountains and our stars; and give you cool drinks from gourds and teach you the old songs and the ways of our people—and, in time, we will pretend that—*(Very softly)*—you have only been away for a day—

(She turns her back to him, thinking. He swings her around and takes her full in his arms in a long embrace which proceeds to passion)

Beneatha (Pulling away). You're getting me all mixed up—

Asagai. Why?

Beneatha. Too many things—too many things have happened today. I must sit down and think. I don't know what I feel about anything right this minute.

(She promptly sits down and props her chin on her fist)

Asagai (Charmed). All right, I shall leave you. No—don't get up. *(Touching her, gently, sweetly)* Just sit awhile and think...Never be afraid to sit awhile and think. *(He goes to door and looks at her)* How often I have looked at you and said, "Ah—so this is what the New World hath finally wrought..."

(He exits. Beneatha sits on alone. Presently Walter enters from his room and starts to rummage through things, feverishly looking for something. She looks up and turns in her seat)

Beneatha (Hissingly). Yes—just look at what the New World hath wrought! ...Just look! *(She gestures with bitter disgust)* There he is! *Monsieur le petit bourgeois noir*—himself! There he is—Symbol of a Rising Class! Entrepreneur! Titan of the system! *(Walter ignores her completely and continues frantically and destructively looking for something and hurling things to floor and tearing things out of their place in his search. Beneatha ignores the eccentricity of his actions and goes on with the monologue of insult)* Did you dream of yachts on Lake Michigan, Brother? Did you see yourself on that Great Day sitting down at the Conference Table, surrounded by all the mighty bald-headed men in America? All halted, waiting, breathless, waiting for your pronouncements on industry? Waiting for you—Chairman of the Board? *(Walter finds what he is looking for—a small piece of white paper—and pushes it in his pocket and puts on his coat and rushes out without ever having looked at her. She shouts after him)* I look at you and I see the final triumph of stupidity in the world!

(The door slams and she returns to just sitting again. Ruth comes quickly out of Mama's room)

Ruth. Who was that?
Beneatha. Your husband.
Ruth. Where did he go?
Beneatha. Who knows—maybe he has an appointment at U.S. Steel.
Ruth (Anxiously, with frightened eyes). You didn't say nothing bad to him, did you?
Beneatha. Bad? Say anything bad to him? No—I told him he was a sweet boy and full of dreams and everything is strictly peachy keen, as the ofay kids say!

(Mama enters from her bedroom. She is lost, vague, trying to catch hold, to make some sense of her former command of the world, but it still eludes her. A sense of waste overwhelms her gait; a measure of apology rides on her shoulders. She goes to her plant, which has remained on the table, looks at it, picks it up and takes it to the window sill and sits it outside, and she stands and looks at it a long moment. Then she closes the window, straightens her body with effort and turns around to her children)

Mama. Well—ain't it a mess in here, though? *(A false cheerfulness, a beginning of something)* I guess we all better stop moping around and get some work done. All this unpacking and everything we got to do. *(Ruth raises her head slowly in response to the sense of the line; and Beneatha in similar manner turns very slowly to look at her mother)* One of you all better call the moving people and tell 'em not to come.
Ruth. Tell 'em not to come?
Mama. Of course, baby. Ain't no need in 'em coming all the way here and having to go back. They charges for that too. *(She sits down, fingers to her brow, thinking)* Lord, ever since I was a little girl, I always remembers people saying, "Lena—Lena Eggleston, you aims too high all the time. You needs to slow down and see life a little more like it is. Just slow down some." That's what they always used to say down home—"Lord, that Lena Eggleston is a high-minded thing. She'll get her due one day!"
Ruth. No, Lena . . .
Mama. Me and Big Walter just didn't never learn right.
Ruth. Lena, no! We gotta go. Bennie—tell her . . . *(She rises and crosses to Beneatha with her arms outstretched. Beneatha doesn't respond)* Tell her

we can still move . . . the notes ain't but a hundred and twenty-five a month. We got four grown people in this house—we can work . . .
Mama (To herself). Just aimed too high all the time—
Ruth (Turning and going to Mama fast—the words pouring out with urgency and desperation). Lena—I'll work . . . I'll work twenty hours a day in all the kitchens in Chicago . . . I'll strap my baby on my back if I have to and scrub all the floors in America and wash all the sheets in America if I have to—but we got to move . . . We got to get out of here . . .

(Mama reaches out absently and pats Ruth's hand)

Mama. No—I sees things differently now. Been thinking 'bout some of the things we could do to fix this place up some. I seen a second-hand bureau over on Maxwell Street just the other day that could fit right there. *(She points to where the new furniture might go. Ruth wanders away from her)* Would need some new handles on it and then a little varnish and then it look like something brand-new. And—we can put up them new curtains in the kitchen . . . Why this place be looking fine. Cheer us all up so that we forget trouble ever came . . . *(To Ruth)* And you could get some nice screens to put up in your room round the baby's bassinet . . . *(She looks at both of them, pleadingly)* Sometimes you just got to know when to give up some things . . . and hold on to what you got.

(Walter enters from the outside, looking spent and leaning against the door, his coat hanging from him)

Mama. Where you been, son?
Walter (Breathing hard). Made a call.
Mama. To who, son?
Walter. To The Man.
Mama. What man, baby?
Walter. The Man, Mama. Don't you know who The Man is?
Ruth. Walter Lee?
Walter. The Man. Like the guys in the streets say—The Man. Captain Boss—Mistuh Charley . . . Old Captain Please Mr. Bossman . . .
Beneatha (Suddenly). Lindner!
Walter. That's right! That's good. I told him to come right over.
Beneatha (Fiercely, understanding). For what? What do you want to see him for!
Walter (Looking at his sister). We going to do business with him.
Mama. What you talking 'bout, son?
Walter. Talking 'bout life, Mama. You all always telling me to see life like it is. Well—I laid in there on my back today . . . and I figured it out. Life just like it is. Who gets and who don't get. *(He sits down with his coat on and*

234

laughs) Mama, you know it's all divided up. Life is. Sure enough. Between the takers and the "tooken." *(He laughs)* I've figured it out finally. *(He looks around at them)* Yeah. Some of us always getting "tooken." *(He laughs)* People like Willy Harris, they don't never get "tooken." And you know why the rest of us do? 'Cause we all mixed up. Mixed up bad. We get to looking 'round for the right and the wrong; and we worry about it and cry about it and stay up nights trying to figure out 'bout the wrong and the right of things all the time . . . And all the time, man, them takers is out there operating, just taking and taking. Willy Harris? Shoot — Willy Harris don't even count. He don't even count in the big scheme of things. But I'll say one thing for old Willy Harris . . . he's taught me something. He's taught me to keep my eye on what counts in this world. Yeah — *(Shouting out a little)* Thanks, Willy!

Ruth.   What did you call that man for, Walter Lee?

Walter.   Called him to tell him to come on over to the show. Gonna put on a show for the man. Just what he wants to see. You see, Mama, the man came here today and he told us that them people out there where you want us to move — well they so upset they willing to pay us not to move out there. *(He laughs again)* And — and oh, Mama — you would of been proud of the way me and Ruth and Bennie acted. We told him to get out . . . Lord have mercy! We told the man to get out. Oh, we was some proud folks this afternoon, yeah. *(He lights a cigarette)* We were still full of that old-time stuff . . .

Ruth *(Coming toward him slowly).* You talking 'bout taking them people's money to keep us from moving in that house?

Walter.   I ain't just talking 'bout it, baby — I'm telling you that's what's going to happen.

Beneatha.   Oh, God! Where is the bottom! Where is the real honest-to-God bottom so he can't go any farther!

Walter.   See — that's the old stuff. You and that boy that was here today. You all want everybody to carry a flag and a spear and sing some marching songs, huh? You wanna spend your life looking into things and trying to find the right and the wrong part, huh? Yeah. You know what's going to happen to that boy someday — he'll find himself sitting in a dungeon, locked in forever — and the takers will have the key! Forget it, baby! There ain't no causes — there ain't nothing but taking in this world, and he who takes most is smartest — and it don't make a damn bit of difference *how*.

Mama.   You making something inside me cry, son. Some awful pain inside me.

Walter.   Don't cry, Mama. Understand. That white man is going to walk in that door able to write checks for more money than we ever had. It's important to him and I'm going to help him . . . I'm going to put on the show, Mama.

Mama. Son—I come from five generations of people who was slaves and sharecroppers—but ain't nobody in my family never let nobody pay 'em no money that was a way of telling us we wasn't fit to walk the earth. We ain't never been that poor. *(Raising her eyes and looking at him)* We ain't never been that dead inside.

Beneatha. Well—we are dead now. All the talk about dreams and sunlight that goes on in this house. All dead.

Walter. What's the matter with you all! I didn't make this world! It was give to me this way! Hell, yes, I want me some yachts someday! Yes, I want to hang some real pearls 'round my wife's neck. Ain't she supposed to wear no pearls? Somebody tell me—tell me, who decides which women is suppose to wear pearls in this world. I tell you I am a *man*—and I think my wife should wear some pearls in this world!

(This last line hangs a good while and Walter begins to move about the room. The word "Man" has penetrated his consciousness; he mumbles it to himself repeatedly between strange agitated pauses as he moves about)

Mama. Baby, how you going to feel on the inside?

Walter. Fine! . . . Going to feel fine . . . a man . . .

Mama. You won't have nothing left then, Walter Lee.

Walter (Coming to her). I'm going to feel fine, Mama. I'm going to look that son-of-a-bitch in the eyes and say—*(He falters)*—and say, "All right, Mr. Lindner—*(He falters even more)*—that's your neighborhood out there. You got the right to keep it like you want. You got the right to have it like you want. Just write the check and—the house is yours." And, and I am going to say—*(His voice almost breaks)* And you—you people just put the money in my hand and you won't have to live next to this bunch of stinking niggers! . . . *(He straightens up and moves away from his mother, walking around the room)* Maybe—maybe I'll just get down on my black knees . . . *(He does so; Ruth and Bennie and Mama watch him in frozen horror)* Captain, Mistuh, Bossman. *(He starts crying)* A-hee-hee-hee! *(Wringing his hands in profoundly anguished imitation)* Yasssssuh! Great White Father, just gi' ussen de money, fo' God's sake, and we's ain't gwine come out deh and dirty up yo' white folks neighborhood . . .

(He breaks down completely; then gets up and goes into the bedroom)

Beneatha. That is not a man. That is nothing but a toothless rat.

Mama. Yes—death done come in this here house. *(She is nodding, slowly, reflectively)* Done come walking in my house. On the lips of my children. You what supposed to be my beginning again. You—what supposed to be my harvest. *(To Beneatha)* You—you mourning your brother?

Beneatha.   He's no brother of mine.
Mama.   What you say?
Beneatha.   I said that that individual in that room is no brother of mine.
Mama.   That's what I thought you said. You feeling like you better than he is today? *(Beneatha does not answer)* Yes? What you tell him a minute ago? That he wasn't a man? Yes? You give him up for me? You done wrote his epitaph too—like the rest of the world? Well, who give you the privilege?
Beneatha.   Be on my side for once! You saw what he just did, Mama! You saw him—down on his knees. Wasn't it you who taught me—to despise any man who would do that. Do what he's going to do.
Mama.   Yes—I taught you that. Me and your daddy. But I thought I taught you something else too . . . I thought I taught you to love him.
Beneatha.   Love him? There is nothing left to love.
Mama.   There is always something left to love. And if you ain't learned that, you ain't learned nothing. *(Looking at her)* Have you cried for that boy today? I don't mean for yourself and for the family 'cause we lost the money. I mean for him; what he been through and what it done to him. Child, when do you think is the time to love somebody the most; when they done good and made things easy for everybody? Well then, you ain't through learning—because that ain't the time at all. It's when he's at his lowest and can't believe in hisself 'cause the world done whipped him so. When you starts measuring somebody, measure him right, child, measure him right. Make sure you done taken into account what hills and valleys he come through before he got to wherever he is.

(Travis bursts into the room at the end of the speech, leaving the door open)

Travis.   Grandmama—the moving men are downstairs! The truck just pulled up.
Mama (Turning and looking at him). Are they, baby? They downstairs?

(She sighs and sits. Lindner appears in the doorway. He peers in and knocks lightly, to gain attention, and comes in. All turn to look at him)

Lindner (Hat and briefcase in hand). Uh—hello . . . *(Ruth crosses mechanically to the bedroom door and opens it and lets it swing open freely and slowly as the lights come up on* Walter *within, still in his coat, sitting at the far corner of the room. He looks up and out through the room to Lindner)*
Ruth.   He's here.

(A long minute passes and Walter slowly gets up)

Lindner (Coming to the table with efficiency, putting his briefcase on the table and starting to unfold papers and unscrew fountain pens). Well, I certainly was glad to hear from you people. *(Walter has begun the trek out of the room, slowly and awkwardly, rather like a small boy, passing the back of his sleeve across his mouth from time to time)* Life can really be so much simpler than people let it be most of the time. Well—with whom do I negotiate? You, Mrs. Younger, or your son here? *(Mama sits with her hands folded on her lap and her eyes closed as Walter advances. Travis goes close to Lindner and looks at the papers curiously)* Just some official papers, sonny.

Ruth. Travis, you go downstairs.

Mama (Opening her eyes and looking into Walter's). No. Travis, you stay right here. And you make him understand what you doing, Walter Lee. You teach him good. Like Willy Harris taught you. You show where our five generations done come to. Go ahead, son—

Walter (Looks down into his boy's eyes. Travis grins at him merrily and Walter draws him beside him with his arm lightly around his shoulders). Well, Mr. Lindner *(Beneatha turns away)* We called you—*(There is a profound, simple groping quality in his speech)*—because, well, me and my family *(He looks around and shifts from one foot to the other)* Well—we are very plain people . . .

Lindner. Yes—

Walter. I mean—I have worked as a chauffeur most of my life—and my wife here, she does domestic work in people's kitchens. So does my mother. I mean—we are plain people . . .

Lindner. Yes, Mr. Younger—

Walter (Really like a small boy, looking down at his shoes and then up at the man). And—uh—well, my father, well, he was a laborer most of his life.

Lindner (Absolutely confused). Uh, yes—

Walter (Looking down at his toes once again). My father almost beat a man to death once because this man called him a bad name or something, you know what I mean?

Lindner. No, I'm afraid I don't.

Walter (Finally straightening up). Well, what I mean is that we come from people who had a lot of pride. I mean—we are very proud people. And that's my sister over there and she's going to be a doctor—and we are very proud—

Lindner. Well—I am sure that is very nice, but—

Walter (Starting to cry and facing the man eye to eye). What I am telling you is that we called you over here to tell you that we are very proud and that this is—this is my son, who makes the sixth generation of our family in this country, and that we have all thought about your offer and we have decided to move into our house because my father—my father—he earned it. *(Mama has her eyes closed and is rocking back and forth as though she were in church, with her head nodding the amen yes)* We don't want to make no trouble for nobody or fight no causes—but we will try to be good neighbors. That's all we got to say. *(He looks the man absolutely in the eyes)* We don't want your money.

(He turns and walks away from the man)

Lindner *(Looking around at all of them).* I take it then that you have decided to occupy.
Beneatha. That's what the man said.
Lindner *(To Mama in her reverie).* Then I would like to appeal to you, Mrs. Younger. You are older and wiser and understand things better I am sure . . .
Mama *(Rising).* I am afraid you don't understand. My son said we was going to move and there ain't nothing left for me to say. *(Shaking her head with double meaning)* You know how these young folks is nowadays, mister. Can't do a thing with 'em. Good-bye.
Lindner *(Folding up his materials).* Well—if you are that final about it . . . There is nothing left for me to say. *(He finishes. He is almost ignored by the family, who are concentrating on Walter Lee. At the door Lindner halts and looks around)* I sure hope you people know what you're doing.

(He shakes his head and exits)

Ruth *(Looking around and coming to life).* Well, for God's sake—if the moving men are here—LET'S GET THE HELL OUT OF HERE!
Mama *(Into action).* Ain't it the truth! Look at all this here mess. Ruth, put Travis' good jacket on him . . . Walter Lee, fix your tie and tuck your shirt in, you look just like somebody's hoodlum. Lord have mercy, where is my plant? *(She flies to get it amid the general bustling of the family, who are deliberately trying to ignore the nobility of the past moment)* You all start on down . . . Travis child, don't go empty-handed . . . Ruth, where did I put that box with my skillets in it? I want to be in charge of it myself . . . I'm going to make us the biggest dinner we ever ate tonight . . . Beneatha, what's the matter with them stockings? Pull them things up, girl . . .

(The family starts to file out as two moving men appear and begin to carry out the heavier pieces of furniture, bumping into the family as they move about)

Beneatha. Mama, Asagai—asked me to marry him today and go to Africa—
Mama *(In the middle of her getting-ready activity).* He did? You ain't old enough to marry nobody—*(Seeing the moving men lifting one of her chairs precariously)* Darling, that ain't no bale of cotton, please handle it so we can sit in it again. I had that chair twenty-five years . . .

(The movers sigh with exasperation and go on with their work)

Beneatha *(Girlishly and unreasonably trying to pursue the conversation)*. To go to Africa, Mama—be a doctor in Africa . . .

Mama *(Distracted)*. Yes, baby—

Walter. Africa! What he want you to go to Africa for?

Beneatha. To practice there . . .

Walter. Girl, if you don't get all them silly ideas out your head! You better marry yourself a man with some loot . . .

Beneatha *(Angrily, precisely as in the first scene of the play)*. What have you got to do with who I marry!

Walter. Plenty. Now I think George Murchison—

(He and Beneatha go out yelling at each other vigorously; Beneatha is heard saying that she would not marry George Murchison if he were Adam and she were Eve, etc. The anger is loud and real till their voices diminish. Ruth stands at the door and turns to Mama and smiles knowingly)

Mama *(Fixing her hat at last)*. Yeah—they something all right, my children . . .

Ruth. Yeah—they're something. Let's go, Lena.

Mama *(Stalling, starting to look around at the house)*. Yes—I'm coming. Ruth—

Ruth. Yes?

Mama *(Quietly, woman to woman)*. He finally come into his manhood today, didn't he? Kind of like a rainbow after the rain . . .

Ruth *(Biting her lip lest her own pride explode in front of Mama)*. Yes, Lena.

(Walter's voice calls for them raucously)

Mama *(Waving Ruth out vaguely)*. All right, honey—go on down. I be down directly.

(Ruth hesitates, then exits. Mama stands, at last alone in the living room, her plant on the table before her as the lights start to come down. She looks around at all the walls and ceilings and suddenly, despite herself, while the children call below, a great heaving thing rises in her and she puts her fist to her mouth, takes a final desperate look, pulls her coat about her, pats her hat and goes out. The lights dim down. The door opens and she comes back in, grabs her plant, and goes out for the last time)

CURTAIN

[1959]

240

LANGSTON HUGHES
[1902–1967]

Of all the artists who shaped literary modernism, Langston Hughes was one of the most prolific and the most important. Dubbed the "Dean of Negro Writing" by his peers, Hughes wrote poems, plays, novels, short stories, articles, and essays. He left an indelible mark on the period through his passionate statements of aesthetic principles and his eloquent pleas for human dignity and equality.

Born in 1902 in Joplin, Missouri, Hughes grew up in Lawrence, Kansas, under the care of his maternal grandmother, Mary Langston. Hughes's mother, Carrie Langston Hughes, was an educated woman who yearned for a career in the theater. His father, James Hughes, was a businessman who left the United States for the more tolerant racial climate of Mexico. After his grandmother's death, Hughes rejoined his mother and gained admission to a top-flight high school in Cleveland, Ohio, where he was one of a handful of black students. Hughes excelled academically, published his first poems, and came to love the work of American poets Walt Whitman and Carl Sandburg. Determined to build on his success after his graduation in 1902, Hughes traveled to Mexico to convince his father to finance his college education. While in Mexico, Hughes began to submit work to the Crisis, the official periodical of the National Association for the Advancement of Colored People (NAACP) edited by W. E. B. Dubois. "The Negro Speaks of Rivers" appeared in the Crisis in 1921, a few months after Hughes's eighteenth birthday.

With the grudging support of his father, Hughes enrolled at Columbia University in New York City. After attending classes for a year, however, Hughes grew restless and dropped out in 1922 to experience more of the "real life" he deemed increasingly important to his art. For the next three years, his adventures rivaled Herman Melville's. He worked a series of menial jobs, signed on as a seaman on a steamship that traveled the west coast of Africa, went to sea a second time bound for Europe, jumped ship, settled in Paris, worked in a nightclub that featured American jazz, and visited Italy. All

241

the while, he wrote and published poems. By the time he returned to America, he had earned a reputation in African-American literary circles as one of the country's most gifted poets. Hughes cemented his literary position in 1925 *by winning first prize in* Opportunity *magazine's poetry contest with "The Weary Blues." The prize brought him to the attention of one of the chief literary entrepreneurs of the New Negro movement, Carl Van Vechten, who arranged a book contract for Hughes with Alfred A. Knopf. Hughes's first volume,* The Weary Blues, *appeared in January 1926 to favorable reviews.*

With a book under his belt, Hughes went back to college at Lincoln University, an all-black college in Pennsylvania. The experience in part gave Hughes the confidence to more aggressively assert his own notions of the aesthetic and political goals of the New Negro movement. Surveying the work of his African American literary peers, Hughes began to believe, like Claude McKay, that some New Negro writers were far too concerned with their reception by white audiences. Bent on "race improvement," eager to be deemed the equal of white authors, some New Negro writers scorned the literary use of what they considered low-brow artistic materials and images of "common" black life. In rising above such things, however, Negro writers, Hughes feared, would lose all touch with the mass black audience that needed them most. Hughes believed that if poetry was to be an agent of social change it must appeal to blacks of all classes, not simply the upper reaches of the black intelligentsia. The art the movement generated should draw on black vernacular materials—jazz and folk takes and spirituals—in order to grant African Americans a sense of racial identity and shared experience that would prove a powerful political tool. Hughes eloquently summarized his thoughts on the New Negro aesthetic in his pivotal essay, "The Negro Artist and the Racial Mountain," that appeared in the Nation *in 1926.*

The poems in Hughes's 1927 volume, Fine Clothes to the Jew, *reflected his manifesto and received harsh reviews from the African-American press for its undue emphasis on the low-brow elements of jazz culture. Undaunted, Hughes turned his talents to other genres, writing a novel (*Not Without Laughter, *published 1930), plays (*Mule Bone, *written with Zora Neale Hurston, and* Mulatto, *completed 1930, produced on Broadway 1935), and short stories (*The Ways of White Folks, *published 1934), all the while honing an increasingly politicized view of his literary work. Spurred in part by the horrors of the Great Depression, Hughes became ever more critical of American capitalism throughout the 1930s. During 1932–33, he traveled in the Soviet Union, penning poems in support of proletarian revolution. In 1937, Hughes was again drawn to a site of leftist political importance when he agreed to cover the struggles of the leftist Spanish Loyalists against the German-backed Fascist insurgents in the Spanish Civil War for a number of* *black newspapers. Upon his return to Harlem in 1938, Hughes founded the politically radical Harlem Suitcase Theater whose first production, his own propaganda drama* Don't You Want to Be Free, *ran for thirty-eight performances.*

Hughes's socialism became more muted during the years of World War II and he rediscovered many of the subjects that occupied his verse during the 1920s. His 1942 volume of verse, Shakespeare in Harlem, *signaled his return to the blues and with* Jim Crow's Last Stand *(1943), his return to the nationally specific issues of segregation and civil rights. Hughes also began to publish a weekly column in the black newspaper, the* Chicago Defender, *in which he spoke out on issues of race and racism through the character of Jesse B. Semple (or Simple), a Harlem everyman who holds forth in a neighborhood bar. Hughes's politics, however, remained an issue in the eyes of both the U.S. Government and Hughes's audience. Throughout the 1940s and 50s, Hughes was attacked by those on the political right for his Communist sympathies and by those on the political left for his apparent abandonment of the proletarian cause. Following WWII, Hughes produced two additional volumes of verse,* Fields of Wonder *(1947) and* One Way Ticket *(1949), both of which helped to pave the way for the volume that many critics deem his masterwork,* Montage of a Dream Deferred *(1951). Drawing on the complex rhythms and dissonances of be-bop jazz, Hughes fashioned a group of poems that functioned as intellectual and emotional improvisations on a single idea: the tragic deferral of universal human dignity and freedom. Hughes referred to the entire volume as a single poem. The lyrics in the volume, he stated, were meant to be read together in order. The result of Hughes's reaching for a larger form was a tour-de-force volume that led to his radical experiment of the next decade, the book-length poem* Ask Your Mama: 12 Moods for Jazz *(1961). A blending of poetry and music, myth and history,* Ask Your Mama *constituted in part Hughes's retrospective ruminations on the complex course of his career.*

Those encountering Hughes for the first time will marvel at the apparent simplicity of his verse. Where other modernists can be bafflingly allusive, Hughes seems surprisingly direct. It is important to remember, however, that Hughes's plain speaking reflects a considered communitarian ethos. He invokes African-American vernacular materials in order to give voice to an oppressed people and forge a group identity out of a shared history of sorrow, and a shared sense of pride. Hughes's poems consistently remind us of the inescapable and painful burden of history while they insist on the need to keep fighting for the joy of life.

The texts reprinted here issue from Arnold Rampersad's 1994 edition of the Collected Poems of Langston Hughes. *Rampersad's edition offers the last published version of each of Hughes's poems. Hughes revised many of his verses throughout his career. As such the versions printed here may differ significantly from the versions that first appeared in print. Variants are given in the notes to the poems.*

For Further Reading

Primary Works

The Weary Blues (New York: Knopf, 1926; London: Knopf, 1926); *Fine Clothes to the Jew* (New York: Knopf, 1927; London: Knopf, 1927); *Not Without Laughter* (New York & London: Knopf, 1930; London: Allen & Unwin, 1930); *Dear Lovely Death* (Amenia, N.Y.: Privately printed at the Troutbeck Press, 1931); *The Negro Mother and Other Dramatic Recitations* (New York: Golden Stair Press, 1931); *The Dream Keeper and Other Poems* (New York: Knopf, 1932); *Scottsboro Limited: Four Poems and a Play in Verse* (New York: Golden Stair Press, 1932); *Popo and Fifina: Children of Haiti*, by Hughes and Arna Bontemps (New York: Macmillan, 1932); *A Negro Looks at Soviet Central Asia* (Moscow & Leningrad: Co-operative Publishing Society of Foreign Workers in the U.S.S.R., 1934); *The Ways of White Folks* (New York: Knopf, 1934; London: Allen & Unwin, 1934); *A New Song* (New York: International Workers Order, 1938); *The Big Sea: An Autobiography* (New York & London: Knopf, 1940; London: Hutchinson, 1940); *Shakespeare in Harlem* (New York: Knopf, 1942); *Freedom's Plow* (New York: Musette Publishers, 1943); *Jim Crow's Last Stand* (Atlanta: Negro Publication Society of America, 1943); *Lament for Dark Peoples and Other Poems* (N.p., 1944); *Fields of Wonder* (New York: Knopf, 1947); *One-Way Ticket* (New York: Knopf, 1949); *Simple Speaks His Mind* (New York: Simon & Schuster, 1950; London: Gollancz, 1951); *Montage of a Dream Deferred* (New York: Holt, 1951); *Laughing to Keep from Crying* (New York: Holt, 1952); *The First Book of Negroes* (New York: Franklin Watts, 1952; London: Bailey & Swinfen, 1956); *Simple Takes a Wife* (New York: Simon & Schuster, 1953; London: Gollancz, 1954); *Famous American Negroes* (New York: Dodd, Mead, 1954); *The First Book of Rhythms* (New York: Franklin Watts, 1954; London: Bailey & Swinfen, 1956); *The First Book of Jazz* (New York: Franklin Watts, 1955; London: Bailey & Swinfen, 1957); *Famous Negro Music Makers* (New York: Dodd, Mead, 1955); *The Sweet Flypaper of Life*, text by Hughes and photographs by Roy DeCarava (New York: Simon & Schuster, 1955); *I Wonder as I Wander: An Autobiographical Journey* (New York & Toronto: Rinehart, 1956); *Simple Stakes a Claim* (New York & Toronto: Rinehart, 1957; London: Gollancz, 1958); *The Langston Hughes Reader* (New York: Braziller, 1958); *Famous Negro Heroes of America* (New York: Dodd, Mead, 1958); *Tamborines to Glory* (New York: John Day, 1958; London: Gollancz, 1959); *Selected Poems of Langston Hughes* (New York: Knopf, 1959); *The Best of Simple* (New York: Hill & Wang, 1961); *Ask Your Mama: 12 Moods for Jazz* (New York: Knopf, 1961); *Fight for Freedom: The Story of the NAACP* (New York: Norton, 1962); *Something in Common and Other Stories* (New York: Hill & Wang, 1963); *Five Plays by Langston Hughes*, edited by Webster Smalley (Bloomington: Indiana University Press,

1963); *Simple's Uncle Sam* (New York: Hill & Wang, 1965); *The Panther & The Lash* (New York: Knopf, 1967).

Secondary Works

Richard K. Bardsdale, *Langston Hughes: The Poet and His Critics* (Chicago: American Library Association, 1977); Nathan Huggins, *Harlem Renaissance* (New York: Oxford University Press, 1971); Hans Ostrom, *A Langston Hughes Encyclopedia* (Westport, Conn.: Greenwood Press, 2001); Audrey Osofsky, *Free to Dream: The Making of a Poet: Langston Hughes* (New York: Lothrop, Lee & Shepard Books, 1996); Arnold Rampersad, editor, *The Collected Works of Langston Hughes* (Columbia: University of Missouri Press, 2001); Arnold Rampersad, *The Life of Langston Hughes*, 2 vols. (New York: Oxford University Press, 1986–1988); C. James Trotman, editor, *Langston Hughes: The Man, His Art, and His Continuing Influence* (New York: Garland, 1995); Steven C. Tracy, *Langston Hughes & the Blues* (Urbana: University of Illinois Press, 1988).

Harlem

LANGSTON HUGHES

What happens to a dream deferred?

Does it dry up
like a raisin in the sun?
Or fester like a sore—
And then run?   5
Does it stink like rotten meat?
Or crust and sugar over—
like a syrupy sweet?

Maybe it just sags
like a heavy load.   10

Or does it explode?

[1951, 1959]

Reprinted from *Selected Poems of Langston Hughes* (1990), by permission of the Copyright Clearance Center, Inc. Copyright © 1990 by Henry Holt & Company.

Ballad of the Landlord

LANGSTON HUGHES

Landlord, landlord,
My roof has sprung a leak.
Don't you 'member I told you about it
Way last week?

Landlord, landlord,   5
These steps is broken down
When you come up yourself
It's a wonder you don't fall down.

Ten Bucks you say I owe you?
Ten Bucks you say is due?   10
Well, that's Ten Bucks more'n I'll pay you
Till you fix this house up new.

What? You gonna get eviction orders?
You gonna cut off my heat?
You gonna take my furniture and   15
Throw it in the street?

Um-huh! You talking high and mighty.
Talk on—till you get through.
You ain't gonna be able to say a word
If I land my fist on you.   20

Police! Police!
Come and get this man!
He's trying to ruin the government
And overturn the land!

Reprinted from *The Poems 1941–1950* (2001), by permission of the Copyright Clearance Center, Inc. Copyright © 2001 by the University of Missouri Press.

Copper's whistle!   25
Patrol bell!
Arrest.

Precinct Station.
Iron cell.
Headlines in press: 30

MAN THREATENS LANDLORD

TENANT HELD NO BAIL

JUDGE GIVES NEGRO 90 DAYS IN COUNTY JAIL

[1940, 1955]

I, Too[♦]

LANGSTON HUGHES

I, too, sing America.

I am the darker brother.
They send me to eat in the kitchen
When company comes,
But I laugh,   5
And eat well,
And grow strong.

Tomorrow,
I'll be at the table[1]
When company comes.   10
Nobody'll dare
Say to me,
"Eat in the kitchen,"
Then.

Besides,   15
They'll see how beautiful I am
And be ashamed—

I, too, am America.

[1925]